Young Children
Reinvent Arithmetic

IMPLICATIONS OF PIAGET'S THEORY

EARLY CHILDHOOD EDUCATION SERIES

Millie Almy, Editor

Young Children Reinvent Arithmetic

IMPLICATIONS OF PIAGET'S THEORY

Constance Kazuko Kamii
with Georgia DeClark

Foreword by Bärbel Inhelder

TEACHERS
COLLEGE
PRESS

Teachers College, Columbia University
New York and London

Published by Teachers College Press, 1234 Amsterdam Avenue,
New York, N.Y. 10027

Library of Congress Cataloging in Publication Data

Kamii, Constance.
   Young children reinvent arithmetic.

   Bibliography: p.
   Includes index.
   1. Arithmetic—Study and teaching (Elementary) .
2. Number concept—Study and teaching (Elementary)
3. Piaget, Jean, 1896–1980. I. DeClark, Georgia.
II. Title.
QA135.5.K186   1984   372.7'2044   84-12784

ISBN 0-8077-2707-5 (paperback)
ISBN 0-8077-2759-8 (cloth)

Manufactured in the United States of America

90 89 88 87 86   3 4 5 6

Contents

Foreword

I would like to express the great pleasure I experienced in reading this new work presented to us today by Constance Kamii. She enjoys a reputation that goes far beyond the frontiers of the United States and South America. In Europe and more particularly in Geneva, she is often asked to present her psychopedagogical research to early childhood educators. With her constant effort and persuasive enthusiasm, she knows how to convince her audience of the interest and necessity of basing the young child's initiation to scientific thought on epistemological foundations.

For years Dr. Kamii has experimented in classrooms in close collaboration with teachers, while participating in the scientific work in progress at the International Center of Genetic Epistemology in Geneva. There she has had the opportunity to assist a creative mind of the caliber of the founder of genetic epistemology, Jean Piaget. With her own perspicacity and finesse, she understood from the very beginning that practical work is more fruitful when it is founded on basic and disinterested research. In Geneva, she learned the method of critical exploration, which consists in getting children to talk by asking them questions guided by theoretical hypotheses and checking the validity of the results. Being bilingual she was able to read the publications in their original language, particularly those on numerical structures and recurrential reasoning not yet translated into English, and numerous papers on work in progress on prenumerical procedures. Thus she was able to avoid the misunderstandings resulting from overly approximate translations of texts that are difficult in their very complexity.

The essential contribution of this new book is that it transposed to actual reality Piaget's central epistemological thesis according to which mathematical thought is, from its most elementary manifestations, the product of the subject's activity that he characterized by the term "reflective abstraction." In reflective abstraction, the subject abstracts the rules of logico-mathematical knowledge from his own coordination of actions, and not from properties of objects. Objects serve as a support for this activity for a long time in the course of development, but they are not the essence of the activity itself. It is the most general coordination of actions of classifying, ordering, and putting into correspondence that form the underpinnings of arithmetical rules and concept of number. These concrete rules are later reflected on more abstract levels and reorganized through reflection. I am delighted to see the clarity and simplicity with which Constance Kamii presented and realized with her colleague, Georgia DeClark, this idea shared by genetic epistemology and psychology on the origins of mathematical thought.

It is one thing to study Piaget's theory and quite another to know how it can be used in a classroom. I am pleased with Dr. Kamii's insistence that educators must justify their objectives on the basis of scientific knowledge about how children invent. She insists that children's ability to *write* correct answers is not a valid objective in beginning arithmetic, and that what is important is their mental activity, that is, their active, autonomous process of reasoning. On the basis of her own research, she convincingly restates Piaget's argument that a classroom that fosters creative, autonomous mental activity in the intellectual realm must also necessarily encourage it in the social and moral realm. She goes on to say that the "how" of the activities presented in this book is much more important than the "what," and illustrates this point with examples from the classroom.

Finally, I want to draw attention to an obvious but often overlooked point in Chapter 11. In evaluating the program, Dr. Kamii emphasizes that a large number of sums correctly known by children by the end of first grade in no way implies a good foundation for further learning in the future.

This book goes counter to present conceptions and practices from beginning to end. Since it has been assumed for centuries that arithmetic must be taught to young children from sources external to them, I expect many educators to have difficulty in accepting the facts and theory presented in this book. For those who want to study what goes on in children's heads, however, in order to find truly new and better ways of providing opportunities for children to construct mathematics at all age levels, this is an important book about how young children might first be introduced to arithmetic.

BÄRBEL INHELDER

Acknowledgments

This book could not have been written without the assistance of many people. The person to whom I owe the greatest intellectual and personal debt is Hermina Sinclair of the University of Geneva. She critiqued many manuscripts and answered my questions over the years, patiently explaining the nature of logico-mathematical knowledge to me.

The teacher who contributed the most to this book is Georgia DeClark. She worked closely with me on classroom activities with skepticism and honesty and is the author of Chapters 9 and 10 as well as the co-author of Chapters 7 and 8. She took great risks, spent months in anguish, and struggled through the painful process of drastically changing her approach to teaching.

Teachers have a great deal of knowledge about what is generally hard for young children and what kinds of activities appeal to them. They also have insightful perspectives of organization of classes and children's personalities. Among those who influenced my thinking are Elaine Bologna of the Summit School in Winston-Salem, North Carolina, and four teachers in the Geneva (Switzerland) public schools—Heidi Mounoud, Gabrielle Serex, Yvonne Cesareo, and Véronique Clerc. Suzanne Stringer, a teacher in the Selma (Alabama) public schools, decided to change her way of teaching after reading an early version of the manuscript and contributed valuable ideas while it was revised.

Among the people who critically read drafts of this book and made helpful suggestions are Jack Easley of the University of Illinois at Champaign-Urbana, Kathleen Gruber of the same institution at Chicago, and Jean Brun of the University of Geneva. My sister, Mieko Kamii, of Wheelock College, read the manuscript in great detail and rewrote many pages. The title of this book owes its existence to Eleanor Duckworth of Harvard University.

I would also like to acknowledge the role of the Social Science Research Council and the National Institute of Mental Health, which enabled me to spend almost four years as a postdoctoral fellow under Jean Piaget, Bärbel Inhelder, Hermina Sinclair, and others at the University of Geneva and the

International Center of Genetic Epistemology. It takes many years to study Piaget's theory, and NIMH supported my efforts when I announced I needed more time. The actual research and the writing of this book were made possible by the Urban Education Research Program of the University of Illinois at Chicago.

Grateful acknowledgment is also made for permission to quote from the following works:

Mieko Kamii. Place Value: Children's Efforts to Find a Correspondence between Digits and Numbers of Objects. Paper presented at the Tenth Annual Symposium of the Jean Piaget Society, Philadelphia, May 29, 1980.

Robert Wirtz. *New Beginnings: A Guide to the Think•Talk•Read Math Center for Beginners*. Monterey, Calif: Curriculum Development Associates, 1980.

Introduction

Piaget's theory is becoming recognized by an increasing number of educators throughout the world as having far-reaching implications for the way we educate children. But it is not immediately obvious how a specific subject like arithmetic should be taught to young children on the basis of this theory. This book addresses the question by focusing mainly on the first grade.

The basic points that can be gleaned from the theory itself are straightforward. They have to do with the nature of logico-mathematical knowledge and the findings that this knowledge is constructed by each child through reflective abstraction and that social interaction is important for children's thinking and the construction of logico-mathematical knowledge.

These theoretical points are in direct conflict with the assumptions of pre-Piagetian math education. The traditional approaches have assumed that math is a subject matter to be internalized by children, that "abstraction" is the same thing as symbolization, and that the internalization of this knowledge is best accomplished through individual exercises and feedback from the teacher and/or objects.

Because Piaget's theory is radically different from previous assumptions, the approach advocated in this book breaks clearly with traditional instruction. I am advocating eliminating all traditional instruction in first grade arithmetic and replacing it with two kinds of activities: situations in daily living (such as voting) and group games.

The use of games for arithmetic is nothing new. Many teachers have been using them for a long time. Games, however, have been used only as supplements to reinforce the learning assumed to take place in lessons and through worksheets and flash cards. Games are also used as rewards and/or fillers for children who have finished their work. What I advocate is promoting games from a secondary to a primary role. After several years of research on group games with preschool and kindergarten children (Kamii and DeVries, 1980), I became convinced that games are a sufficient and much better means for learning first grade arithmetic than lessons and worksheets.

Young children literally *reinvent* arithmetic. For centuries educators have believed that young children learned arithmetic by having it taught or by discovering it. Yet in reality children have been learning most of it in spite of instruction—by constructing it from within and/or by rote. Piaget made a distinction between invention and discovery. The example of discovery he gave was Columbus's discovery of America. America already existed before its discovery. The example he gave of an invention, by contrast, was that of the automobile, which did not exist before its invention. He argued that logico-mathematical knowledge is invented by each child, that is, it is constructed by each child from within. It cannot be discovered or learned by transmission from the environment, except for the conventional mathematical signs (such as " = ") and the notational system, which constitute the most superficial part of arithmetic.

As Kohlberg and Mayer said, "The most important issue confronting educators and educational theorists is the choice of ends for the educational process. Without clear and rational educational goals, it becomes impossible to decide which educational programs achieve objectives of general import and which teach incidental facts and attitudes of dubious worth" (1972, p. 449). In this book, I present the essential points of Piaget's theory in Part 1[1] and go on to the objectives of primary arithmetic in Part II. (Some readers prefer to start with Part II and read Part I later.) On the basis of constructivism, a scientific theory about how human beings acquire moral values and knowledge, Piaget conceptualized moral and intellectual autonomy as the aim of education. Within this broad goal (discussed in Chapter 3), I develop more specific objectives for first grade arithmetic such as numerals and place value (Chapter 4), addition (Chapter 5), and subtraction (Chapter 6). In these chapters, I argue that many objectives in arithmetic now prescribed for first grade are more appropriate for the second and third years of elementary school. Parts III and V—on activities, principles of teaching, and evaluation—all flow from the objectives thus defined.

A strength of this book is the involvement of Georgia DeClark, the teacher with whom I worked. She is the author of Part IV and the co-author of Part III. In well over a decade of curriculum research, I had come to the conclusion that it was essential to experiment with teachers because they have a vast amount of knowledge and experience, and a perspective researchers lack. To develop a practical program that can be used by other teachers, it is essential for researchers to work in classrooms with teachers who know their pupils.

In 1980 I decided that it was necessary for me to work with a student in or a graduate of the master's degree program in early childhood education at

---

1. To simplify discussions of complex theoretical matters, I have used only masculine pronouns. I do not intend this usage to reflect stereotyped concepts of children or adults.

the University of Illinois at Chicago, since this program trained experienced teachers in the use of Piaget's theory. Georgia DeClark was a student in this program and was teaching first grade in a public school in Glen Ellyn, a Chicago suburb. Georgia had already worked through the difficult and painful process of changing from the kind of authority figure she had originally been trained to be, to a person who reduced her power as much as possible. I visited her class and found a highly autonomous group of children who could play games on their own when they were not busy with the official curriculum. (The children from her class mentioned in this book were given fictitious names. In making up these names, we kept the actual sex and name initial of each child.)

When I asked Georgia what she thought about developing a first grade arithmetic program with me by throwing out all traditional instruction and using, instead, only situations in daily living and games, her response was "It is not that I don't believe you and Piaget, but I am not convinced enough. I can't promise to go through with what you want me to do, but I will give it a try and see how far I can go." Her school was using a well-known math series that she felt was unsatisfactory, but she was not ready to drop all the traditional math she felt she was employed to teach.

The agreement we made before the beginning of the 1980–81 school year was that, regardless of how I thought children should be taught, the ultimate decisions were hers to make. I told her that I would be happy if she could work in the way I wanted her to, but that whatever she taught would give me interesting things to study. The reader will see in Chapter 4 that I had indeed found highly interesting things about place value in Georgia's class.

We began with the games described at the beginning of Chapter 10. By October, Georgia could see that the children were mentally much more active in games than they had been during the previous five years, when she used workbooks. We ended up making all the decisions together about each game. When I thought of a new game, I always asked her what she thought of it. When it passed her test, I knew the game was worth trying. The close collaboration of a theorist and practitioner with a good theory is deeply satisfying and mutually enriching.

By April Georgia had given four worksheets (without consulting me!). Each time she gave one, she was reassured that almost all the children could do it with ease. She could also see that the one or two children who could not complete the worksheets were also those who could not play games and that worksheets would not have helped these individuals. Another reassuring factor was the findings from the January testing. As can be seen in Chapter 5, we tested the children in October, January, April, and June with two dice with a numeral on each side. We showed 3 and 3 on the dice, for example, and asked children how many points they would have if they got these numbers. As can be seen in Table 5.1, the children's ability to give correct sums immediately from memory improved spectacularly between October and January. Upon seeing these data, Georgia began to say, "This IS convincing! It IS true that kids learn in this way. But I still have to grow at my own speed."

I strongly believe in teachers' autonomy. Curriculum change is too often imposed from above, and teachers are recycled overnight to be the mere executors (if not the executioners) of someone else's decision. I think teachers have to believe in what they are doing, and as I insisted elsewhere (Kamii, 1981a), they must have the scientific training necessary to be able to experiment, evaluate results, and make curriculum decisions for them-selves. Just as children in most public schools are not encouraged to say, "I am not convinced," teachers are not encouraged to say so when they are skeptical. When people are encouraged to think, to study, and to express their disagreement, they generally arrive at the truth sooner than when their opinions are not valued. Chapter 9 is a poignant account of an honest teacher who struggled through a revolution within herself.

How Georgia has put Piagetian principles into practice in her teaching is shown in the account in Chapter 8 of the moment-to-moment interaction as she played one of the games with her students. This account is based on a videotape, which is available to interested readers as are two other tapes and the transcribed accounts from them. Additional information is given in Chapter 8.

Pertinent to the discussion in this book on teaching arithmetic to young children are two earlier books—*Group Games in Early Education* (Kamii and DeVries, 1980) and *Number in Preschool and Kindergarten* (Kamii, 1982). The former discusses the unique desirability of group games (Chapter 2) and the issue of competition (Chapter 11)—important points that are not repeated in the present volume. *Number in Preschool and Kindergarten* is useful for teachers who want to know what arithmetic looks like before first grade. But arithmetic is only a small part of a total curriculum, and the reader interested in other aspects is referred to "Piaget for Early Education" (Kamii and DeVries, 1977) and *Physical Knowledge in Preschool Education* (Kamii and DeVries, 1978). Piaget's epistemological framework can be found in the Appendix of *Group Games*.

The present book is written for teachers of young children, but it is also addressed to administrators, curriculum specialists, and evaluators. I, there-fore, hope it will be used in courses on methods of teaching elementary mathematics, early childhood education, educational psychology, and evalu-ation.

The final point I wish to make here is that education must stop being dictated by the pendulum that keeps returning to what did not work before. Rather than going back to "basics," we must move forward with what we now know about how human beings acquire knowledge and moral values.

Young Children
Reinvent Arithmetic

IMPLICATIONS OF PIAGET'S THEORY

Part I

THEORETICAL FOUNDATION

CHAPTER 1

Piaget's Theory
of Number

The approach advocated in this book begins with Piaget's theory of number, according to which *number is a mental structure* that each child constructs out of a natural ability to think rather than learns from the environment. Furthermore, since any number is built by the repeated addition of 1, its very construction can be said to include addition.

The purpose of this chapter is to clarify this theory of number before discussing the importance of social interaction in connection with this theory in the next chapter. Two experimental tasks will be discussed in detail to provide the empirical evidence for the theory. They are the conservation task and one that involves the dropping of beads into two glasses. Findings from two other tasks will also be presented to show that addition, too, grows out of the child's natural ability to think. These findings led me to hypothesize that addition does not need to be taught to first graders and that it is more important to provide opportunities for children to engage in numerical reasoning.

Since Piaget's theory can be understood only in the epistemological context within which he worked, I will begin by discussing his position in relation to empiricism and rationalism.

REVIEWING EMPIRICISM, RATIONALISM, AND PIAGET'S CONSTRUCTIVISM

Piaget is often believed to have been a psychologist, but he was actually a genetic epistemologist. Epistemology is the study of the nature and origins of knowledge, expressed in such questions as "How do we know what we think we know?" and "How do we know that what we think we know is true?" Historically, two main currents have developed in response to these questions, the empiricist and the rationalist currents.

Empiricists (such as Locke, Berkeley, and Hume) argued in essence that knowledge has its source outside the individual and that it is internalized through the senses. They further argued that the individual at birth is like a clean slate on which experiences are "written" as he grows up. As Locke expressed it in 1690, "The senses at first let in particular ideas, and furnish the yet empty cabinet, and the mind by degrees growing familiar with some of them, they are lodged in the memory . . ." (1947, p. 22).

Rationalists such as Descartes, Spinoza, and Kant did not deny the importance of sensory experience, but they insisted that reason is more powerful than sensory experience because it enables us to know with certainty many truths that sensory observation can never ascertain. For example, we know that every event has a cause, in spite of the fact that we obviously cannot examine every event in the entire past and future of the universe. Rationalists also pointed out that since our senses often deceive us (e.g., perceptual illusions), sensory experience cannot be trusted to give us reliable knowledge. The rigor, precision, and certainty of mathematics, a purely deductive discipline, remains the rationalists' prime example in support of the power of reason. When they had to explain the origin of this power, rationalists ended up by saying that certain knowledge or concepts are innate and that they unfold as a function of maturation.

Piaget saw elements of truth and untruth in both camps. As a scientist trained in biology, he was convinced that the only way to answer epistemological questions was to study them scientifically rather than by speculation. With this conviction, he decided that a good way to study the nature of empirical knowledge and reason in man was to study the development of knowledge in children. His study of children was thus a means to answer epistemological questions scientifically.

While Piaget saw the importance of both sensory information and reason, his sympathy lay on the rationalist side of the fence. His sixty years of research with children was motivated by a desire to prove the inadequacy of empiricism. The conservation of number task, which is discussed next, should be understood in light of this background.

THE CONSERVATION OF NUMBER TASK

Conservation of number is the ability to deduce (through reason) that the quantity of the collection remains the same, when the empirical appearance of the objects is changed. Let us review the method and findings for this task (Inhelder, Sinclair, and Bovet, 1974, pp. 275-277).[1]

---

1. From the description given, the interviews might appear rather standardized. Each interview must be adapted to the particular subject, especially with regard to the latter's understanding of the terms used in quantification.

I. Method
  A. Materials: 20 red counters, 20 blue counters.
  B. Procedure
      1. Equality: The experimenter lays out one row of about eight blue counters (at least seven)[2] and asks the child to put out the same number of red ones, saying, "Put out as many of your red counters as I've put blue ones . . . (exactly the same number, just as many, no more, no less)."

      The child's response is recorded in his protocol. If necessary, the experimenter then puts the red and blue counters in one-to-one correspondence and asks the child whether or not the two rows have the same amount.

      2. Conservation: The experimenter modifies the layout in front of the child's watchful eyes by spacing out the counters in one of the rows or by moving them together (as shown in Figure 1.1). The following questions are then asked: "Are there as many (the same number of) blue ones as red ones, or are there more here (blue) or more here (red)? How do you know?"

      3. Countersuggestion: If the child has given a correct conservation answer, the experimenter says, "Look how long this line is. Another child said there are more counters in it because this row is longer. Who is right, you or the other child?"

      If the child's answer was wrong, on the other hand, the experimenter reminds him of the initial equality: "But don't you remember, before, we put one red counter in front of each blue

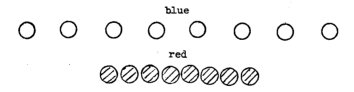

FIGURE 1.1   The arrangement of the objects when the child is asked if there are as many blue ones as red ones, or more blue ones, or more red ones.

___

2. Piaget referred to small numbers up to 4 or 5 as "perceptual numbers" because small numbers such as "oo" and "ooo" can easily be distinguished at a glance, perceptually. When seven objects are presented, however, it is impossible to distinguish "ooooooo" from "oooooooo," for example, by perception alone. Small numbers greater than 4 or 5 are called "elementary numbers."

one. Another child said that there is the same number of red and
blue ones now. Who do you think is right, you or the other child?"

II. Findings

    A. At level I, the child cannot make a set that has the same number.
Needless to say, therefore, he cannot conserve the equality of the
two sets either. Some of these children put out all the red counters
linearly as shown in Figure 1.2a. They stopped putting out counters
only because there were no more left to put out. Figure 1.2b shows a
more advanced response within level I. The children who do this do
not put out the same number of red ones as blue ones but carefully
use the spatial frontiers of the rows as the criterion for deciding the
"sameness" of the two quantities. (When they have not yet built the
beginning of the mental structure of number shown in Figure 1.4b,
children use the best criterion they can think of, which in this case is
the spatial frontiers of the two sets.)

    B. At level II, which is found at four to five years of age, the child can
make a set that has the same number but cannot conserve this
equality.[3] When he is asked the conservation question, he says, for

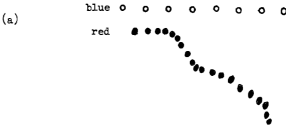

FIGURE 1.2.
Two attempts within level I to make a
set that has the same number.

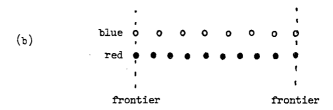

---

    3. The ages mentioned are approximate. These vary with the cultural and educational
settings of the subjects.

example, "There are more red ones because the blue ones are all squashed together."

C. Level III children are conservers. They give correct answers to all the questions, are not swayed by countersuggestions, and give one or more of the following arguments to explain why they think the two rows have the same quantity.
  1. "There are just as many blue ones as red ones because it was the same much before, and we haven't taken anything away, they've just been squashed up" (the *identity* argument).
  2. "We could put all the red ones back the way they were before, so there aren't more blue ones or red ones" (the *reversibility* argument).
  3. "Here the red ones are in a long row, but there's space in between the counters, so that makes it the same" (the *compensation* argument).
D. Conservation is not achieved overnight, and between levels II and III is an intermediate level. Intermediate level children give the correct answer to only one of the questions when one row is made longer and the other row is subsequently made longer, or they hesitate and/or keep changing their minds ("There are more blue ones . . . no, red ones . . . they're both the same. . . ."). Even when these children give correct answers, they cannot justify them adequately.

Why can't the child conserve at level II, and how does he become able to conserve later? To answer this question, it is necessary to discuss Piaget's theory of number in the context of the distinction he made among three kinds of knowledge: physical, logico-mathematical, and social (conventional) knowledge. He distinguished them according to their ultimate sources and modes of structuring. Number is an example of logico-mathematical knowledge, which I will discuss below, first in contrast with physical knowledge and then with social (conventional) knowledge.

LOGICO-MATHEMATICAL AND PHYSICAL KNOWLEDGE

Physical and logico-mathematical knowledge are the two major types, or poles, of knowledge distinguished by Piaget. Physical knowledge is knowledge of objects in external reality. The color and weight of a chip are examples of physical properties that are *in* objects in external reality, and can be known by observation. The knowledge that a chip will fall when we let go of it in the air is also an example of physical knowledge.

Logico-mathematical knowledge, on the other hand, consists of relationships constructed by each individual. For instance, when we are presented with a red chip and a blue one, and think that they are different, this difference is an example of the foundation of logico-mathematical knowledge. The chips are indeed observable, but the difference between them is not. The difference is a *relationship* created mentally by the individual who puts the two objects into this relationship. The difference is neither *in* the red chip nor *in* the blue one, and if a person did not put the objects into this relationship, the difference would not exist for him.

Other examples of relationships the individual can create between the chips are "similar," "the same in weight," and "two." It is just as correct to say that the red and blue chips are similar as it is to say that they are different. The relationship an individual puts the objects into is up to that individual. From one point of view the two chips are different, and from another point of view they are similar. If the individual wants to compare the weight of the two chips, he is likely to say that the objects are "the same" (in weight). If, on the other hand, he wants to view the objects numerically, he will say that there are "two." The two chips are observable, but the "twoness" is not. Number is a relationship created mentally by each individual.[4]

The child goes on to construct logico-mathematical knowledge by coordinating the simple relationships he created earlier between objects. For example, by coordinating the relationships of "same," "different," and "more," the child becomes able to deduce that there are more beads in the world than red beads and that there are more animals than cows. It is likewise by coordinating the relationship between "two" and "two" that he comes to deduce that $2 + 2 = 4$, and that $2 \times 2 = 4$.

Piaget recognized external and internal sources of knowledge. The source of physical knowledge (as well as social knowledge) is partly[5] external to the individual. The source of logico-mathematical knowledge, by contrast, is internal. This statement will be clarified by the following discussion of two kinds of abstraction through which the child constructs physical and logico-mathematical knowledge.

---

4. I hasten to say that 2 is not a good number to choose to illustrate the logico-mathematical nature of number because 2 is a perceptual number (see note 2). Yet 2 can also be a logico-mathematical number for an adult who has constructed the entire system of logico-mathematical numbers. I chose the number 2 in this example in spite of the problem of perceptual numbers because, with two counters, I can illustrate other simple relationships such as "different," "similar," and "the same in weight."

5. My reason for saying "partly" will become clear when I discuss empirical and reflective abstraction.

Construction by Empirical and Reflective Abstraction

Piaget's view about the logico-mathematical nature of number is in sharp contrast with math educators' view that is found in most texts. One typical text (Duncan, Capps, Dolciani, Quast, and Zweng, 1972) states, for example, that number is "a property of sets in the same way that ideas like color, size, and shape refer to properties of objects" (p. T30). Accordingly, children are presented with sets of four pencils, four flowers, four balloons, and five pencils, for example, and are asked to find the sets that have the same "number property."This exercise reflects the assumption that children learn number concepts by abstracting "number properties" from various sets in the same way that they abstract color and other physical properties from objects.

In Piaget's theory, the abstraction of color from objects is considered very different in nature from the abstraction of number. The two are so different, in fact, that they are distinguished by different terms. For the abstraction of properties from objects, Piaget used the term *empirical* (or *simple*) abstraction. For the abstraction of number, he used the term *reflective* abstraction (*abstraction réfléchissante*).

In empirical abstraction, all the child does is focus on a certain property of the object and ignore the others. For example, when he abstracts the color of an object, the child simply ignores the other properties such as weight and the material with which the object is made (plastic, wood, metal).

Reflective abstraction, in contrast, involves the construction of relationships between/among objects. Relationships, as stated earlier, do not have an existence in external reality. The similarity or difference between one chip and another does not exist *in* one chip or the other, nor anywhere else in external reality. This relationship exists only in the minds of those who can create it between the objects. The term *constructive* abstraction might be easier to understand than *reflective* abstraction to indicate that this abstraction is a veritable construction by the mind rather than a focus on something that already exists in objects.

Having made the theoretical distinction between empirical and reflective abstraction, Piaget went on to say that, in the psychological reality of the young child, one cannot take place without the other. For example, the child could not construct the relationship "different" if he could not observe different properties in objects. Similarly, the relationship "two" would be impossible to construct if the child thought that discrete objects behave like drops of water (which can combine to become one drop). Conversely, the child could not construct physical knowledge if he did not have a logico-mathematical framework that enabled him to put new observations into relationship with the knowledge he already has. To note that a certain fish is red, for example, the child needs a classificatory scheme to distinguish "red" from "all other colors." He also needs a classificatory scheme to distinguish "fish" from all the other kinds of objects he already knows. A logico-mathematical framework (constructed by reflective abstraction) is thus necessary for empirical abstraction because children could not "read" facts from external reality if each fact remained an isolated bit of knowledge, bearing no relationship to the knowledge already built in an organized fashion.

While reflective abstraction thus cannot take place independently of empirical abstraction during the sensory-motor and preoperational periods, it later becomes possible for reflective abstraction to take place independently. For example, once the child has constructed number (by reflective abstraction), he will become able to operate on numbers and do 5 + 5 and 5 × 2 (by reflective abstraction).

The distinction between the two kinds of abstraction may seem unimportant while the child is learning small numbers, say, up to 10. When he goes on to larger numbers such as 999 and 1,000, however, it becomes clear that it is impossible to learn every whole number all the way to infinity from sets of objects or pictures! Numbers are learned not by empirical abstraction from sets that are already made but by reflective abstraction as the child constructs relationships. Because these relationships are created by the mind, it is possible to understand numbers such as 1,000,002 even if we have never seen or counted 1,000,002 objects, in or out of a set.

The Construction of Number as the Synthesis of Order and Hierarchical Inclusion

Number according to Piaget is a synthesis of two kinds of relationships the child creates among objects (by reflective abstraction). One is order, and the other is hierarchical inclusion.

I will begin by clarifying what Piaget meant by order. All teachers of young children have seen the common tendency among children to count objects by skipping some and counting some more than once. When given eight objects, for example, a child who can recite "One, two, three, four . . ." correctly up to ten may end up claiming that there are ten things by "counting" as shown in Figure 1.3a. This tendency shows that the child does not feel the logical necessity of putting the objects in an order to make sure he does not skip any or count the same one more than once. The only way we can be sure of not overlooking any or counting the same object more than once is by putting them in an order. The child, however, does not have to put the objects literally in a spatial order to put them into an ordered

FIGURE 1.3.
Two ways of counting objects: (a) The
way many four-year-olds count. (b)
The mental ordering of the objects.

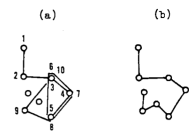

NOTE: Reprinted from C. Kamii, *Number in Preschool and Kindergarten* (Washington, D.C.:
National Association for the Education of Young Children, 1982).

relationship. What is important is that he order them mentally as shown in
Figure 1.3b.

If ordering were the only mental action on objects, the collection would
not be quantified, since the child could consider one object at a time rather
than a group of many at the same time. For example, after counting eight
objects arranged in an ordered relationship as shown in Figure 1.4a, the
child usually states that there are eight. If we then ask him to show us the
eight, he sometimes points to the last one (the eighth object). This behavior
indicates that, for this child, the words "one," "two," "three," and so on are
names for individual elements in the series, like "John," "Marie," "Suzy," . . .
"Peter." When asked how many there are, therefore, the child says what
amounts to "Peter." The name "Peter" stands for the last individual in the
series and not for the entire group. To quantify the collection of objects, the
child has to put them in a relationship of hierarchical inclusion. This
relationship, shown in Figure 1.4b, means that the child mentally includes
"one" in "two," "two" in "three," "three" in "four," and so on. When
presented with eight objects, he can quantify the collection numerically only
if he can put all the objects into a single relationship thus synthesizing[6] order[7]
and hierarchical inclusion.

---

6. A definition of synthesis is the reciprocal assimilation of two schemes—the scheme of
ordering, and that of hierarchically including 1 in 2, 2 in 3, and so on.

7. While it is necessary to order the objects to make sure that none is skipped or counted
more than once, the specific order becomes irrelevant once an object has been counted. Once it
has been counted, the object becomes included in the category of "those already counted," just
like any other object, and it does not matter whether the particular object was the third, fourth,
or fifth in the order.

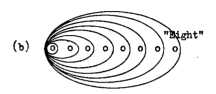

FIGURE 1.4.
The term "eight" used to refer (a)
only to the last element and (b) to the
entire group of objects.

Young children's reaction to the class-inclusion task[8] helps us understand
how difficult it is to construct the hierarchical structure. In the class-
inclusion task, the child is given several objects, for example, six miniature
dogs and two cats of the same size and is asked, "What do you see?" so that
the examiner can use words from the child's vocabulary. The child is then
asked to show "*all* the animals," "*all* the dogs," and "*all* the cats" with the
words that he used (e.g., "doggy"). Only after ascertaining the child's
understanding of these words does the adult ask the following class-inclusion
question: "Are there more dogs or more animals?"

Four-year-olds typically answer, "More dogs," whereupon the adult asks,
"Than what?" The four-year-old's answer is, "Than cats." In other words, the
question the examiner asks is "Are there more dogs or more animals?" but
what young children "hear" is "Are there more dogs or more cats?" Young
children hear a question that is different from the one the adult asked
because once they have mentally cut the whole (animals) into two parts (cats
and dogs), the only thing they can think about is the two parts. For them, at
that moment, the whole no longer exists. They can think about the whole,
but not when they are thinking about the parts. In order to compare the
whole with a part, the child has to do two opposite mental actions at the
same time—cut the whole into two parts and put the parts back together
into a whole. This, according to Piaget, is precisely what four-year-olds
cannot do.

---

8. The class-inclusion task aims at determining the child's ability to coordinate the quantitative and qualitative aspects of a class and a subclass. For example, the child who says that there
are more dogs than animals is not coordinating the quantitative and qualitative aspects of the
class (animals) and a subclass (dogs).

Class inclusion is similar to the hierarchical structure of number but different. Class inclusion
deals with qualities such as those that characterize dogs, cats, and animals. In number, on the
other hand, all qualities are irrelevant, as a dog and a cat are both considered as 1. Another
difference between number and class inclusion is that in number there is only one element at
each hierarchical level. In a class, there is usually more than one element.

By seven to eight years of age, most children's thought becomes mobile enough to be reversible. Reversibility refers to the ability to mentally do opposite actions simultaneously—in this case, to cut the whole into two parts and reunite the parts into a whole. In physical, material action, it is not possible to do two opposite things simultaneously. In our heads, however, this is possible when thought has become mobile enough to be reversible. It is only when the parts can be reunited in the mind that a child can "see" that there are more animals than dogs.

Piaget thus explained the attainment of the hierarchical structure of class inclusion by the increasing mobility of children's thought. This is why it is important for children to put all kinds of contents (objects, events, and actions) into all kinds of relationships. When children put all kinds of contents into relationships, their thought becomes more mobile, and one of the results of this mobility is the logico-mathematical structure of number shown in Figure 1.4b.

LOGICO-MATHEMATICAL AND SOCIAL KNOWLEDGE

Piaget's theory of number is also in contrast with the common assumption that number concepts can be taught by social transmission like social (conventional) knowledge, especially through teaching children how to count. Examples of social (conventional) knowledge are the fact that Christmas comes on December 25, that a tree is called "tree," that grown-ups sometimes greet each other by shaking hands, and that tables are not to stand on. The ultimate sources of social knowledge are conventions worked out by people. The main characteristic of social knowledge is that it is largely arbitrary in nature. The fact that some people celebrate Christmas while others do not is an example of the arbitrariness of social knowledge. There is no physical or logical reason for December 25 to be considered any different from any other day of the year. The fact that a tree is called "tree" is likewise completely arbitrary. In another language, the same object is called by another name, since there is no physical or logical relationship between an object and its name. It follows that, for the child's acquisition of social knowledge, input from people is indispensable.

The preceding statement does not imply that input from people is all that the child needs to acquire social knowledge. Like physical knowledge, social knowledge is knowledge of content and requires a logico-mathematical framework for its assimilation and organization. Just as the child needs a logico-mathematical framework to recognize a red fish as such (physical knowledge), he needs the same logico-mathematical framework to recognize a "bad word" as such (social knowledge). To recognize a bad word, the child needs to make dichotomies between "bad words" and "words that are OK" and between "words" and "everything else." The same logico-mathematical framework is used by the child to construct both physical and social knowledge.

People who believe that number concepts should be taught by social transmission fail to make the fundamental distinction between logico-mathematical and social knowledge. In logico-mathematical knowledge, the ultimate source of knowledge is the child himself, and nothing is arbitrary in this domain. For example, 2 + 3 gives 5 in all cultures, regardless of the base or notational system used. Different cultures have different notational systems, but the underlying numerical relationships among oo, ooo, and ooooo are the same everywhere. To cite another example of the universality and nonarbitrary nature of logico-mathematical knowledge, there are more edible objects than a specific kind of food in all cultures.

The words "one, two, three, four" are examples of social knowledge. Each language has a different set of words for counting. But the underlying idea of number belongs to logico-mathematical knowledge, which is universal.

Piaget's view is thus in contrast with the belief that there is a "world of numbers" into which each child must be socialized. To be sure, there is consensus about the sum of 2 + 3, for example, but neither number nor addition is "out there" in the social world, to be transmitted from people. Children can be taught to give the correct answer to 2 + 3, but *they cannot be taught directly the relationships underlying this addition.* By the same token, even two-year-olds can see the difference between a pile of three blocks and one of ten blocks. But this does not imply that number is "out there" in the physical world, to be learned by empirical abstraction.

WHY CONSERVERS CONSERVE

Let us return to the question posed earlier: How do children become able to conserve number? The answer is that children become able to conserve when they have constructed in their heads the logico-mathematical structure of number shown in Figure 1.4b, at least to some extent. Those who have constructed this structure can impose it on the rows of different length. Those who have not can base their judgments only on perceptual features. To them, "going spatially beyond the frontier" means "more."

Because number is a mental structure that takes a long time to construct, we see the sequence of development presented earlier. At level I, the child cannot even make a set that has the same number. At level II, he becomes able to do this because he has begun to construct the logico-mathematical (mental) structure of number shown in Figure 1.4b. However, this emerging structure is not strong enough yet to enable him to conserve the numerical equality of the two sets. By level III, he has constructed a numerical structure that has become powerful enough to enable him to view the group of objects numerically, rather than spatially.

The real significance of this and other conservation tasks lies in the light they shed on epistemological issues. This task is one of the multitude that demonstrated the limitations of empiricism. Empirical knowledge must be interpreted and corrected by reason. The task also proved that number is something each human being constructs from within, and not something that is socially transmitted. No child was taught to conserve number before Piaget invented the conservation task.

Many interpreters of Piaget's theory erroneously assimilate conservation into empiricist assumptions. For example, Ginsburg and Opper (1979) describe the conservation of number as "the child's ability to recognize that the number property of a set remains invariant despite irrelevant changes such as the mere physical arrangement of the set" (p. 149). The expression "the child's ability to recognize that" implies that there is something "out there" to be recognized. This is an example of empiricist thinking about all knowledge as having its source in external reality. Furthermore, number is not a "property of a set" which "remains invariant" in the external world by itself. Number is an idea, and if the number remains invariant, this invariance takes place in the child's head. Moreover, while the spatial arrangement of the set is irrelevant to adults, it is highly relevant to young children who have not constructed the mental structure of number.

In another passage, Ginsburg and Opper state: "If number is seen to change whenever mere physical arrangement is altered, then the child fails to appreciate certain basic constancies or invariants in the environment" (p. 140). Nonconservers do not think that number changes. Because they have not yet constructed number in their heads, they simply cannot think about it. All they can think of is quantity, which they judge on the basis of space. Conservation is not an "appreciation" of "certain basic constancies or invariants *in the environment*" (italics are mine). Furthermore, nonconservers do not think number changes "*whenever* mere physical arrangement is altered" (italics are mine). Some arrangements do not elicit nonconserving responses as readily as others. For example, the arrangement shown in Figure 1.5 does not elicit nonconserving responses as the two rows in Figure 1.1.

It is very difficult for educators to accept the idea that number is constructed by each child on his own, without any instruction. Therefore, I would like to describe a rather different study that shows children's construction of number at an even earlier age than revealed by the conservation task. While the two tasks are different, they both demonstrate that numerical

FIGURE 1.5. An arrangement that does not involve the direct comparison of frontiers.

reasoning has its roots in a more general ability—the ability to reason logically.

THE TASK INVOLVING THE DROPPING OF BEADS

Inhelder and Piaget (1963) gave young children two glasses of different shapes. One glass was wide and short, while the other one was thin and tall. The researchers then asked each child to put a bead into one glass with one hand and, simultaneously, another bead into the other glass with the other hand. After the child repeatedly dropped beads into the glasses with one-to-one correspondence, the adult asked whether the two glasses had the same number of beads. As long as the levels looked about the same, the children replied that the two glasses had the same number. There came a point, however, when the levels became too different for some children to think that the two glasses had the same number. Some, on the other hand, were sure that the number was the same. Some children who could not answer the conservation question could answer correctly the ones about the number of beads. This task was given with many variations such as the two that follow:

1. Putting one (or more) bead(s) into one of the glasses before dropping the others with one-to-one correspondence, that is,

$$1+1+1+1+1+1+1+1+1+1+1+1+1+1+1+1+1+1+1+1$$
$$1+1+1+1+1+1+1+1+1+1+1+1+1+1+1+1+1+1+1+1$$

2. Putting the extra one(s) in the middle by asking the child to wait and
   watch the adult drop the extra one(s) as shown here:

Child $1+1+1+1+1+1+1+1+1+1$ $+1+1+1+1+1+1+1+1+1$
Adult $1+1+1+1+1+1+1+1+1+1+1+1+1+1+1+1+1+1+1+1$

It is extremely interesting to listen to children who base their judgments
on empirical knowledge. The two collections can look the same when an
extra bead is put only into one glass. Four-year-olds say, usually, that the
two glasses have "the same much" and when asked "How do you know?"
they reply, "Because I looked." Upon being asked to describe how the beads
were dropped, they can usually give all the empirical facts correctly ("Then
you told me to stop, and you put one in your glass. . . . Only you put an extra
one in your glass, and I watched 'cause you told me to wait. . . . Then we got
going again. I put one in my glass every time you put one in yours. . . ."
Empirical knowledge is thus one thing; ability to reason logically is quite
another.

The method and findings from the aforementioned task are outlined below
for those who wish to use it.

I. Method
   A. Materials
      1. Five glasses: two identical ones, a narrow one having the same
         height, an even narrower one having the same height, and a
         wider, shorter one.
      2 A large quantity of wooden beads.
      3. Two cardboard boxes big enough to hide each glass when placed
         upside down over it. A hole was made in the bottom of each box so
         that the child could drop beads into the glasses that were hidden
         by the boxes.
   B. Procedure
      1. The interviewer first ascertained that the child understood the
         words that would be used in the task, such as "the same amount
         ("the same number," or "the same much")," "more," and "less."
      2. The child was then asked to drop one bead into each of two visible
         glasses, and the experimenter sometimes said "bing . . . bing . . .
         bing . . ." to insist on the simultaneity of the one-to-one corre-
         spondence. The following three sets of questions were asked as
         the child continued to drop beads, first into identical glasses, and
         then into two glasses differing in width.
         a. When the collections were large enough to make perceptual
            judgment impossible (i.e., when the collections were greater
            than five), the experimenter asked whether or not the two

glasses had the same amount (and, of course, asked "How do you know?").

b. After the addition of some more beads, the boxes were placed over the glasses to hide them, and the experimenter asked from time to time whether the two glasses had equal or unequal amounts.

c. The experimenter then asked if the amounts would be the same or different if the child continued to drop beads "all afternoon" or "for a long, long time."

II. Findings

A. Table 1.1 gives the ages at which three levels were found. At level I, the child thought the two glasses had the same amount as long as the glasses were identical. As soon as the narrow glass was introduced, however, these children said that the narrow one contained more because its level was higher. When the glasses were hidden under the boxes, they typically said, "When we can't see the beads any more, we can't know whether there's the same amount in the glasses." As for the question about the result of continuing for a long time, they either said that they could not know or gave the correct answer by perseveration, without being able to justify what they said.

B. Level II was an intermediary level characterized by oscillation and hesitation.

C. At level III, all the questions were answered correctly with certitude and logical explanations. One five-year-old (5;9, or five years and nine months) even said, "Once we know, we know for forever (that the two glasses will have the same amount)!"

TABLE 1.1. The Relationship Between Ages and Levels in the Task of Dropping Beads

Age (N = 66)	Level		
	I	II	III
5	5%	35%	60%
6	0	7	93
7	0	9	91

This task clearly demonstrates that number develops out of the child's natural logic. The level I child reveals the absence of ability to deduce the answer logically when he says that he cannot know the answers when he cannot see the beads. This kind of statement about the necessity of empirical observation is made both when the glasses are hidden and before the collections are made. The level I child does not know the answers and thinks, furthermore, that the answers are not knowable. To the level III child who has developed his ability to reason logically with one-to-one correspondence, however, the answers are obvious.

This task convincingly shows that number is not constructed by empirical abstraction from sets. It also shows that the description or explanation often given of conservation is wrong. To some people, as stated earlier, conservation is the "ability to recognize that the number property of a set remains invariant despite irrelevant changes such as the mere physical arrangement of the set" (Ginsburg and Opper, 1979, p. 149). This statement may give the impression of "explaining" conservation, but it does not explain the achievement of level III in the other task. The logico-mathematical structure shown in Figure 1.4b accounts for both achievements. If a child has this hierarchical mental structure of number, he can use it in a variety of different situations such as the two tasks already discussed. A child who has not constructed this mental structure can rely only on empirical information—on the frontier of the line of objects in the conservation task, and on the apparent quantity of beads in the second task.

The two tasks presented above show that number concepts grow out of the child's natural ability to think. They also show that addition exists in the very construction of number, since the child builds number by repetitive addition of 1.

THE TASK INVOLVING DIFFERENCES OF 1

I would like to discuss two more tasks indicating that addition in arithmetical inferences and set partitioning, too, grows out of the child's natural ability to think. We will see in the following task that if the child makes a series of stacks (stacks A through G in Figure 1.6) with 1 more chip in each succeeding stack, he can infer at age six that to make L equal to N, he has to add 2 to L (Gréco, 1960).

I. Method
   A. Material: Thin chips or Formica rectangular plaques that can be stacked as shown in Figure 1.6.

FIGURE 1.6.   The stacks used to explore children's thinking about differences of 1.

B. Procedure
1. The making of stacks: The child was asked to make a series of stacks by putting one (chip or plaque) out, then two to the right, then three, four, five . . . and to continue up to seven or eight as shown in Figure 1.6. While the child was making these "small stacks," the experimenter made the "big ones" without telling the child that L had eleven. The child was told only that each succeeding stack had one more than the preceding stack.
2. The recognition of the numerical order
   a. Verbalization: The child was asked how many were in A, B, C, . . . , F (or G). He was then asked to count the number in one of the "big stacks" chosen at random such as N. (Care was taken not to choose L at this point.) After the child counted fourteen in N, for example, he was asked how many he thought were in the next one (O) and to verify his guess if necessary.
   b. Equalization: Two adjacent stacks were picked up (A and B, for example, and then B and C, F and G, L and M, and P and Q), and the child was asked how many chips had to be added to the smaller stack to make it have the same number as the larger one.
3. Anticipation of differences of 2
   a. Anticipation without verification: The experimenter picked up A and C, saying, "Let's take this stack, and not the one that comes right after it but the one that comes afterwards." The child was then asked how many had to be added to A to make it have as many as C. Other couples such as the following were then selected for the same kind of question: E and G, L and N, and O and Q. No verification was allowed at this point, and the child was asked to explain his reasoning.
   b. Anticipation followed by verification: The experimenter announced the repetition of the same thing as before (A + $\square$ = C, E + $\square$ = G, L + $\square$ = N, and O + $\square$ = Q), with the additional request that the child verify his guesses this time,

and explain any discrepancy between his anticipation and observation.

4. Anticipation of differences greater than 2: Similar questions were asked about couples such as B and E, B and F, and L and O.

II. Findings: Table 1.2 shows the relationship between the five levels found and the ages of the children. Four of the five levels are described below. (At level 0, the children did not even understand the questions posed.)

A. At level I, the children considered the series of stacks as qualitatively increasing quantities with irregular differences between adjacent stacks. Some children thought the differences increased as the stacks became larger. Others believed that the differences decreased with increasing numbers. The following is an excerpt of one child's responses:

> NANO (5;7).[9] Each time he observed a difference of 2, he anticipated a difference of 3 for the following couple.[10] Surprised after observing a difference of 2 between D and F, he said, "It's funny. It's always 2." But he expected a difference of 3 between E and G because "this time there are more." He expected a difference of "4 or 5" between L and N, "maybe 6" between M and O, and "6, because there are a lot" between O and Q. (Gréco, 1960, p. 172)

Whether the differences increased or decreased, they were estimated with a global impression of the series, and the child based his reasoning more on the size of the individual collections than on the differences between them.

B. At level IIA, the child anticipated a difference of 2 between stacks of the "small series" (A to G), but not between terms of the "big series" (L to Q). In other words, he could reason on the differences between small stacks, but level-I thinking persisted when he went on to larger numbers.

---

9. Piaget gave part of the child's name and his age at the beginning of each protocol he cited. "NANO" is thus part of the child's name, and "5;7" means five years and seven months of age.

10. The anticipation of a difference of 2 after repeated observation of differences of 2 is an example of empirical generalization. Piaget (1978) made a distinction between *empirical* generalization and *reflective* generalization. In empirical generalization, the child merely generalizes from what he observed before. In reflective generalization, he generalizes on the basis of reasoning, or theoretical understanding. For example, once the child understands that the difference between D and F is 2 because there is a difference of 1 each between D and E and between E and F, he can apply this understanding to figure out how many he needs to add to F to make it have the same number as H. Children usually become able to make an empirical generalization before becoming able to make a reflective generalization. NANO here is not even able to generalize empirically from past experience.

TABLE 1.2.   The Relationship Between Ages and Levels in the Task with Differences of 2

Age	N	Level				
		0	I	IIA	IIB	III
4;6 – 5	10	4	6			
5 – 5;6	15	1	9	4	1	
5;6 – 6	15		4	4	7	
6 – 6;6	10		1	2	6	1
6;6 – 7	10			1	4	5
7 – 7;6	5			1		4
7;6 – 8;6	5				1	4
Totals:	70	5	20	12	19	14

C. At levels IIB and III, the child anticipated a difference of 2 between "big stacks" as well. The only difference between levels IIB and III was that the higher-level child could give a precise justification of his anticipation. The majority of kindergarten children were at level IIB as can be seen in Table 1.2.

Level IIA is instructive, as it shows the progressive structuring of number. The child gradually constructs this mental structure shown in Figure 1.4b. He may thus be able to reason on differences of 1 between small terms, but not between terms larger than seven or eight. On the basis of this and many other studies, Piaget (Gréco, Grize, Papert, and Piaget, 1960) concluded that the following four "slices" exist at ages six to seven: (1) numbers from 1 to 7 or 8; (2) those from 8 to 14 or 15; (3) those from 15 to 30 or 40; and (4) those above 30 or 40. The progressive structuring of number means that if a child can conserve number when eight objects are used, for example, he cannot necessarily be expected to conserve when fifteen, thirty, or more objects are used.

The differences between B and E, B and F, and L and O are still hard at age nine. Piagetian research thus shows that numerical reasoning is made possible by children's natural logic, and that numerical reasoning is sometimes easier than expected by common sense and sometimes much harder.[11]

A TASK IN WHICH THE WHOLE WAS DIVIDED INTO TWO PARTS

I would like to present one more task. It shows the additive composition of number and the fact that the child constructs set partitioning (e.g., 8 = 4 + 4, 3 + 5, 2 + 6, and 1 + 7), too, through his own ability to think. In this situation the child was told that a whole (8) would remain the same but that it would be divided differently on two successive days (Piaget and Szeminska, 1941).

I. Method: The child was told that he would have four pieces of candy for his morning snack and four for his afternoon snack. The experimenter went on to say that he (the child) was to have the same number on the next day, but since he was less hungry in the morning than in the afternoon, he would eat only one in the morning and all the others in the afternoon. Beans were placed in front of him as shown in Figure 1.7 to illustrate each statement. As can be seen in the top part of this figure, the set for the second day (IIa) was first arranged like the one for the first day (I), with two subsets of 4. While saying that the child would eat "only one in the morning and all the others in the afternoon," the experimenter moved 3 from one subset to the other (see IIb in Figure 1.7). The question then put to the child was whether he would have the same number of pieces on both days.

II. Findings

A. This task literally gave the answer to the child, as he was explicitly told that he would have the same number the next day! He was also shown the identical arrangement of 4 + 4 in IIa, before 3 were moved to the other subset. Yet, level I children said that the number was not the same on the two days! The first child below focused on the subset of 7, while the second child compared the subsets on the left-hand side (4 versus 1). The two wholes were right in front of the child, but he could think only of the parts at level I.

11. An example of how much harder numerical problems can be than expected by common sense is found in Christofides-Henriques and Maurice (1982). The authors asked children between the ages of six and twelve to divide chips into two piles so that one pile (A) would have 3 more than the other (B), and B would have 2 less than A. Ten-year-olds tried hard for a long time to obtain the desired result, and only some of them realized the impossibility of the task after many attempts.

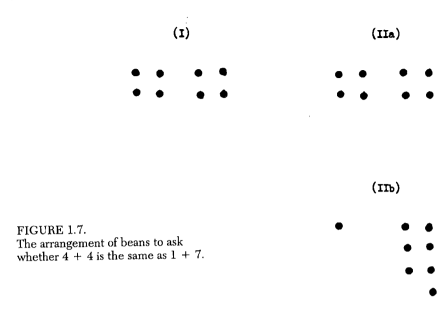

FIGURE 1.7.
The arrangement of beans to ask
whether 4 + 4 is the same as 1 + 7.

GIN (5;9): Is there the same amount to eat on both days, there (I) and
there (IIb)?—*No, there's more there (IIb).*—Why?—*There's a big lot (7),
and a little lot(1). There (I) there are 4 and 4.*—But are those (7) and that
(1) together the same as those (I)?—*No, because there are more there (7).*
        AN (6;11): Is there the same amount there (I) and there (IIb)?—*No.
There's 1 there (IIb) and there are 4 there (I).*—How many were there
before here (IIb)? (The two sets of 4 were arranged again, then, before the
child's eyes, 3 were taken from the first subset and added to the 4 of the
second.) Aren't they the same, these (IIb) and those (I)?—*No. Now there's
only 1 here (IIb) and there are 4 there (I).*—Could we make them into 4
and 4 again here (IIb)?—*Yes* (doing so).—Will you have the same amount
to eat on both days (4 + 4 and 4 + 4)?—*Yes.*—And now (changing again
to 7 + 1)?—*No, because there are less here* (IIb). (Piaget and Szeminska,
1941, p. 187)

B. At level II, the children compared the wholes and gave the correct
   answer, but based their judgment on empirical techniques. Instead
   of reasoning logically, they either made a one-to-one correspondence
   or counted the beans.
C. At level III, the children answered immediately with certitude that
   the number was, of course, the same. In discussing this task, Piaget
   particularly emphasized the part-whole relationship involved in
   addition.

COMMENTS AND CONCLUSIONS

Piaget and his collaborators at the International Center of Genetic Episte-mology have conducted a host of other studies on number, and most of them have not been translated into English. The research most relevant to arithmetic in the primary grades can be found in Volumes XI, XIII, and XVII of the Etudes d'Epistémologie Génétique, but many others have been published in scattered books and journals. To those who are not convinced that children construct logico-mathematical knowledge on their own, with-out any instruction, I recommend a recent book by Sinclair, Stambak, Lézine, Rayna, and Verba (1982). In a chapter entitled "Babies and Logic" the authors show in great detail how babies, long before the age of two, spontaneously put objects into logical relationships.

In conclusion, the most important points with respect to first grade arithmetic that can be made from the aforementioned research are as follows:

1. Number is not empirical in nature. The child constructs it through reflective abstraction from his own mental action of putting things into relationships.
2. Number concepts cannot be taught. While this may be bad news for educators, the good news is that number does not have to be taught, as the child constructs it from within, out of his own natural ability to think.
3. Addition does not have to be taught either. The very construction of number involves the repeated addition of "1."

This theory is fundamentally different from the empiricist assumptions on which the teaching of first grade arithmetic has been based. The theory also enables teachers to understand why certain children do not seem to "pick up" arithmetic, no matter how well and how many times something is explained. Educators are under the illusion that they are teaching arithmetic when all they are really teaching are the most superficial aspects such as specific sums (4 + 4 = 8, 4 + 5 = 9, . . .) and the conventional meaning of written signs (e.g., 4 and +). Arithmetic is not a body of knowledge that must be taught through social transmission. It must be constructed by each child through reflective abstraction. If the child cannot construct a relation-ship, then all the explanation in the world will not enable him to understand the teacher's statements.

In the next chapter, we will turn to the importance of social interaction for the development of logico-mathematical knowledge.

CHAPTER 2

The Importance
of Social Interaction

How do children develop their natural ability to think logically, to construct number, and to invent arithmetic? Part of the answer lies in social interaction, or more specifically in the mental activity that takes place in the context of social exchanges. In this chapter I first discuss the importance of social interaction for the development of logico-mathematical knowledge. In the second part I go on to specify two types of activities teachers can use in classrooms to stimulate the construction of logico-mathematical knowledge through the exchange of points of view.

THE IMPORTANCE OF SOCIAL INTERACTION FOR THE
CONSTRUCTION OF LOGICO-MATHEMATICAL KNOWLEDGE

Two Recent Sets of Studies

Piaget (1947) stated that social interaction is indispensable for the child to develop logic. Very young children are egocentric and feel no obligation to be coherent when they talk. The obligation not to contradict oneself, to reason logically, to make true statements, and to use words in commonly (culturally) understood ways grows out of social interaction. Piaget wrote, "The child first seeks to avoid contradicting himself when he is in the presence of others" (p. 163). The desire to "make sense" and to exchange points of view with other people undergirds the child's growing ability to think logically.

Two relatively recent studies demonstrated the importance of social interaction, and by extension the unimportance of direct instruction, for the construction of logico-mathematical knowledge. One was conducted by Perret-Clermont (1980), and the other was undertaken by Inhelder, Sinclair, and Bovet (1974).

PERRET-CLERMONT'S WORK

Perret-Clermont studied the effects of exchanges of ideas among children in small groups. In one of the experiments, she gave fruit juice in an opaque pitcher to a nonconserver and asked him to give exactly the same amount to drink to two other children. The two children receiving the juice were given glasses of different shapes, one (B) being wider and shorter than the other (A). A third glass (A'), which had the same dimensions as glass A, was then casually given as something to use if it was helpful. (Another glass, which was identical to A and A', was also available.) The children were told that they could drink their juice when they agreed that the two with different glasses (A and B) had exactly the same amount.

The children usually began by pouring the liquid into A and B. (No one used A and A' first, to transfer the content of A' into B afterwards.) The exchange of opinions continued for about 10 minutes, accompanied by many actions. For example, one child might pour some liquid from B back into the pitcher, asserting that B had more. Another might then insist on pouring some into B again to reestablish the same level. The third child might then suggest that the content of B should be emptied into A'.

Whether the group consisted only of nonconservers, or a nonconserver was in the majority or minority of the threesome, significantly more children in the experimental groups made progress on the posttest and/or the second posttest than did subjects in the control groups. (The second posttest was identical to the first one but was given about a month later. The only difference between the control and experimental groups was that the latter had had the 10-minute session just described.)

The pretest and posttests consisted not only of the conservation of liquid task by also of tasks involving the conservation of number, quantity of clay, and length. Among the significant findings of this study were the following:

1. More than 70 percent of those who made progress in the conservation of liquid task also made progress in conserving the quantity of clay. The benefit of social interaction can thus be inferred to extend beyond the specific content of liquid in containers. The clashes among children seemed to have stimulated their ability to coordinate other relationships as well.
2. The children who showed progress in the posttest were those that the pretest revealed were either conservers or intermediary cases in the conservation of number task. Social interaction thus facilitates the development of a higher level of logical thinking only when there already exist in children's heads the as yet uncoordinated elements that need to be coordinated in order to produce that higher level.

INHELDER, SINCLAIR, AND BOVET'S WORK

Cognitive conflict in conservation. Perret-Clermont built on the work of Piaget's close collaborators, Inhelder, Sinclair, and Bovet. Their learning experiments were conducted to better understand the constructive process involved in the child's advancing from one level to another, not to see if it was possible to accelerate development. They gave classical tasks such as the conservation of liquid and class inclusion tasks to individual children rather than to small groups. When a child reacted by putting various elements into inadequate relationships, the adult tried to create cognitive conflict between one point of view (one relationship) and another by raising a question and/or calling the child's attention to a relevant factor that was not taken into account. Their reason for trying to induce cognitive conflict in children was that conflict is a characteristic of an intermediary level before a higher-level coordination is made (what Piaget called "équilibration majorante," or "augmentative equilibrium"). The researchers thus neither taught "right" answers nor corrected "wrong" ones.

One task involved a situation created to produce cognitive conflict using the apparatus shown in Figure 2.1. Three pairs of cylindrical glass containers were held in place on a board. The top two pairs (A, A', B, and B') had faucets that the child could manipulate to let juice flow into the containers below. The pairs at the top and bottom (A, A', C, and C' with a diameter of 5 cm and a height of 7 cm) remained in place, but glass B' (which was identical to B) was sometimes replaced with a narrower glass E (with a diameter of 3 cm) or a wider one (having a diameter of 7 cm).

With the narrow container (E) in the middle as shown in Figure 2.1, the child was asked, among other things, to let all the liquid in A empty into B.

FIGURE 2.1.
The apparatus with which some children learned
to conserve the quantity of liquid.

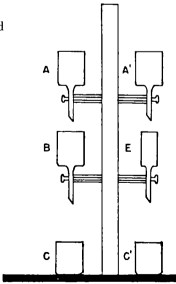

He was then asked to let the juice flow from A' to E, and make E have the same amount as B. Afterwards, he was asked if there would be the same amount to drink in C and C' if he emptied B and E into them. The child then checked his prediction against empirical fact.

Two types of behavior were seen in this situation. The child either made the level equal in B and E (thereby having some liquid left in A' and unequal amounts in C and C') or emptied all of A' into E (thereby getting unequal levels in B and E and the same amount in C and C'). Whatever the child did, he was never told that he was "right" nor was an "error" ever corrected. The adult only asked what the child thought, why C and C' turned out to have different levels, what could be done to make them have the same amount, and so on.

Of the 19 children who were at an intermediary level on the pretest, 16 made impressive progress, and 10 turned out to be solid conservers on the second posttest. However, of the 15 children who were nonconservers on the pretest, only 2 made some progress. These were the lowest-level children on the pretest, subjects who were sure, without any hesitation, that one of the glasses had more. Low-level children do not feel any conflict between thinking that two containers, A and A', have the same amount, and thinking that E has more, when A' is emptied into it (E). Hesitation and uncertainty are signs of conflict, that is, a higher level than when the child makes absolutely no connection between thinking that $A = A'$ and $E > B$.

Educators should make note of two points of this study:

1. Children do not need any direct teaching to make progress in the logico-mathematical realm. Being confronted with a conflicting idea often results in higher-level thinking.
2. The progress a child makes is a function of the level already attained. The children who show progress on the posttest are those who are already at a relatively high, intermediary level on the pretest.

Cognitive conflict in class inclusion. I would like to cite another example from Inhelder and others (1974) of a more purely logico-mathematical task, that is, class inclusion.[1] The experimenter gave a collection of plastic fruit to a doll, for example, two apples and four peaches. The child was then asked to give to another doll "more apples, because she likes apples very much, but

---

1. The conservation of liquid task involves physical as well as logico-mathematical knowledge because it requires logical reasoning about a physical content. The class inclusion task involves mostly logico-mathematical knowledge because it concerns relationships among objects, and the specific properties of the objects do not matter. What matters is the part-whole relationship between a class and a subclass.

the two dolls have to have the same number of fruit so they will both be happy." This task was designed to make the comparison of a subclass (apples or peaches) and a class (fruit) easier by asking the child to make a second collection in which the relative size of the subgroups was changed.[2]

The following five hierarchical levels were found in children's responses during the learning sessions:

Ia. The child gave a collection identical to the experimenter's, as if he had heard "Give the same thing to the other doll."
Ib. He responded to only one part of the request, that is, "Give more apples," and gave four apples and no peaches to the second doll.
II. He gave more apples but the same number of peaches to the second doll, four apples and four peaches.
III. He gave more apples and compensated qualitatively for this addition by giving four apples and three peaches.
IV. He gave six apples, thereby eliminating the problem of compensation. Six apples are indeed "more apples and the same number of fruit!"
V. He gave three, four, five, or six apples and compensated numerically for this addition by giving three, two, one, or zero peaches respectively.

People who conduct experiments in the United States usually pay attention only to the number of correct answers children give on the pretest and posttest. Inhelder and the other researchers in Geneva, by contrast, took great pains to analyze the constructive process of learning in each child during each session. As can be seen in the hierarchical levels, children constructed logico-mathematical knowledge by progressively coordinating relationships. At level I, the child thought either of "the same number of fruit" or of "more apples," and the two remained completely independent of each other. At level II, he considered both, but without compensating for "more apples" by reducing the number of peaches. At level III, compensation began to appear, but it was only intuitive and qualitative and not yet precise. Level IV was a very clever solution because the child simplified the problem by giving only apples to his doll. Finally at level V, he became able to compensate precisely for the addition of apples by reducing the number of peaches by the correct number.

This and a host of other studies show that each level of being "wrong" is a

---

2. Note that both in this task and the previous one, the child was asked to *do* something (rather than only to *say* something). This physical action is crucial—not because manipulation as such is important but because the child has to think actively when he has to produce a desired result. Children think hard when they have to decide *how* to produce a desired result, and it is this active thinking that is important in the construction of logico-mathematical knowledge.

necessary step toward the construction of the next level. Children's "wrong" ideas are not errors to be eliminated but relationships to be coordinated better at the next level. For example, level III is numerically wrong, but it is an enormous advance over level II, and a necessary step for the attainment of level V.

Inhelder and others clarified Piaget's theory of learning and demonstrated, once again, the inadequacy of empiricism. Children do not acquire logico-mathematical knowledge through transmission, association, or reinforcement as empiricists believe.

Pedagogical Implications of These Studies

In Inhelder, Sinclair, and Bovet's experiments, each child interacted individually with an adult. In these experiments, the authors proved that a Socratic question or the presentation of a conflicting viewpoint, without any direct teaching, was sufficient for a child to construct higher-level, logico-mathematical knowledge. Perret-Clermont built on this work by having children confront each other's differing ideas, without the intervention of an adult. She showed that this confrontation facilitated children's construction of more advanced ideas.

In arithmetic and more specifically in addition, children who arrive at different sums (for example, $8 + 5 = 12$ and $8 + 5 = 14$) might be asked to explain to one another how they arrived at their answers. The ensuing dialogue, encouraged by the teacher, would allow the children to think about the adequacy of one or another solution or way of arriving at a solution. Such an exchange would accomplish two things: It would encourage children to think, for the purpose of proving or defending their solutions to their peers, and it would prevent the development of the idea` that math is arbitrary, incomprehensible, and something to be memorized. For such an exchange to happen, teachers would have to seriously consider the question of how an atmosphere for children's thinking is created, as distinct from how a classroom is managed for specific learnings.

Insofar as peers and adults constitute the child's social environment and thus the objects of his social interaction, they influence his construction of logico-mathematical knowledge in very important ways. They fuel the child's mental activity by such indirect means as saying something that casts a doubt in *his* mind about the adequacy of an idea. They also do things that become *for him* an impetus for making a new relationship.

People, however, are not the source of feedback for logico-mathematical knowledge. That source is wholly internal to the child. It is the internal coherence of *his* system of thought that is the source of feedback in logico-mathematical knowledge. In the above situation with apples and peaches, for example, the child at level I, II, or III was often impervious to statements such as "I don't understand (how you gave more apples and the same number of fruit)," unless he was on the verge of making the next coordination. In a game of Twenty Questions,[3] likewise, if the object to be guessed is known not to be an animal, and a child asks "Is it a dog?" there is no way of convincing him that this question is silly, unless he is already at a level that is close to making the logical relationship among "animals," "objects other than animals," and "dogs."

As stated in Chapter 1, logico-mathematical knowledge develops through reflective abstraction, i.e., through the child's own coordination of relationships created by him. Thus, the child who thinks that there are more dogs than "animals" (i.e., cats), when presented with six dogs and two cats and asked if there are more dogs or more animals, does so because he is coordinating the relationships that *he* created among the objects. For him, at this time, there are only dogs and cats because the superordinate class "disappears" when he thinks about dogs. Later, when he becomes able to think simultaneously of wholes and of parts (of animals as well as of dogs and cats), he achieves these points of view by coordinating the relationships he made into a hierarchical one. He then becomes able to say with the force of logical necessity that there are more animals than dogs.

When Piaget argued about the importance of coordinating viewpoints, he was not talking about externally observable coordinations. The confrontation of points of view is important for the development of logico-mathematical knowledge because it puts the child in a social context that encourages him to think about other points of view in relationship to his own. In Perret-Clermont's study, the children knew that the glasses A and A' were the same. But it did not occur to them before an argument that the way to make A and B have the same amount was to pour liquid into A and A' first. By coordinating this relationship $(A = A')$ with $A' = B$, they deduced that $A = B$. This was a new relationship made by a child that was facilitated by the social context. The other children who were persuaded by this idea agreed not because the relationship was transmitted to them, but because *they* made a new relationship $(A = B)$ with the ones they had created before. The children who simply could not understand the explanation given to them were those that could not make these connections.

There is a world of difference between social transmission and the stimulation of thinking through the confrontation of viewpoints. Social

---

3. Twenty Questions is played in the following way: "It" thinks of something, and the other players try to guess what it is by asking questions. "It" answers with a "yes" or a "no." Since the guessers can ask no more than twenty questions, they do well to ask them in terms of categories, such as "Is it an animal?" If the answer is "No," young children often ask "Is it a dog?"

knowledge requires the transmission of information from people. Children could not possibly know on their own that "can" is spelled with "c" but "kangaroo" is spelled with a "k." Logico-mathematical knowledge, on the other hand, does not require such input from people. As we saw in Chapter 1, children construct number, addition, and class inclusion on their own, through reflective abstraction, without any social transmission. There is absolutely nothing arbitrary in logico-mathematical knowledge, and this is why the exchange of viewpoints without transmission of knowledge is sufficient for its construction.

Arithmetic is now taught through transmission, as if it were social knowledge. If a child writes 4 + 2 = 5 , for example, teachers usually mark this answer as being wrong. To the extent that this direct feedback from an external source in authority precludes all discussion among children, it is undesirable, for it crushes children's initiative and confidence in their own ability to think.

Next, we will focus on two kinds of situations that the teacher can create to stimulate mental activity (reflective abstraction) in children through social interaction.

TWO KINDS OF SITUATIONS IN THE CLASSROOM

Situations in daily living and group games provide opportunities for children to think. (Try to think of other possibilities.[4])

There are many instances in a day in the life of a classroom when voting might occur. In one case, when a class tried to decide whether to continue an activity or not, 13 children voted in favor of continuing it. One child immediately said, "We don't need to vote for the other choice." The teacher, Georgia DeClark, who consciously looked for this kind of numerical problem in daily living took the time to ask the child how he knew that it was unnecessary to vote for the other choice. He explained, "13 + 13 = 26, and we only have 24 kids today." Many children did not understand his reasoning, and the teacher asked if the class wanted to vote for the alternative. The children who did not understand were glad to avail themselves of this empirical method. Those who understood it lost no time in saying, "We told you 13 was the winner."

Teachers usually do not take the time to discuss this kind of remark because they are afraid of taking time away from the curriculum! But

---

4. This is a difference between a "method" of teaching and the use of a scientific theory in education. When a book does not give a method or recipe, its author expects other people to have their own ideas about how to use general principles in their practice.

children are emotionally involved and mentally active in situations such as these, and when they are involved and interested, they learn faster. The repetitive, mechanical exercises found in workbooks are less likely to provoke such mental activity.

Group games such as Double War can encourage children to think, to compare, and to debate. This game is played like War, except that the sum of two cards is compared with the sum of the opponent's two cards, and the person who has the greater total picks up all four cards. Cards from two decks with values up to 4 can be used at the beginning of the year ($4 \times 8 =$ 32 cards), and the deck can be enlarged later. The cards are dealt to two players, with two piles for each. The children turn the two top cards over and compare the two sums. The person who has more cards at the end wins.

These kinds of games offer advantages such as the following over workbooks:

- *They give the child his own reason for doing arithmetic.* A third grade teacher of an inner city public school once told me that her group of "slow" learners did not seem to remember from one day to the next the combinations that made a total of 7 ($6 + 1$, $5 + 2$, and $4 + 3$). I suggested the following card game called Sevens:[5] Values up to 6 are used, and the top three cards of the deck are turned up. Children take turns trying to pick up two cards that make a total of 7. If it is impossible to make this total (when a 3, 2, and 6 are turned up, for example), the next player starts a pile for a fourth card. As cards are picked up, they are replaced with those from the deck. The player who has more cards than anybody else at the end wins.

  To the teacher's surprise, some of the children came back the next day remembering all the combinations. These children were not willing to learn sums for the teacher, but they were willing to learn them to be able to play with their friends.

- *Feedback comes from peers and from oneself.* Many children and adults become convinced that math is particularly hard, incomprehensible, and mysterious. When I walk around first grade classrooms while children are working on workbooks, and stop to ask individual children how they got a particular answer, they typically react by reaching for the eraser and start erasing the answer, even if it is perfectly correct! This behavior shows that already in first grade these children have lost confidence in their own ability to figure things out. Children who lack confidence in their own ability to think will not develop that ability.

---

5. See Chapters 7 and 10 for other comments about this game.

In games, feedback comes from other children and oneself. For example, if a child in the above game of Sevens cannot see two cards that make a total of 7, the others have a chance to say something. In games, children check each other's thinking and learn that they *can* figure things out for themselves.

Children become mentally more active when there is the possibility of outdoing their opponents, or of being outdone by them. When worksheets are used, teachers often have to correct the same errors day after day. The reason is that this feedback is both distant and delayed. In games, by contrast, immediate feedback comes directly from their friends.

Games have other advantages over worksheets. Those will be presented in Chapter 7 after a discussion of the goals and objectives of first grade arithmetic in Chapters 3 to 6.

COMMENTS AND CONCLUSIONS

The social climate and the situation that the teacher creates are crucial to the development of logico-mathematical knowledge. Since logico-mathematical knowledge is constructed by the child, through reflective abstraction, it is important that the social environment encourage reflective abstraction. Piaget argued that every child of normal intelligence is able to learn arithmetic. Arithmetic is something children can reinvent and not something that has to be transmitted to them. If children can think, they cannot help but construct number, addition, and subtraction.If math is so difficult for so many children, it is generally because it is imposed too early, and without adequate awareness of how children think and learn. To quote Piaget:

> Every normal student is capable of good mathematical reasoning if attention is directed to activities of his interest, and if by this method the emotional inhibitions that too often give him a feeling of inferiority in lessons in this area are removed. In most mathematical lessons the whole difference lies in the fact that the student is asked to accept from outside an already entirely organized intellectual discipline which he may or may not understand, while in the context of autonomous activity he is called upon to discover[6] the relationships and the ideas by himself, and to re-create them until the time when he will be happy to be guided and taught. (1948, pp. 98-99)

---

6. Piaget should have used the term "invent" here instead of "discover." Refer to the Introduction for a discussion of his use of these terms.

While educators have come to recognize the undesirability of whole-class instruction, they have gone to the other extreme, still within the empiricist tradition, of individualizing instruction with programmed booklets, self-correcting materials, teaching machines, and computers used like workbooks.[7] Isolating children in order to pour knowledge systematically and efficiently into their heads is undesirable. In the logico-mathematical realm, the confrontation of points of view serves to enhance children's ability to reason at increasingly higher levels. Peer interaction should, therefore, be maximized.

In school, children are seldom asked what they honestly think. They are not encouraged to have opinions of their own and to defend their points of view. If a child thinks that $8 + 5 = 12$, he should be encouraged to defend his idea until *he* decides that another solution is better. It is important to encourage children to have their own opinions and to let *them* decide when another idea is better. Wrong ideas have to be modified by the child. They cannot be eliminated by the teacher. Besides, the nature of logico-mathematical knowledge is such that every teacher can be certain that children will arrive at correct answers, if they argue long enough among themselves.

This is not to say that children do not learn from workbooks and transmission. They do, and they usually acquire the truth faster by being told than by constructing it themselves. But we must think about learning in a larger context than the memorization of sums and the ability to produce high test scores. In other words, we need to see autonomy as the ultimate aim of education and that is what we will turn to in the next chapter.

---

7. Inhelder, Sinclair, and Bovet (1974) avoided the programmed approach that aims at eliciting correct answers. Here is what they said about programmed learning: It "runs counter to the idea that for true learning to occur the child must be intellectually active" (p. 26).

Part II:

OBJECTIVES

CHAPTER 3

Autonomy:
The Aim of Education
for Piaget

If teachers' primary concerns are to have orderly, quiet classrooms, they will react to disputes that involve two children in certain ways. If, on the other hand, their main concerns are to produce autonomous citizens who can think for themselves in all kinds of situations, they will react to the same dispute differently. The handling of disputes is usually not discussed in a book on arithmetic. But the ways in which conflicts among children are resolved, from the standpoint of what the teacher allows as well as what the children can manage, make an enormous difference to the way children can learn arithmetic.

Let me share an incident. I tried to introduce card games such as War and Concentration (described in Chapter 7) in a first grade classroom in Chicago. The teacher of this class assumed that it was her responsibility to control, direct, organize, and police her pupils. She dutifully divided the class into small groups to play the games. But the groups quickly dissolved as fights broke out among the children, and what was to have been a rich activity degenerated into screaming, shouting children and torn cards. I concluded that the kind of teaching I advocated was not possible unless the teacher understood the importance of autonomy as the broad aim of education.

The socio-affective and intellectual climate of a classroom heavily influences the way children learn or do not learn any academic content. Some teachers create such an authoritarian, coercive climate that I marvel at children's willingness even to go to school. Many others create a climate that is conducive to learning. But even this general atmosphere can be improved upon when the teacher has understood autonomy.

The most important but neglected question in education is how objectives are conceptualized. For Piaget (1948, Chapter 4), the long-range goal of education was autonomy. This stands in sharp contrast to educators' preoccupation with means, such as how to teach the three R's. We must ask if our objectives are justifiable in light of the scientific evidence about how children learn. Controversies about methods cannot be resolved without a clear conceptualization of objectives. For example, programmed learning may look scientific and produce higher test scores, but we must ask ourselves how adequate its scientific foundation is and what test scores mean in light of our broad goals.

In this chapter, I will first clarify what Piaget meant by *autonomy* and then discuss autonomy as the aim of education. In subsequent chapters I will discuss more specific objectives usually found in first grade arithmetic, such as addition, subtraction, and place value.

WHAT IS AUTONOMY?

Autonomy means being governed by oneself. It is the opposite of heteronomy, which means being governed by someone else. Autonomy has a moral aspect and an intellectual one. Let us first consider its moral aspect.

Moral Autonomy

Moral autonomy refers to the ability to make moral judgments and decisions for oneself, independently of the reward system, by taking into account the points of view of the other people concerned. In his research Piaget (1932) asked children between the ages of six and fourteen whether it was worse to tell a lie to an adult or to another child. Young, heteronomous children consistently replied that it was worse to tell a lie to an adult. When asked why, they explained that adults can tell when a statement is not true. Older children, in contrast, tended to answer that sometimes one almost has to lie to adults, but it is rotten to do it to other children. This is an example of moral autonomy. For autonomous people, lies are bad independently of the reward system, adult authority, and the possibility of being caught.

Piaget made up many pairs of stories and asked which one of two children was the worse. The following is an example of such a pair:

> A little boy (or a little girl) goes for a walk in the street and meets a big dog who frightens him very much. So then he goes home and tells his mother he has seen a dog that was as big as a cow.

> A child comes home from school and tells his mother that the teacher had given him good marks, but it was not true; the teacher had given him no marks at all, either good or bad. Then his mother was very pleased and rewarded him. (Piaget, 1932, p. 148)

Young children systematically manifested the morality of heteronomy by saying that it was worse to say, "I saw a dog as big as a cow." Why was it worse? Because dogs are never as big as cows and adults do not believe such stories. Older, more autonomous children, on the other hand, tended to say that it was worse to say, "The teacher gave me good marks," *because* this lie is more believable.

Figure 3.1 shows the developmental relationship between autonomy and heteronomy. In this figure, time is represented along the horizontal axis from birth to adulthood. The vertical axis represents the proportion of autonomy in relation to heteronomy, from 0 percent to 100 percent autonomy. The dotted line shows the ideal development of an individual. All babies are born dependent and heteronomous. Ideally, the child becomes increasingly more autonomous, and correspondingly less heteronomous, as he grows older. In other words, to the extent that the child becomes able to govern himself, he is governed less by other people.

In reality, most adults do not develop in this ideal way. The great majority stop developing at a low level (the solid line in Figure 3.1). Piaget (1948) noted that it is a rare adult who has developed the morality of autonomy. This observation can easily be confirmed in our daily life. Newspapers are full of stories about corruption in government and about theft, assault, and murder.

What makes some adults morally autonomous?   The important question for educators and parents is what causes some children to become morally autonomous adults. Piaget's answer to this question was that adults reinforce

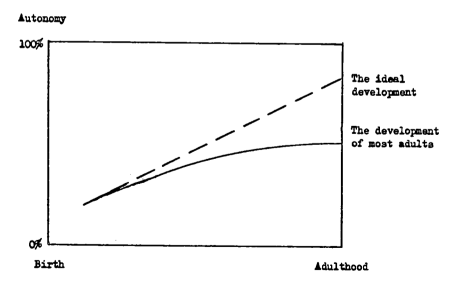

FIGURE 3.1.   Developmental relationship between heteronomy and autonomy.

children's natural heteronomy when they use reward and punishment, and they stimulate the development of autonomy when they exchange points of view with children.

When a child tells a lie, for example, the adult might deprive him of dessert or make him write fifty times, "I will not lie." The adult can also refrain from punishing the child and instead look him straight in the eye with great skepticism and affection and say, "I really can't believe what you are saying because. . . ." Such a response invites the child to think and encourages the exchange of points of view that contributes to the development of his autonomy. The child who can see that the adult cannot believe him can be motivated to think about what he must do to be believed. The child who is raised with many similar opportunities can, over time, construct for himself the conviction that it is best in the long run for people to deal honestly and truthfully with each other.

Punishment leads to three possible outcomes. The most common one is calculation of risks. The child who is punished will repeat the same act but try to avoid being caught the next time. Adults can be overheard saying, "Don't let me catch you doing that again!" Sometimes, the child stoically decides in advance that even if he is caught in a forbidden act, the price will be worth paying for the pleasure he will have. The second possibility is blind conformity. Some compliant children become perfect conformists because conformity assures them of security and respectability. When they become complete conformists, children do not have to make decisions any more, as all they have to do is obey. The third possible outcome is revolt. Some children are perfectly "good angels" for years but decide at a certain point that they are tired of pleasing their parents and teachers, and that the time has come for them to begin living for themselves. They may even engage in various behaviors that characterize delinquency. These behaviors may look and feel like autonomous acts, but there is a vast difference between autonomy and revolt. Revolt is generally rooted in anger directed at repression, real or imagined. Autonomy has roots that are quite different.

Punishment reinforces children's heteronomy and prevents them from developing autonomy. While rewards are more pleasant than punishments, they, too, reinforce children's heteronomy. Children who help parents only to get money, and those who study only to get good marks are governed by others, just like children who are "good" only to avoid being punished. Adults exercise power over children by using rewards and punishments, and it is these sanctions that keep them obedient and heteronomous.

If we want children to develop the morality of autonomy, we must reduce our adult power by refraining from using rewards and punishments, and encourage them to construct for themselves their own moral values. For example, the child has the possibility of thinking about the importance of honesty only if he is not punished for telling lies and is, instead, confronted with the fact that other people cannot believe or trust him.

The essence of autonomy is that children become able to make decisions for themselves. Autonomy is not the same thing as complete freedom. Autonomy means being able to take relevant factors into account in deciding what the best course of action might be. There can be no morality when one considers only one's own point of view. If one takes other people's points of view into account, one is not free to tell lies, break promises, or be inconsiderate.

Punishment versus sanctions by reciprocity. Piaget was realistic enough to say that in the reality of life, it is impossible to avoid punishment altogether. Streets are full of cars, and we obviously cannot allow children to touch stereo sets and electric outlets. Piaget, however, made an important distinction between punishment and sanctions by reciprocity. Depriving a child of dessert because he told a lie is an example of punishment, as the relationship between a lie and dessert is completely arbitrary. Telling him that we cannot believe what he said is an example of sanction by reciprocity. Sanctions by reciprocity are directly related to the act we want to stop and to the adult's point of view, and they have the effect of motivating the child to construct rules of conduct for himself by coordinating viewpoints.

Piaget gave six examples of sanctions by reciprocity. I would like to relate four of the six examples:

1. *Exclusion from the group.* When a group is listening to a story and a child disrupts the group, the teacher often says, "You can either stay here without bothering the rest of us, or I must ask you to go to the book corner and read by yourself." Whenever possible, the child must be given the possibility of deciding when he can behave well enough to return to the group. Mechanical time limits serve only as punishment, and children who have served the required time often feel perfectly free to commit the same misdeed again.
2. *Appeal to the direct and material consequence of the act.* I have already given an example of this type of sanction in connection with children's lies.
3. *Depriving the child of the thing he has misused.* Sometime ago, I was in a classroom of four- and five-year-olds for three days in succession. The room was rather small for a class of about twenty-five children, and a third of its floor space was set aside for block constructions which stayed up throughout my visit. I was surprised that the elaborate constructions stayed up for three days, and that children were extremely careful not to disturb anybody else's work when they went to the block area from time

to time to modify their products. When I asked the teacher how she got the children to be so careful, she explained that she was very strict at the beginning of the year and did not let children go in the block area if they knocked anything over. Later, she said, she negotiated with individual children the right to go in that area when they knew that this right had to be earned. The teacher's goal here was not just to produce a particular behavior, but to create the possibility for all the children to use blocks autonomously. The teacher wanted to create a situation in which the children could trust their classmates to respect their productions.

4. *Restitution.* For example, if a young child spills paint on the floor, an appropriate reaction may be to say, "Would you like me to help you clean it up?" Later in the year, it may be enough just to ask, "What do you have to do?"

  One day, in a kindergarten class, a child came up to the teacher crying because his art project had been damaged. The teacher turned to the class and said that she wanted the person who broke the object to stay with her during recess so that she could help him repair it. The child responsible for the breakage could see the point of view of the victim and was encouraged to construct for himself the rules of restitution and of being careful. When children are not afraid of being punished, they are perfectly willing to come forward and make restitution. The teacher helped the child repair the broken object and told him that next time something similar happened, she wanted him to tell her so that she could help him fix the object again.

Piaget pointed out that all the preceding sanctions by reciprocity can quickly degenerate into punishment if there is no relationship of mutual affection and respect between the adult and the child. Mutual respect is, in fact, essential for the child's development of autonomy. The child who feels respected for the way he thinks and feels is more likely to be respectful of the way other people think and feel.

Piaget's theory about how children learn moral values is fundamentally different from empiricist and common sense views. The common sense view is that the child acquires moral values by internalizing them from the environment. According to Piaget, children acquire moral values not by internalizing or absorbing them from the environment but by constructing them for themselves, through interaction with other people. For example, no child is taught that it is worse to tell a lie to an adult than to another child. Yet young children construct this belief out of what they have been told. Likewise, no child is taught that it is worse to say "I saw a dog as big as a cow" than to say "The teacher gave me good marks." But young children make such judgments by putting into relationships the things that they have been told. Fortunately, most of them go on to construct more complex relationships and end up believing it is worse to say "The teacher gave me good marks."

It is probably safe to say that most of us have had the experience of being punished. To the extent that we also had the possibility of coordinating viewpoints with others, we had the possibility of becoming more autonomous and independent of the clutches of the reward system.

I said at the beginning of this section that autonomy has both a moral and an intellectual aspect. Let us now turn to its intellectual aspect.

Intellectual Autonomy

As in the moral domain, intellectual autonomy also means being governed by oneself and making decisions for oneself. While moral autonomy involves questions of right or wrong, intellectual autonomy involves questions of true or false. Heteronomy in the intellectual realm means merely following somebody else's view. An extreme example of intellectual autonomy can be found in the story of Copernicus, to whom the heliocentric theory is attributed. Copernicus published his account of the heliocentric theory at a time when most others believed that the sun revolved around the earth. He was laughed at and scorned but was autonomous enough to remain convinced of the validity of his idea. Had he been an intellectually heteronomous person, he might have succumbed to the pressure of others' views. More generally, an intellectually heteronomous person unquestioningly believes what he is told, including illogical conclusions, slogans, and propaganda.

A more commonplace example of intellectual autonomy can be seen in the child who used to believe in Santa Claus. When the little girl was about six, she surprised her mother one day by asking, "How come Santa Claus uses the same wrapping paper as we do?" Her mother's "explanation" satisfied her for a few minutes, but she soon came up with the next question: "How come Santa Claus has the same handwriting as Daddy?" This child had her own thoughts, which were different from what she had been taught.

Children may accept adults' explanations for the moment. However, they continue to think about those explanations and construct relationships among those bits of knowledge and other things that they know. Thus the acquisition of knowledge cannot be described as the direct internalization of information from the environment. When the little girl in our example put Santa Claus into relationship with everything else she knew, she began to feel that something had seriously gone awry.

In school, children are too often discouraged from thinking autonomously. Let me illustrate what I mean. Elementary school teachers expend a good deal of effort making up worksheet exercises for children to do. From the child's point of view, math thus becomes "answering the teacher's questions for which he, the teacher, has the answers," since it is the adult who issues the questions and marks the answers as right or wrong. In first grade arithmetic, if a child writes $8 + 5 = \underline{12}$, most teachers will mark it as being wrong. Thus arithmetic becomes one more area in which truth and reason are confused with adult authority. Inferences about truth that should be made by the child come ready made, instead, from the teacher's head. Similarly, judgments about morality that should be arrived at through deliberation emanate, instead, from the teacher's authority.

Recall the observation (reported in Chapter 2) of children reaching for their erasers the moment they were asked how they had arrived at a particular answer. Typically, they began erasing like mad, even when their answers were perfectly correct. Even in first grade many children already have learned to distrust their own thinking. Children who are discouraged from thinking autonomously will construct less knowledge than those who are mentally active and confident.

If a child says that $8 + 5 = \underline{12}$, a better reaction would be to refrain from correcting him and encourage children who got different (correct as well as incorrect) answers to explain their thinking to one another. Alternatively, the teacher can ask the child, "How did you get 12?" Children often correct themselves as they try to explain their reasoning to someone else. The child who tries to explain his reasoning has to make sense to the other person. While thus trying to coordinate his point of view with another viewpoint, the child often realizes his own mistake.

Now that we have clarified what Piaget meant by moral and intellectual autonomy, we will turn to a view of autonomy as the aim of education.

AUTONOMY AS THE AIM OF EDUCATION

Figure 3.2 shows autonomy as the aim of education in relation to the goals of education as currently defined by most educators and the public. I will first discuss the part of each circle that does not overlap with the other and then proceed to the intersection of the two.

The shaded part of the circle to the right stands for the implicit and the explicit, intended and unintended heteronomous goals of education as it exists today. This education requires a great deal of memorization to pass one examination after another. All of us who succeeded in school achieved this distinction by memorizing an enormous number of "right" answers without understanding or caring about them. All of us remember the relief we felt at being free to forget the things we memorized for the purpose of

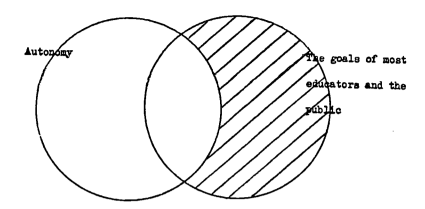

FIGURE 3.2.   The relationship between autonomy and the goals of most educators and the public.

passing a test. We made these efforts mostly because we were good, obedient achievers in a system that reinforced our heteronomy.

The result of this kind of education is what McKinnon and Renner (1971) and Schwebel (1975) found in their research on college freshmen's ability to think logically at the formal operational level. These college students were those who were successful enough in elementary and high school to enter the university. McKinnon and Renner reported that only 25 percent of their subjects were capable of solid logical thinking at the formal level. Schwebel's report of 20 percent is even worse.

McKinnon and Renner asked what kind of education these university students received in high school. They concluded that high schools do not teach students to think logically, and if high school teachers do not emphasize logical thinking, we must ask who trained these teachers. Their answer: the universities. In other words, schools underemphasize thinking from beginning to end. If university students cannot think logically at the formal operational level, they are limited in their ability to think critically and autonomously.

In both the intellectual and moral realms, today's schools regrettably reinforce children's heteronomy and unwittingly prevent them from developing autonomy. Schools use grades, gold stars, the detention hall, merits and demerits, and awards to enforce adults' rules and standards.

The part of the circle labeled "autonomy" that does not overlap with the other circle stands for intellectual and moral autonomy. The ability to think logically at the formal level belongs here.

The intersection of the two circles stands for goals of today's schools that unwittingly result in learnings that are useful for the development of autonomy. The ability to read and write, to do arithmetic, to use maps and charts, and to situate events in history are examples of such learnings from school. *If autonomy is the aim of education, attempts must be made to increase the area of overlap between the two circles.*

Let us return to the incident described at the beginning of this chapter concerning the impossibility of playing games in a first grade class in Chicago. Most adults handle disputes by separating children, telling them to stop fighting, or deciding how the underlying conflict should be resolved. These interventions make the problem disappear for the moment, but they do not help children become more autonomous in the long run. A teacher who has autonomy in mind as the broad aim figures out a way for the children to work out a mutually acceptable solution. For example, if the fight resulted from the fact that one child always insisted on dealing the cards, the teacher might say to all the children, "Can you think of a way that would be fair to everybody?" He will then allow ample time for the parties to agree on a rule. Children respect the rules *they* make for themselves.

A teacher who has autonomy in mind as the aim of education takes the time necessary to help children exchange points of view because, as can be seen in Figure 3.1, the more autonomous a child becomes, the more possibility he will have of becoming even more autonomous. Once children learn to negotiate solutions at age two, three, four, five, or six, they will always be able to use this ability and build on it. If they do not, they will continue to get into fights.

The teacher who protests that he does not have this kind of time because he has a curriculum to cover needs to reexamine his thinking. By not taking the time necessary to help children learn to negotiate solutions, he unwittingly perpetuates the occurrence of fights. Furthermore, children who can play games peacefully learn sums all by themselves, saving the teacher time in the long run.

An Example of Autonomy in a Classroom

The ability to respect other people's feelings and ideas is important not only in relation to conflicts but also with respect to learning cognitively. Taylor (1983) describes the following example of teaching an academic content in the context of autonomy as the broader aim. A teacher divided her second-grade class of 28 children into six small groups, each with a leader, and put the following problem on the board:

$$107$$
$$+117$$

She gave the groups several minutes to decide on a solution, and when the time was up, the representative of each group went to the board and put an answer on it.

Group I had decided that the problem could be solved by adding the 1's in the hundreds place, then the 0 and the 1 in the tens place (writing 2 and 1 in the respective columns), and since 7 + 7 was 14, they would write 14 in the ones place. Their answer was thus 2114.

The second group objected to this solution, saying that 14 was a two-digit number that could not be written in the ones place. They decided that only the 4 should be allowed there, giving a total of 214.

Group III disagreed and said that only the 1 in the 14 should be written because the 1 was more important than the 4, and that the answer was 211.

The fourth group decided that this must be a problem involving "carrying" and got 224 as the answer.

The other two groups had solutions that were already on the board. Individual pupils then offered well-reasoned arguments in favor of one answer or to show that one was inadequate. The inventor of the version under attack then defended it vigorously. The arguments thus continued with intensity until the end of the 45-minute period. By that time, the only thing the class could agree on was that it was impossible to have four different correct answers.

The children eventually constructed the "correct" algorithm. Many pupils offered wrong ideas along the way, but they were encouraged to defend their opinion until *they* were convinced that they were wrong. Children learn by *modifying* old ideas, according to constructivism, rather than simply by accumulating new bits of information. This procedure differs greatly from traditional instruction. In traditional instruction, children are assumed to learn by internalizing knowledge; therefore, teachers simply correct the errors and present right answers, believing that the learner will then absorb this wisdom. Many teachers know that this is not what happens, but they go on correcting the same error day after day. A debate about the superiority of one answer or another is good because it encourages children to think critically and honestly by putting different opinions into relationship. In such a debate, children modify old ideas when *they* are convinced that a new one is better.

The teacher in the preceding example taught an academic content in the context of trying to foster the development of moral and intellectual auton-omy. I say "moral autonomy" because children can develop it only if their ideas are taken seriously into account in making decisions. I say "intellectual autonomy" because children can develop it only when all ideas, including wrong ones, are respected. Furthermore, children mobilize their intelli-gence and the totality of their knowledge when they have to take a stand and confront other opinions. This kind of coordination of viewpoints is, therefore, far better than traditional methods that only aim at getting students to give "right" answers. Whether we teach grammar, math, physics, or history, we teach it very differently when our broader aim is the development of autonomous thinking.

AN AIM BASED ON A SCIENTIFIC THEORY—COMMENTS

Goals and objectives in education have traditionally been derived from people's values, from what Kohlberg and Mayer (1972) called the "bag of virtues" approach. Many people valued "life adjustment" a few decades ago, but the pendulum has now swung to the other extreme of "back to basics." Some people insist that curiosity and creativity are more important than knowing many facts, but others hold the opposite view.

Because hierarchies of values are influenced by personal taste and/or fashion, it is impossible to establish criteria for deciding which values are best. Although autonomy as the aim of education does not completely avoid the issue of values, it is powerful because it is derived from a scientific theory.

In Chapter 2, I referred to Inhelder, Sinclair, and Bovet (1974) and Perret-Clermont (1980), who empirically demonstrated that the coordination of points of view leads to the construction of higher-level, logico-mathematical knowledge. Piaget (1932) went further and hypothesized that the coordination of viewpoints leads to the *construction* of autonomy.

Constructivism is very different from the empiricist belief according to which knowledge and moral values must be given to the child from the outside. The constructivist view is that if children coordinate points of view, or relationships, they will develop their natural intelligence, and this development can tend only toward autonomy. The history of science amply supports constructivism. Science was not given to scientists from the outside. It was, and continues to be, created by scientists through the exchange of viewpoints among them. Science evolves only in one direc-tion—toward a higher level that integrates previous knowledge. This process of construction is in a way similar to the development of an embryo. Embryos develop in one direction—toward increasing differentiation and coordination.

Some critics may object that Piaget's theory is not the only scientific theory about how children learn and that equal consideration must be given to other theories such as behaviorism. For others (including myself), Piaget's theory has surpassed behaviorism not by eliminating it but by integrating it into a larger, more powerful whole. Piaget showed that physical and psychological reward and punishment explain heteronomy, but not autonomy. Piaget's theory can thus explain everything that behaviorism can, but the converse is not the case.

Behaviorism is still useful for teaching motor skills such as penmanship, typing, and swimming, and specific surface bits of knowledge such as the multiplication tables and vocabulary in a foreign language. While behaviorism is adequate for these kinds of specific, simple learnings, it is not adequate to explain the acquisition of more general, deeper, and powerful ideas, such as the logic of multiplication or the values undergirding people's defiance of particular reward systems.

Piaget wrote about autonomy half a century ago and explicitly advocated it as the aim of education in 1948. The approach to first grade arithmetic suggested in this book is not another "method" to reach the same, traditional goals of first grade arithmetic; instead it relies on a fundamental redefinition of goals and objectives based on a revolutionary scientific theory.

CHAPTER 4

Numerals and Place Value as Objectives

This and the following two chapters (on addition and subtraction) are devoted to a discussion of specific objectives generally found in first grade arithmetic. These objectives are usually based on adults' reasoning rather than on children's ways of thinking. Teachers need to be acquainted with what is cognitively possible in first grade and what is not. In this chapter I will argue that the reading and writing of numerals are appropriate objectives for first grade, but that place value is not.

THE READING AND WRITING OF NUMERALS

As stated in Chapter 1 number is constructed through reflective abstraction. Once the child has constructed the idea of eight through reflective abstraction, he can *represent* it either with symbols such as " ⌀ ⌀ ⌀ ⌀ ⌀ ⌀ ⌀ ⌀ " and "ooooooo," or with signs such as the spoken word "eight" and the graphic mark "8" (see Figure 4.1). A symbol in Piaget's theory is a signifier that bears a figurative resemblance to the thing represented and can be invented by the child. Symbols, therefore, do not need to be taught. A sign, by contrast, is a conventional signifier. Signs bear no similarity to the thing represented and are parts of systems devised to communicate some message to others. The word "eight" and the numeral "8" are signs, which require social transmission.

Math educators seem to believe that children progress from (a) the "concrete" level of objects to (b) the "semiconcrete" level of pictures and to (c) the "abstract" level of numerals. They seem to suggest that this is a sequence of learning in the sense that experience at each level facilitates the acquisition of the next. This belief is manifested by the pictures such as those in Figure 4.2 found at the beginning of most first grade arithmetic books. This sequence of objectives from the concrete to the semiconcrete and then to the abstract is based on a theory that fails to distinguish between "abstraction" and "representation."

While pictures of objects may be colorful and aesthetically pleasing to

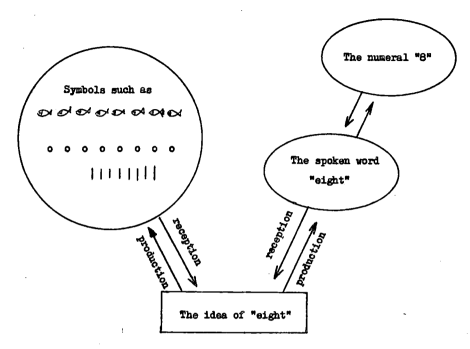

FIGURE 4.1.   Representing the idea of eight with symbols and signs.

children, they do not constitute "semiconcrete number" any more than the same quantity of objects constitute "concrete number." Number is an idea that, when constructed (see Chapter 1), is *imposed on the objects* by the child. Once the child has constructed the idea of "eight," he can produce a variety of symbols, including pictures, without any teaching. The child's production and reception of symbols is shown on the left-hand side of Figure 4.1 as a process different from his learning of conventional signs. Hence the pictures that can be found in first grade texts are unnecessary both for the construction of number concepts and for the learning of numerals.

Young children like to count and to read and write numerals. They generally do not have trouble acquiring this social, conventional knowledge in first grade. Therefore, these objectives are appropriate. Sinclair, Siegrist, and Sinclair (1982) found in Geneva, Switzerland, that even without formal instruction, most kindergarten children write numerals when asked to represent graphically up to eight identical objects such as pencils or toy cars.

As indicated in Figure 4.1 the numeral "8" is a graphic representation of the spoken word "eight." Children's learning of how to read and write 8 in no way depends upon the omnipresent pictures that fill the pages of workbooks and other teaching aids made for young children.

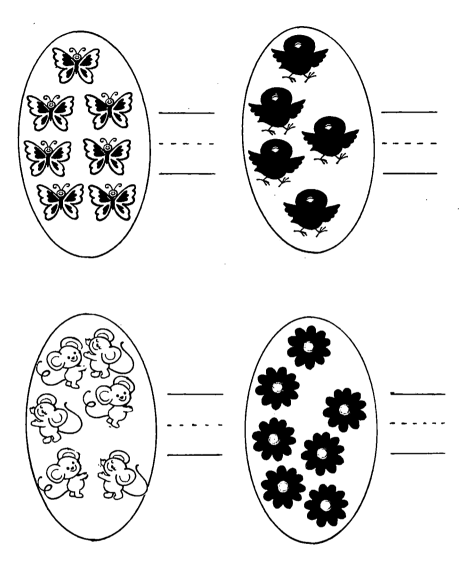

FIGURE 4.2. The use of pictures in a typical math workbook.

Numeration goes up to 99 in most first grade arithmetic texts. First graders enjoy saying and writing large numbers, and there is no reason to prevent them from going as far as they want to. First graders can generate written numbers essentially by repeating a cyclical order. Once they learn the order of the digits from 0 to 9, they can write a 1 in the tens column and repeat the same order until they reach 19. They can then write a 2 in the tens column and repeat the same order from 0 to 9 and so on. When they reach 9 in the tens column, all they have to do is start a third column and go through essentially the same procedure. My position here is that it is impossible for first graders to understand that the 2 in 26 means 20. However, it is very easy for them to recognize 26 as being smaller than 62. The reason is that first graders know with certainty which number comes afterwards in the spoken and written sequence.

An exception to these statements about the ease with which first graders learn to write numerals up to 100 is the production of signs for the "teens." Many first graders write 31 for thirteen. They make these errors because they build their system of writing based in part on their knowledge of how the number series is uttered. It is unfortunate that in English the counting (spoken) words from eleven through nineteen correspond so poorly with the Arabic written system. From the standpoint of the child who is learning phonics for reading and spelling for writing at the same time he is learning how to write numerals, it is confusing that the two systems (alphabetic writing and ideographic digits) follow such different rules for composition. After all, *both* can stand for spoken words, and *both* can be read. Just as children learn which verbs (such as "thought" instead of "thinked") and nouns (such as "feet" instead of "foots") are exceptions to general grammatical rules, they learn through social transmission that the counting words for the teens are not written as they sound.

PLACE VALUE

The undesirability of teaching place value in first grade was revealed in Mieko Kamii's (1980, 1981, 1982) research in the Boston area and my own in and around Chicago. I will begin with Mieko's description of one task.

> The child was shown a Tinkertoy car and was asked, "How many wheels does a car need?" Then a box containing twelve more identical wheels was opened and the wheels were dumped out in front of the child (thus making sixteen wheels altogether). The child was asked, "Can you figure out a way to tell how many cars we could outfit with all those wheels?" Note was taken of what the child did with the wheels (lining them up, or grouping them into sets of four, or counting them without touching them, etc.). Then the child was given a large (12″ × 18″) sheet of paper and drawing materials (markers and crayons) and was asked to make a drawing "so that if someone else came along and looked at your drawing, they could tell that we could make that many cars with all those wheels." After the wheels were drawn, the child was asked to write two numbers, "for how many wheels you drew in all," and "for how many cars we could make."
>
> Using a different color each time, I drew a series of circles around the

child's digits and numerals. The first was around the 6 and the second was around the 1 in 16. I asked after (drawing) each circle, "Do you think this part of your sixteen has anything to do with the amount of wheels that you've drawn here? Can you take this marker and show me in your drawing?" Then I drew a circle around the whole 16 and finally a circle around the 4, and I asked each time, "Do you think that that has anything to do with what you've drawn?" (M. Kamii, 1980, pp. 6–7)

This procedure may seem· unnecessarily complicated, but it was part of a larger study with children between four and nine years of age. Its purpose was to find out about the development of children's ability to make groups of objects and represent them with pictures and numerals, and to study the interaction between individually constructed and socially transmitted signifiers.

Only the findings concerning place value will be presented here (M. Kamii, 1982, pp. 145–148). As can be seen in Table 4.1, five levels were found, with most of the seven-year-olds at levels III and IV. Following is a description of each level:

- *Level I*. For children at this level, number squiggles are marks that are linked to objects in the real world on which they are found. For example, 6 can stand for Channel 6.
- *Level II*. Children at level II try to find some kind of correspondence between the squiggles they have written and something else on their paper that may be quantitative. For example, one child made a correspondence between the *colors* used in writing squiggles and drawing objects.

TABLE 4.1.   The Relationship Between Ages and Levels in Interpreting the Digits in 16

Level	Age					
	4 N=12	5 N=15	6 N=12	7 N=17	8 N=12	9 N=12
V				13%	18%	42%
IV			55%	56	82	50
III	25%	62%	36	31		8
II	42	31				
I	33	7				

- *Level III*. Number squiggles, and particularly single digit numerals, *can* stand for quantities of objects represented. But other ideas operate at the same time, resulting in confusion and inconsistency of responses. The notion that single and two digit numerals refer to specific amounts (cardinality) is one among several ideas that are not fully differentiated. Here are three examples:
  1. Two digit numerals cannot be "dissected" into their constituent digits. The number "disappears" when it is broken down into its written parts.
  2. The 6 in 16 means the sixth wheel, or the whole numeral 16 means the sixteenth wheel.
  3. The 6 in 16 refers to six wheels, but the 1 in 16 means one car (i.e., six of something and one of something else).
- *Level IV*. Whole two digit numerals *consistently* stand for the totality of the objects represented, but the individual digits are transformed into numerals in their own right and are treated in one of the following two ways:
  1. 6 in 16 signifies six objects, and 1 in 16 stands for one object. The fact that nine objects remain unaccounted for is of no concern to these children.
  2. 6 in 16 stands for sets of six, and 1 in 16 for sets of one object.
  In neither case does the child sense a necessary relation between the numerical parts (six objects and ten objects) and the numerical whole (sixteen objects) being represented.
- *Level V*. The individual digits making up a two digit numeral stand for amounts that are determined by the place or position in which the digits occur. The mechanisms leading to this understanding of place value consist of a synthesis of three gradually constructed ideas:
  1. Notational rule—1 in 16 stands for 10 because it is written in the 10's place.
  2. Numerical part-whole relationships—1 in 16 stands for 10 because 6 and 10 add up to 16.
  3. Multiplication—1 in 16 stands for 10 because $1 \times 10 = 10$.

The author concluded:

> The children's responses suggest that place value is too difficult for first graders, and extremely confusing for second and even third graders to understand. Grouping objects and dealing with large quantities is one problem, but coordinating grouped quantities with the numeration system is quite another. When the group sizes are small, many first graders and almost all second graders easily structure objects ($n = 16$ or 23) into groups (group sizes of four and five) and accurately represent their results

in symbolic form (drawings). They understand that a multi-digit numeral is made up of separate digits (written parts) and that the numeral as a whole represents the cardinal value of the whole. But they remain troubled with the suggestion that the *notational parts* have a specific relation to the *numerically quantified whole*. Third graders (eight-year-olds) often talk about ones and tens and hundreds, but only two out of twelve subjects in this age group marked the 1 in 16 as standing for ten of the drawn wheels. Of the nine-year-olds roughly half (five out of eleven children) indicated that the 1 in 16 indeed represents ten of the sixteen wheels. (M. Kamii, 1980, pp. 12–13)

The reason for the difficulty of place value can be understood by referring to a theory of number with a body of specific research findings accumulated over half a century. As stated in Chapter 1, six- and seven-year-olds are still in the process of constructing the number system (through reflective abstrac-. tion) with the operation of + 1. The base-10 written system requires the mental construction of 1 (1 collection of 10) out of 10 (units) and the coordination of the two-level hierarchical structure shown in Figure 4.3. It is impossible to construct the second level while the first one is still being built. As we saw in Chapter 1, the child cannot create the hierarchical structure of numerical inclusion before the age of seven or eight, when his thought becomes reversible.[1]

Furthermore, the base-10 system (or any other base system) involves multiplication. The 2 in 26 means 2×10. Multiplication is usually not introduced until the third grade. In first and second grade, children think additively and would write "10 + 10 + 10 . . ." if asked to represent groups of 10 in the way they honestly thought (Perret, Theurillat, Jeanneret, Lorimier and Schwaerzel, 1981). It is easy for first graders to make groups of ten objects empirically. But it is quite another thing to think multiplicatively of 26 as $2 \times 10 + 6$.

Even counting objects by 10's goes counter to the way most first graders think. I made systematic observations of pairs of children playing a guessing game in Georgia DeClark's class. They were to look at successive heaps of chips varying in number from 20 to 50 for a fraction of a second, and then write down how many they thought they had seen. The children's guesses were generally close, usually within ± 10 of the actual number. The chips

---

1. Class inclusion is different from number in that the hierarchical structure involves qualitative differences among objects, and there is usually more than one element in a class. For example, dogs, cats, and animals have qualitative differences, but in number, all the elements are the same. They are all "ones." In number, each level in the hierarchical structure contains only one element. In class inclusion, by contrast, a class usually contains more than one element, and a class of one is an exception.

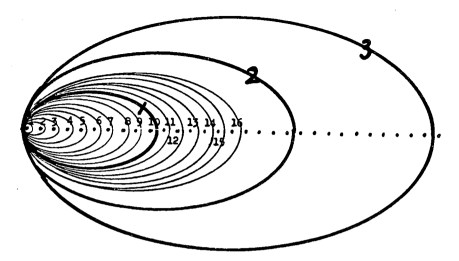

FIGURE 4.3. The two-level hierarchical structure necessary to understand each of two digits.

were then counted and the person who came closer to the correct number would win.

The pairs of children often found two different quantities by counting the same pile of chips. Taking advantage of this situation, I showed them "my idea" of making counting easier and more accurate by making groups of ten and counting by 10's. When I asked the children if they thought this was a good idea, almost all of them reacted with a blank or puzzled look! Before counting the chips again to find the correct number, many of them mixed up the groups of ten *thoroughly,* as if they felt the necessity of homogenizing the chips that had been rendered uncountable by being separated into small groups. Only the few advanced children were willing to count by 10's.

Drawing circles around groups of ten (or fewer) objects is easy for first graders. Counting the number of circles and saying "2 tens and 6 ones" is also easy for them. The decoding of any two digit number is likewise easily learned. First graders can draw the correct number of sticks when presented with "34," "43," and so forth. All these are "skills," or tricks, that are taught in almost all first grade arithmetic programs under the illusion that this is how children learn place value.

To begin with, place value is not a skill. In fact, arithmetic is not a collection of skills. Educators must be clear about what kind of learning a child is engaged in and how that learning occurs. Such knowledge is necessary for conceptualizing appropriate principles of teaching. Skills generally involve motoric performance and can be perfected through practice. Learning to write numerals, therefore, is partly a skill. Learning to add, subtract, and multiply, however, involves logico-mathematical thinking, and thinking is not a skill. Thinking does not develop and cannot be perfected through mere practice. "Tens and ones" can be taught only after the child's construction of ones. By the same token, the "hundreds" can be taught only after the construction of tens and ones. Mentally making a 1 out of a hundred and coordinating it hierarchically with the structure of tens and ones is an enormous task.

Finally, the difficulty of place value can be understood in light of the fact that our system of notation with 0 as a place-holding numeral was invented relatively late in history. Who was responsible for this elaboration of the Arabic notational system, or when this occurred, is a matter of speculation. It can only be said that this happened sometime after the sixth century but before the twelfth (M. Kamii, 1982). The history of systems of notation is beyond the scope of this chapter, and the reader is referred to Danzig (1967), M. Kamii (1982), and Smith and Karpinski (1911).

I became curious about what first graders might do in Chicago. Having observed many lessons on place value in one high-level first grade class in a Chicago public school (first graders in the school were tracked into high-, middle-, or low-level groups), I decided to give a simplified version of Mieko Kamii's task. The procedure was as follows:

1. I put sixteen chips out and asked the child to count them and to make a drawing of "all these." The children made drawings either in a line or in a bunch as shown in Figure 4.4a.
2. The child was asked to write "sixteen with numbers" on the same sheet, to show that there were sixteen chips.
3. The child was asked what "this part" meant, as I circled the 6 in 16 as shown in Figure 4.4a and asked him to indicate in the drawing what 6 meant (Figure 4.4b).
4. The child was asked what "this part" meant, as I circled the 1 in 16 as in Figure 4.4a and asked him to indicate it in the drawing (Figure 4.4c).
5. Finally, the child was asked what "the whole thing" meant as I circled 16 and probed into the relationships among 16, 1, and 6. For example, when a child circled the entire group of objects as shown in Figure 4.4d, I asked why "these" (the nine left-over chips) were not circled.

Table 4.2 gives a summary of the findings. Roughly half of the children (N = 13, or 45 percent) were found to be in what M. Kamii called "level IV," where they thought each digit represented units. While 2 of the 17 seven-year-olds in her sample understood place value, none of the Chicago first graders did.

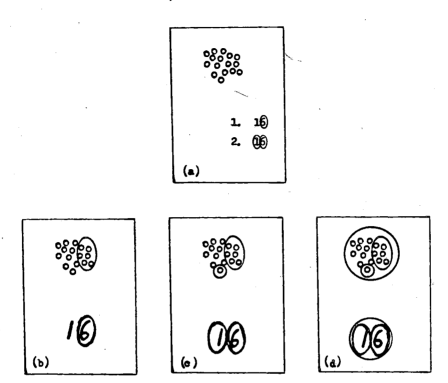

FIGURE 4.4.   Children's understanding of the 6 and the 1 in 16.

Table 4.2 shows children's pathetic efforts to make sense of the high-pressure teaching I had observed. Consider the second example of this table in which two children said that the numeral 6 stood for six chips, that the numeral 1 stood for one chip, and that "the whole [written] thing" (16) stood for the nine objects that had not been circled—a particularly poignant effort to account for all the objects drawn. Note that, in spite of all the hours spent making groups of ten objects and saying "2 tens and 3 ones," and so on, none of the children said that the 1 in 16 stood for 10. I became convinced that the lessons I had observed only taught tricks. As long as the children knew to pull tricks out of a certain drawer, they could think of tens and ones. When the lesson was over and I, a frequent visitor who came only at math time, tested the children without telling them which drawer to pull out, they went back to the way they honestly thought.

I talked about Mieko Kamii's research and mine in a class one day at the University of Illinois at Chicago. Georgia DeClark was in this class and politely but firmly reacted with the following: (1) I am not really convinced

TABLE 4.2.   What the Digits in 16 Meant to a Group of First Graders

	N Total=29	Percent
"16" does not stand for all the objects drawn.	7	24
Each digit represents <u>units</u>, and "16" stands for 6+1. ⊙ooooo⊙oooooooooo 6 1 16	1	
Each digit represents <u>units</u>, and "16" stands for the remaining 9. 6 1 16 (ooooo⊙oooooooooo)	2	
Each digit represents an ordinal position, and "16" stands for the 16th object. 1 6 16 (⊙ooo⊙oooooooooo⊙)	3	
Each digit represents a kind of ordinal position, and "16" means "1" connected to "6." 1 16 (⊙ooo / ooooo / ooooo⊙) 6	1	
"16" stands for all the objects drawn.		
Each digit represents <u>units</u>.	14	48
a. Mutually exclusive groups (M. Kamii's level IV) 6 1 (ooooo⊙oooooooooo) 16	13	
b. "1" is part of "6." 6 (⊙ooooooooooooooo) 16 1	1	
Each digit represents an ordinal position.	6	21
a. Starting from the same end 1 6 (⊙ooo⊙oooooooooo) 16	5	
b. Starting from opposite ends 6 1 (ooooo⊙oooooooooo⊙) 16		
Others (o o ⊙⊙o o o o o / o o ⊙⊙o o o) 16 1 5	2	7

by these findings, and (2) I have to teach place value anyway because it is part of the curriculum I am expected to cover.

This was an ideal situation for an experiment because the teacher believed that she could teach place value. I suggested to Georgia that she teach place value to her group of first graders in her traditional way, and then allow me to administer a posttest when she was sure the children had learned it. Georgia agreed and invited me to come and observe the lessons she gave.

I had observed many first graders engaged in similar lessons. Georgia's class was different in that her children seldom made errors during the lessons. They came up to the board, drew circles around ten objects, wrote the correct numbers for tens and ones, and correctly wrote and interpreted two digit numerals.

When Georgia was confident that the children had mastered place value, she invited me to give the posttest. I sat in a corner of the classroom and asked one child after another to come, so that Georgia could watch individual children if she wanted to. The number of children who said the 1 in 16 stood for ten chips was zero! The great majority were again found to be at what Mieko called "level IV."

I became curious about older children in the same school and in the junior high school they went to afterwards and decided to test students in grades 4, 6, and 8 as well. The proportion of children who circled ten chips to show what the 1 in 16 meant was 51 percent for grade 4 (N = 35), 60 percent for grade 6 (N = 48), and 78 percent for grade 8 (N = 41). These findings are remarkably similar to those from the Boston area. Note that this was in an affluent Chicago suburb, where an overwhelming proportion of the population is well educated, achievement oriented, and white. When I discussed the findings with two math teachers in the junior high school, they were not surprised. They said that some children never seem to get place value. I wondered what might have happened if these children had not been taught tricks such as "regrouping" prematurely.

It is my conviction that premature instruction, be it in place value or other aspects of the curriculum, is injurious to children's making sense of a discipline. Given what we know about the developmental course of children's thinking, we ought to ask ourselves whether it would not be wiser to delay place value instruction until children have solidly constructed the number series (by repetition of the + 1 operation) and can partition wholes in many different ways (part-whole relationships). The "we" includes curriculum developers, textbook writers, school administrators, and teachers, both in universities and in elementary schools.

CHAPTER 5

Addition
as an Objective

Addition is easy and natural for most first graders. In this chapter, addition is viewed as an appropriate objective for them, provided it focuses on children's mental action of adding rather than on the fact of producing written and/or correct answers. The first part of the chapter, "Addition Without Pencils," centers on the mental action of adding. In the second part, "Addition with Pencils," we see why this is an undesirable goal—although the ability to produce written answers is the objective of most math series used widely today, both in vertical form:

$$\begin{array}{r} 4 \\ +2 \\ \hline \end{array}$$

and in horizontal form:

$$4 + 2 = \underline{\hspace{1cm}}$$

We will also see why missing addends:

$$4 + \underline{\hspace{1cm}} = 6 \quad \text{and} \quad \underline{\hspace{1cm}} + 2 = 6$$

and the addition of two-digit numbers:

$$\begin{array}{r} 21 \\ +13 \\ \hline \end{array}$$

are premature in first grade. In the third part of the chapter, "Story Problems," I show that the solving of "word problems" should take place concurrently with the learning of sums rather than subsequently as applications of them.

ADDITION WITHOUT PENCILS

Although I agree with traditional math educators that it is good for children to know sums by heart, I do not agree that the objective in first grade should be that children know "addition facts." For me, the objective should be that children engage in the mental action of operating on numbers and remember the results of these actions. If they engage in this kind of action (2 + 5, for example), they will naturally produce the result of this action (7, for example), and if they repeatedly engage in this action, they will inevitably remember the result.

Another point of disagreement with empiricist math educators concerns the sequencing of objectives. Most first grade arithmetic programs aim at sums through 5 or 6 first, then through 9 or 10, and then through 12 and 18, in increasing magnitude. This sequence may make sense to adults, but it does not correspond to the actual order of acquisition according to research. Each of these points is elaborated below in this section.

Remembering the Relationships Made Through One's Own (Mental) Actions

There is a vast difference between the objective of remembering the relationships made through one's own (mental) actions and the goal of knowing "addition facts." When the knowing of "facts" is the objective, children are taught techniques to get "facts," and are drilled to internalize them. For example, I once wondered why first graders so often wrote 2 + 5 = 5. The reason, I found out, was that they put two blocks out for the first addend, then three more for the second addend (that is, five, including the first two), and counted the total! For these children, addition was not necessarily the joining of two distinct sets (see Figure 5.1a). They were dutifully executing a technique, or "skill," taught by their teacher but learned at their level. They were not engaged in the (mental) action of adding, and were merely exercising a skill that had been taught (prematurely) to get at "facts" empirically.

The objective in first grade should be that children add numbers by using their own logic. A child who adds numbers (such as 2 and 5) in his own way will obtain a result (usually 7). If he does not know what to do, he has no business working on addition. If he has the logic of addition and repeats the same action day after day in interaction with other people, he will inevitably remember the result, without any adult pressure. This objective flows out of Piaget's theory of number (discussed in Chapter 1), autonomy as the broad aim of education (discussed in Chapter 3), and his theory of memory (to be discussed shortly). The child who uses his own ability to think learns addition without being told how to do it and becomes confident in his own ability to figure things out. When he can thus reinvent arithmetic, there is nothing mysterious or hard about it. Traditional arithmetic, by contrast,

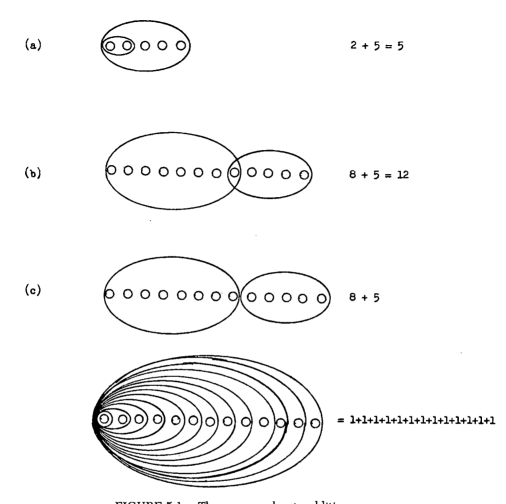

(a)   2 + 5 = 5

(b)   8 + 5 = 12

(c)   8 + 5

                                                                    = 1+1+1+1+1+1+1+1+1+1+1+1

FIGURE 5.1.   Three approaches to addition.

reinforces the child's natural heteronomy through a teacher who decides
what "facts" are to be learned, when, and how, and which answers are
correct.

   To know how to make decisions in the classroom, it is essential for the
teacher to understand that the objective for the child to remember the sums
he made is very different from the empiricist goal of knowing "addition
facts." To clarify this difference, I would like to show that there are no such
things as "addition facts," and that memory is not the simple "storage" and
"retrieval" of "facts."

There are no such things as "addition facts."   In Piaget's theory, there is
no such thing as an "addition fact." A fact is empirically observable.[1] Physical
and social knowledge involves facts but not logico-mathematical knowledge.
The fact that a ball bounces when it is dropped is observable (physical
knowledge). The fact that a ball is not appreciated in the living room is also
observable (social knowledge). But logico-mathematical knowledge consists
of relationships, which are not observable. Although four balls are observable, the "four-ness" is not. When we add 4 to 2, we are putting into an
additive relationship two numerical quantities that each of us constructed,
by reflective abstraction; $4 + 2$ *equals* 6 is a relationship, not a fact. A fact is
empirically verifiable, but a relationship is not.[2]

I make this point not to quibble about words but to insist on teachers'
understanding their own objectives in a precise way. Unless they differentiate relationships from facts, they cannot understand that "addition facts" are
wrong ends, and that feedback from adults is the wrong means to reach
illusory ends.

The difference between an observable fact and a relationship can be seen
clearly in the class-inclusion task discussed in Chapter 1. All the dogs, cats,
and animals are observable in this task, and four-year-olds can usually say,
successively, that there are four dogs, two cats, and six animals. What they
cannot do is to put the parts into a simultaneous relationship with the whole.
This is why they say that there are more dogs than "animals" (i.e., cats).
Observation of facts is one thing, and the logico-mathematization of what is
observable is quite another thing. Try explaining to a four-year-old who
cannot class-include that there are more animals than dogs. There is
occasionally an advanced child who is on the threshold of constructing the
hierarchical relationship, but most of them react with a puzzled, blank,
unconvinced look. The reason for the puzzled look is that in the logico-
mathematical realm, truth can come only from the coherence of the system
of relationships in the child's head. In this domain, truth cannot come
directly from external, observable sources.

Some may be saying, "But observation and manipulation are necessary in
beginning arithmetic." I agree. But observation and manipulation are the
least important parts of numerical thinking. Three examples are given below

---

1. According to my dictionary, a fact is "a truth known by actual experience or observation."
A fact is sometimes opposed to theory. Questions of fact are also opposed to questions of law.

2. To be sure, $4 + 2$ can be known by counting, which is an empirical procedure. See the
example cited in Chapter 2 about the difference between *counting* and *knowing by deduction*
whether thirteen votes for one alternative is greater than the number who would vote for the
other alternative.

to illustrate this point. The first one has already been given; it involves putting objects out to solve an addition problem. The second example concerns counting on fingers, and the third one deals with "counting-all" as opposed to "counting-on." We will see in each example that what is important is the child's thinking, rather than the fact of observing or manipulating objects.

I have already described how first graders often write absurd answers like $2 + 5 = 5$. The reason they do is that they are taught how to manipulate objects to get correct answers, rather than how to think. Children who are encouraged to think may make errors, but they do not make completely illogical errors like $2 + 5 = 5$. It is logically impossible to add 5 to a natural number and get 5. The teaching of mindless observation and manipulation is dangerous because it stops children from thinking. Observation and manipulation are useful only in the context of the child's own logical thinking.

I go on to the second example. Fuson (1982) observed that in doing $8 + 5$ by counting on fingers, about a third of the six-year-olds in her sample got 12 as the answer because they said "eight-nine-ten-eleven-twelve" as they extended the first, second, third, fourth, and fifth fingers. The first set disappeared as a distinct one in their minds as the children thought about the second set (see Figure 5.1b). The children were observing and manipulating (symbolic) objects, but observation and manipulation can occur only in the service of the child's thinking—at his level. Observation and manipulation do not *cause* higher-level thinking.

The example given above illustrates "counting-on." Before becoming able to count-on, young children go through a long period of "counting-all." Counting-all means putting out eight objects, for example, then five objects, and counting all of them all over, from one to thirteen, instead of counting on from eight (i.e., nine-ten-eleven-twelve-thirteen). The long persistence of counting-all shows that addition is not learned through observation and manipulation. To add two numbers, the child has to mentally make one whole (8, for example), then another whole (5, for example), and then put them together mentally to make a new, homogeneous whole in which the previous wholes disappear in a sense but continue to exist in another sense. The reason for having to count from "one" may simply be that the child does not know the string of number words well enough to start in the middle. But it may also be that the child is unable to coordinate the part-whole relationship among the sets. If he cannot make the part-whole relationship among the sets, he mentally changes all the elements into ones as shown in Figure 5.1c. In other words, he changes $8 + 5$ to $1+1+1+1+1+1+1+1+1+1+1+1+1$.

Educators who believe that addition is a "skill"[3] to get "facts" often conceptualize counting-on as an objective and try to teach it directly and behaviorally. Counting-on is a poor objective because it unwittingly aims at depriving the child of a process of thinking he has to go through before getting to that level. If children are left alone to add numbers on their own, they *will* figure out a way that is appropriate for them. If they do not figure out a way, this means that addition is too hard for them and ought not to be imposed on them. If they count-all, most first graders will sooner or later give this up, just as toddlers give up crawling when they become able to walk.

It is important for children to construct sums through their own mental action, not only because these are relationships that each child has to construct for himself but also because we want the child to remember them. Since the reader needs to know Piaget's theory of memory to understand this statement, it is presented briefly below.

Piaget's theory of memory.   Piaget's theory of memory is very different from the empiricist belief that "facts" are "stored" and "retrieved." According to Piaget, a fact is "read" differently from reality by children at different levels of development because each child interprets it by assimilating it into the knowledge he has already constructed. In other words, a fact is always a reconstruction by an individual at his level of development. If children come to know facts by reconstructing them, it follows that they can remember only what they were able to assimilate in the first place. Different children at different levels of development can thus be expected to remember different "facts." The following study conducted by Pierre Mounoud and Piaget illustrates this point (Piaget and Inhelder, 1968). The children were shown the model that can be seen in Figure 5.2, and were asked to recreate it from memory. Four levels of immediate recall were found in relationship to the child's general level of development in logic.

I. Method
   A. Materials
      1. A model (Figure 5.2) consisting of three rows of blue chips glued onto cardboard (three and three in row A; one, two, and three in row B; and one and five in row C)
      2. Six red chips

---

3. A skill is a motor behavior such as typing, penmanship, and swimming. Calling addition a skill is symptomatic of a way of thinking that fails to differentiate between thinking (which is not directly observable) and behavior (which can be observed).

Blue chips

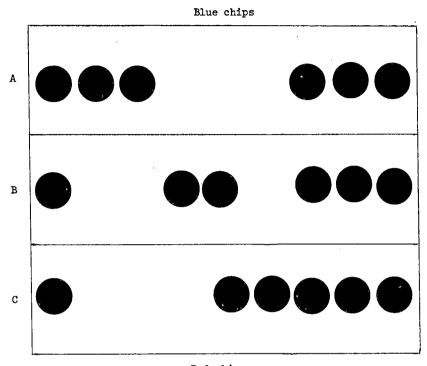

Red chips

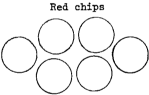

FIGURE 5.2.   The materials used in the memory task.

3. A large number of chips of a different color (at least eighty)
4. Paper and pencil
B. Procedure
  1. Comparing the quantity in the three rows
     a. The child was first asked to cover up all the blue chips in row B
        by putting a red one on each blue chip of the model.
     b. He was then asked whether it was possible to cover up all the
        blue chips in row A with the same red ones. After the
        anticipation, he was asked to verify it.
     c. The same procedure as "b" above was repeated for row C.

        d. The child was asked:
           i. If R (the number of red chips) = B (the number in row B).
           ii. If R (the number of red chips) = A (the number in row A).
           iii. If R (the number of red chips) = C (the number in row C).
           iv. If A = B = C.

2. Recall of the model from memory: The model was removed, and the child was asked for (a) a verbal description or a drawing of the model and (b) a reproduction with chips. The model was never shown again after this exposure, and the child was asked to do both (a) and (b) two more times: a week later, and after several months.

3. Conservation of number: During the second session (a week after exposure to the model) the child was given the conservation of elementary number task with eight to ten eggs and egg cups.

II. Findings: The 29 children interviewed between the ages of 4;0 and 6;6 were grouped into the following four categories according to whether or not they made the following three kinds of relationships: The numerical equality of the three rows, the coincidence of the extremities, and the subdivision of the rows into subgroups.

Level I. At this level, at age four, the rows differed greatly in number (12, 8, and 9, for example, or 4, 13, and 15), and their extremities were uneven. Most of the rows were divided into subsets, but their density varied from one subset to another.

Level II. The characteristics of this level were the opposite of the previous level's. The children at level II were concerned with the numerical equality of the rows, but they judged it globally by the spatial frontiers of the extremities. They did not make subsets, and made long rows of 15, 13, and 13; or even of 21, 26, and 23; or short ones of 7, 5, and 6.

Level III. The children showed progress toward numerical equality by making two of the three rows the same in number (4, 4, and 8, for example, or 5, 5, and 8). They made the extremities of the rows even, like the children at level II, but made subgroups, unlike the level II children. However, neither the sets nor the subsets were numerically the same as the model. The children divided a row of 5 into 1 and 4, for example, or a row of 4 into 1 and 3, remembering the general idea of subsets, and not the exact numbers.

Level IV. The criterion for this level was the numerical equality of all three rows. Only one child, the oldest, reproduced the model exactly. The other seven at level IV gave 3 + 3, 2 + 4, and 1 + 5; or 3 + 3, 1 + 4 + 1, and 1 + 5, and so on.

These levels illustrate the statement that, even in immediate recall, children often remember "facts" that are different from what has been shown. Even an "input" is thus an assimilation into previously constructed knowledge, and not a simple recording of facts.

Furthermore, a child's level of immediate recall was closely related to his level of development in logico-arithmetical knowledge as indicated by the conservation task. Five of the six children at the lowest level on the memory task were also at the lowest level on the conservation task. The fourteen solid conservers divided themselves into levels III and IV in immediate recall. They either remembered that all three rows had six chips or that two of the three rows had the same number.

The relationship between level of numerical thinking and level of recall can also be seen in children's ability to notice and/or deduce that $A = B = C$. The percents of children who said that the numbers in the three rows were the same were 0, 50, 88, and 100 respectively at levels I, II, III, and IV of the memory task.

A particularly interesting phenomenon emerged in long-term memory: Two patterns that did not exist in the model appeared among 41 percent of the children several months later, namely, *seriation* (6, 5, 4, 3, 2, and 1 (in 6 rows); 8, 7, and 6 (in 3 rows); or 4, 6, and 9) and *symmetry* (4, 1, 4; 2, 1, 2; and 3, 1, 3; or imperfect symmetry such as 3, 3; 2, 1, 2, 2). The appearance of these patterns is highly significant and attests to the tendency of the human mind to organize knowledge by putting the bits into relationships. Knowledge is indeed not a collection of unrelated bits, and memory is not the mere retrieval of facts that have been stored.

The educational implication of Piaget's theory of memory is that it is important for children to construct sums through their own mental actions of putting numbers into relationships. When they do, they can remember a coherent network of relationships much better than arbitrary sets of numbers. The study described here shows that even arbitrary sets of numbers are remembered better by children who can put them into relationships. While sums, too, can be remembered by rote, it is much easier for children to remember them in relation to one another. For example, the "doubles" (2 + 2, 3 + 3, etc.) are easy for first graders to commit to memory. They can remember $5 + 6 = 11$ much better in relation to $5 + 5 = 10$ than all by itself. By putting $5 + 6$ into relationship with $5 + 5$, the child can deduce, with the force of logical necessity, that $5 + 6$ *must be 10 + 1*.

Putting $5 + 6$ into relationship with $5 + 5$ is what the child has to do for himself, inasmuch as no one else can do this for him. This is why it is important for children to construct sums through their own mental action of putting numbers into relationships. Children who put numbers into more and more relationships can be counted on to construct an increasingly more coherent and larger network of relationships. The sequence of objectives discussed below is intended to facilitate the child's construction of such a network.

The Sequence of Objectives

After defining the goal as the child's own construction of sums, the teacher needs to sequence the activities he makes available for children to choose from. The difficulty level of the available materials can obviously not be the same in September, January, and May.

As stated earlier, most first grade arithmetic programs in existence today begin addition by defining sums up to 5 or 6 as the first objective, and then sums to about 9 or 10, 12, and 18. The objectives thus continue to be sequenced according to the magnitude of the *sum*, in spite of the research that has shown difficulty to depend on the size of the *addends* (Suydam and Weaver, 1975, p. 58). For example, $5 + 1 = 6$ is easier to remember than $3 + 2 = 5$.

The following sequence of objectives is based on the magnitude of the addends that corresponds to the way children learn. This information should help teachers in deciding which games to make available in the classroom.

Adding addends up to 4. The first set of objectives is based on the fact that small numbers are the easiest. Four is a number arrived at by observing children in the card game of Double War (see Chapter 7). This number seemed to be the minimum necessary to make the game interesting in Georgia's class, but three may be a better number for other classes in which children's general level of development is lower.

Adding addends up to 6. The basis for the second set of objectives is that first graders like dice games, and dice go up to 6. Addends up to 5 may have been a cognitively better objective, but dice are used by older children and adults, and it seemed motivationally better to let first graders play like older children. If 6 seems too big, the teacher may want to change the 6 on each die to another number.

Adding doubles (2 + 2, 3 + 3, etc.) up to 10 + 10. The third set of objectives is based on Suydam and Weaver's (1975) review of research and my own research. Suydam and Weaver stated that the doubles and combinations in which 1 is added to a number appear to be memorized more easily than the other combinations. (If children construct the number series on their own with the operation of $+ 1$, it is not surprising that they become able to give the sum of any number and 1 with ease. In other words, it is superfluous to define these combinations as objectives.)

The preceding three sets of objectives were defined also on the basis of the research done in Georgia's class that confirmed the findings from previous studies. We tested the children individually and orally in October, January, April, and June, with two dice bearing numerals. A list of written questions such as 9 + 1 was also used in June, when addends greater than 6 were presented. Tables 5.1 and 5.2 include only the percentages of children who gave correct answers immediately from memory. The combinations of addends are arranged in the first column in order of difficulty at the time the test was first given, from the easiest (known by 96 percent of the children) to the hardest (known by 0 percent). It will be recalled that these children received no formal instruction in school. The following observations can be made:

1. The doubles (indicated with ovals in the first column of Table 5.1) were among the easiest to commit to memory. Interestingly, 2 + 2 was memorized first, and followed by 5 + 5, 3 + 3, and 4 + 4, in that order. In other words, 5 + 5 yields a bigger sum, but it is easier to remember than 3 + 3 and 4 + 4. We see in Table 5.2 giving the findings on addends greater than 6 that 10 + 10 is likewise easier to remember than 9 + 9, and that 9 + 9 is in turn easier than 8 + 8. The ease with which first graders deal with 5 and 10 may be related to the number of fingers they have on each hand.
2. The combinations in which 1 is added to a number are also easy. A larger sum like 6 + 1 can thus be easier than a smaller one such as 2 + 3.
3. The next in difficulty are any number + 2. Although 2 + 6 yields a larger sum than 2 + 3, the two do not differ in difficulty.
4. Commutativity comes out of children's natural logic. 4 + 1 and 1 + 4 are about the same in difficulty, and 6 + 2 and 2 + 6 are likewise similar. This observation confirms Gréco's (1962) finding that children figure out the commutativity of addition around seven to eight years of age, through their own ability to think logically.

My reasons for defining the doubles as an objective are not only because they are easy to memorize but also because they become points of reference for children to use to deduce and remember other sums. As stated earlier, many children get the answer to 5 + 6 from their knowledge of 5 + 5.

Set partitioning of sums already known, and of 10. In this fourth set of objectives, set partitioning refers to making a set with two subsets in a variety of ways. For example, 10 can be made with 9 and 1, 8 and 2, 7 and 3, and so on. In set partitioning, children think in the direction opposite to

TABLE 5.1.   Percentage of First Graders Giving the Correct Answer Immediately: Addends 1 to 6

			Oct. N=25	Jan. N=26	April N=24	June, 1981 N=24
(2 + 2)			96%	100%	100%	100%
(5 + 5)			96	100	96	100
(3 + 3)			88	96	96	100
6 + 1	+ 1		80	96	86	100
4 + 1	+ 1		76	88	86	100
(4 + 4)			72	81	96	96
1 + 4	1 +		72	85	71	100
1 + 5	1 +		56	88	83	96
(6 + 6)			28	58	75	88
2 + 3		2 +	28	58	79	100
4 + 2		+ 2	28	50	75	88
3 + 2		+ 2	28	58	71	88
2 + 6		2 +	28	50	63	88
2 + 4		2 +	24	42	67	75
5 + 3			24	35	54	63
6 + 2		+ 2	20	62	63	88
2 + 5		2 +	16	50	67	88
4 + 5			12	31	54	75
5 + 2		+ 2	8	58	75	100
5 + 4			8	46	58	71
5 + 6			8	35	50	50
3 + 4			8	39	46	71
3 + 6			8	35	42	63
6 + 3			4	35	58	79
6 + 5			4	12	50	54
3 + 5			4	35	46	63
4 + 6			4	23	42	67
4 + 3			0	31	42	71

TABLE 5.2.   Percentage of First Graders
Giving the Correct Answer Immediately: Addends 7 to 10

	June, 1981 N = 24
9 + 1	100%
7 + 2	100
1 + 10	100
10 + 10	100
2 + 8	88
7 + 3	83
9 + 2	79
9 + 9	63
8 + 5	54
8 + 8	54
7 + 7	50
5 + 7	50
7 + 8	38

NOTE: The thirteen combinations reported here
are the only ones given to the children.

addition. In addition, they combine two wholes into a higher-order whole.
In set partitioning, by contrast, they separate a whole into two parts.

To partition sets, children have to think about all the old sums in a new
way. As we will see in the next chapter on subtraction, $6 = 4 + 2$ and $4 + 2$
$= 6$ are very different mental processes for children in the preoperational
period, when their thought is not yet reversible. Furthermore, knowing that
$6 = 3 + 3$ (a double), $4 + 2$, *or* $5 + 1$ requires the construction of new
relationships involving compensation. Compensation in this context means
knowing that an increase in one addend necessitates a corresponding
decrease in the other.

Ten was introduced as a new sum in the fourth set of objectives for two
reasons: It is relatively easy, and the set partitioning of 10 is particularly
useful for handling larger addends. To do $8 + 6$, for example, many children
spontaneously think of $(8 + 2) + 4$ by knowing that $8 + 2 = 10$, and that 6
$= 2 + 4$. Much later, when they engage in subtraction, they often do $14 -$
6 by regrouping the numbers around 10 and changing the problem either to
$(14 - 4) - 2$ or to $(10 - 6) + 4$.

Thinking about 6, 7, 8, and 9 as 5 + 1, 5 + 2, 5 + 3, and 5 + 4, and adding addends up to 10. The fifth set of objectives comes from Japan. Hatano (1980, 1982) reported that many Japanese educators under the leadership of Gimbayashi (1969) advocate the use of 5 as an intermediate higher-order unit, so that children can think of larger addends from 6 to 9 as 5 + 1, 5 + 2, 5 + 3, and 5 + 4. Hatano further reported that Japanese children add numbers by mentally regrouping them around 5 and 10, rather than by "counting-on" as American children usually do. To do 8 + 7, for example, some regroup the numbers around 10 into (8 + 2) + 5, while others regroup them around 5 into (5 + 5) + 3 + 2.

The desirability of using 5 as an intermediate higher-order unit can be supported from a Piagetian perspective with two arguments:

1. The child constructs the number series progressively from small numbers to larger ones. Since 6 to 10 are large numbers that are much harder for young children to think about than perceptual numbers (up to 4 or 5, as stated in Chapter 1), it is desirable for them to think about 6 to 10 as 5 + 1, 5 + 2, 5 + 3, 5 + 4, and 5 + 5.
2. The child can remember better the knowledge he constructs out of, and in relation to, what he already knows, than the knowledge he acquires by accumulating isolated bits. Counting is a way of getting each answer separately, without putting it into relationship with previous knowledge. Mental regrouping, by contrast, is a way of producing new knowledge in relation to what is already known. (An example of mental regrouping has already been given in the desirability of the child's deriving the answer to 5 + 6 from his knowledge of 5 + 5.)

It seems important for children to have a choice of ways to regroup numbers. To do 7 + 8, for example, it is desirable that they have the following four choices at their disposal:

$$(7 + 7) + 1 \qquad \text{Regrouping around a double}$$
$$\left.\begin{array}{l} (7 + 3) + 5 \\ (8 + 2) + 5 \end{array}\right\} \quad \text{Regrouping around 10}$$
$$(5 + 5) + 2 + 3 \quad \text{Regrouping around 5}$$

Conclusion

The conceptualization of objectives given here is intended to enable children to find ways that are comfortable for them when they come across a problem. While certain combinations are easy for all children (e.g., 5 + 5, 10 + 10, and any number + 1), different individuals have different strategies for generating new knowledge from what they already know. For example, some children prefer to do 8 + 5 by working around 10: (8 + 2) + 3, while others prefer to work around 5: (5 + 5) + 3. Children also shift strategies from one problem to the next. For example, they may work around 10 to do 8 + 7: (8 + 2) + 5, and around a double to do 7 + 6: (6 + 6) + 1. As for 6 + 3, it often gets structured through multiples of 3: 3, 6, 9. It is, therefore, desirable to encourage them to work out their own mental regroupings and to avoid teaching the "right" way.

It should be obvious that mental regrouping also facilitates memory by facilitating the construction of a network of relationships. Children who have constructed 8 + 5 through mental regrouping can reconstruct it quickly when the problem reappears in the future. Those who use counting can be expected to have more trouble committing this sum to memory.

Some third and fourth graders tenaciously continue to use counting instead of mentally regrouping the addends. This is probably the result of poor teaching in the earlier grades that taught them the mindless technique of counting and the fear of getting a wrong answer. Since counting is the surest way of getting the correct answer, children who are afraid of being wrong develop an emotional dependency on it.

The objective of the child's remembering the relationships made through his own (mental) actions was discussed without any allusion to writing mathematical signs. The ability to write mathematical signs in equations and vertical addition is the objective of most math series widely used today, and I would like to explain below why I am opposed to this goal.[4]

ADDITION WITH PENCILS

As stated in Chapter 4, math educators fail to make a distinction between abstraction and representation. For them, therefore, higher-level arithmetic means arithmetic in writing, and it is important to get children to become able to write answers to questions such as

$$2 + 4 = \underline{\hspace{1cm}} \text{ and } \begin{array}{r} 2 \\ +4 \\ \hline \end{array}$$

Furthermore, they see the ability to fill in missing addends $(2 + \underline{\hspace{1cm}} = 6$ and $\underline{\hspace{1cm}} + 4 = 6)$ as a perfectly reasonable objective. I will show next why the ability to write answers to these kinds of questions is not a desirable

---

4. This statement is not in contradiction with what I stated in Chapter 4. I advocated the writing of numerals there to represent numerical quantities. This is not the same thing as the writing of numerals to represent addition and the result of this operation.

objective for first graders. Since Chapter 4 stated that place value is premature in first grade, it should not be surprising that the position taken here is also opposed to the vertical as well as horizontal addition of two digit numbers, even without "carrying."

The Results of Addition

Worksheets containing addition problems are given day after day to get first graders to become able to deal with mathematical signs. All these are unnecessary and even harmful when used as the main staple of children's intellectual diet. I say "unnecessary" because once children know sums, they can fill in the answers with the greatest of ease, even if they do not see a single worksheet like this all year long. I say "harmful" for the following reasons:

1. These worksheets interfere with children's possibility of remembering sums because when they think about how to write "7," for example, they cannot simultaneously think about the combination of "2, 5, and 7."
2. These worksheets encourage children to work in a mindless, mechanical way by focusing their attention on the production of written answers. Many children think nothing of writing $7 + 2 = \underline{7}$ after counting on their fingers, and going through the same mechanical procedure all over to do $2 + 7 = \underline{}$ immediately afterwards. In doing $3 + 4 = \underline{}$, too, when the purpose of the activity is to produce written answers, children tend to count-all or count-on mechanically instead of thinking about the question in relation to what they already know well such as $3 + 3$.
3. These worksheets reinforce children's heteronomy because the teacher alone decides which ones are to be completed and/or which answers are correct.
4. These worksheets preclude the possibility of social interaction, which was emphasized in Chapters 2 and 3.

Wirtz (1980), who objected strenuously to making first graders write mathematical signs, developed a beginning arithmetic program called "TTR," which stands for "Think, Talk, Read." Although I do not agree entirely with his approach, I am in complete agreement with his statement that having children write arithmetic has the effect of separating it from thinking logically. Below are two examples of this separation. The first one comes from the home of a fourth grader, and the second one, from a second grade classroom.

Joe brought home a note from his fourth grade teacher asking for someone to help him with basic addition combinations. "Joe is still counting on his fingers. That's too slow in fourth grade. He is falling behind. Can someone help him practice with flash cards?"

His father was surprised. . . . But he made some "flash cards" presenting basic addition facts.

When Joe saw the card asking "3 + 7 = ____," he counted on his fingers—"eight, nine, ten," and announced "ten." His father congratulated him on getting the right answer and for counting from the larger number. "But Joe, you're in fourth grade and you ought to remember that by now."

Joe continued to count on fingers and his father's impatience was building until they came to "5 + 5 = ____." Joe smiled and said "ten" without using his fingers.

An "entry point"! So his father quickly found "5 + 6 = ____" and put two cards side by side. . . . Before Joe had time to respond, his father said "Now you know that 5 + 5 = 10; and you know that 6 is 1 more than 5; so if 5 + 5 = 10, how much is 5 + 6?" Joe gave his father a puzzled look and then counted on his fingers to find the answer—"eleven."

His father was incredulous. "Joe, look at these two cards. Don't you see anything similar between 5 + 5 and 5 + 6?" "Yes," Joe replied, "they both begin with a five." . . . Had he been tuned in, the father would have wondered at the expression "a five." While he might have expected "they both begin with five," Joe had said "they both begin with *a five*." Perhaps we ought to write his words down as "a 5" because Joe was looking at "marks on paper". . . . And, as marks on paper, the numerals "5" and "6" are quite unrelated.

During the first week of school in September, Margaret Grow, a second-grade teacher, wrote 19 + 3 = ____ (in vertical notation) several times on the chalkboard and asked for volunteers. There were plenty—but no one wrote "22." There were three different outcomes:

a.	b.	c.
19	19	19
+ 3	+ 3	+ 3
16	/12	112

Margaret Grow asked Helen to tell her about 19 + 3 = 16. "Well, I see the plus-sign, but whenever 9 and 3 are in the same column, it's 'take away' . . . and 9 take away 3 is 6."

The teacher asked Henry to explain his example (marked 'b' above).

"Nine and 3 is 12 and 1 and nothing is 1, but it's bigger than the 1 in the other column, so I made it bigger."

"How do you read it, Henry?"

After considerable study: "One hundred and twelve, I guess."

Most had written 112 as in example "c."

Margaret Grow got the attention of the group and asked, "If you had 19 cookies and I gave you 3 more, would you have 112 cookies?" They giggled and laughed. "Of course not!"

> Children come to school unwilling to be involved in nonsense, except in fun. By second grade, these children were willing to write nonsense and think nothing of it. This accomplishment of schooling has been characterized as "destroying the intellectual integrity of children" (W. W. Sawyer). Instead of arithmetic, they had learned to play a very complex "marks on paper game" quite unrelated to any real world experiences. (Wirtz, 1980, pp. 6–7)

Classroom teachers in grades two to four are very familiar with the kinds of phenomena described by Wirtz. It is important to evaluate first grade arithmetic by observing what happens to children in the long run. By merely counting the number of correct answers given on tests at the end of first grade, educators remain blind to the large-scale intellectual harm resulting from pencil pushing. Arithmetic must be rooted in children's honest thinking. There is something very wrong with the kind of instruction that produced the examples Wirtz cited.

Missing Addends

Teachers all over the world know that questions such as $2 + \underline{\quad} = 6$ and $\underline{\quad} + 4 = 6$ are hard for first graders. Many first grade teachers such as O'Hare (1975) have expressed the view that "of all the concepts presented in first grade math programs, I believe that the missing addend is the one which children find most difficult" (p. 35). O'Hare went on to give the example of a child who completed $4 + \underline{\quad} = 9$ by writing 13 in the blank. This is the typical error not only in the United States but also in various parts of Europe and Latin America, where I have spoken with teachers of young children.

First graders add the two numbers in $2 + \underline{\quad} = 6$ because addition is natural for them, and they cannot make the hierarchical relationship necessary to *read it into the equation*. While $2 + \underline{\quad} = 6$ seems no harder to adults to read than $2 + 4 = \underline{\quad}$, the latter is much easier for young children. It is easier because it can be read by thinking unidirectionally in a way that is natural at ages six to seven. I say "unidirectionally" because making one set $(1 + 1)$, making another set $(1 + 1 + 1 + 1)$, and joining them always involves increasing the size of the initial group.

We can get out of marks written on paper only the meaning that our intelligence enables us to put into them. As will be discussed shortly, meaning is what *we* put into written signs, not what automatically comes from them. To read a hierarchical relationship in the equation shown in Figure 5.3, the child's thought has to go in two opposite directions, simultaneously. As we saw in the class-inclusion task in Chapter 1, this is precisely what most children cannot do at six to seven years of age. They can

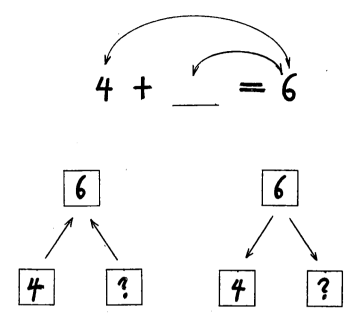

FIGURE 5.3. The two-directional thinking necessary to read a hierarchical relationship in an equation with a missing addend.

think about the parts (two and four, or "cats" and "dogs") and the whole (six,
or "animals") successively, but not simultaneously because their thought is
not mobile enough to be reversible.

Writers of first grade arithmetic series go on imposing missing addends,
unaware of the steady output from Piagetian research since the publication
of *The Child's Conception of Number* in 1941. Young children's difficulty
with the inclusion relationship was described in this book and further
elaborated in Inhelder and Piaget (1959).

It is possible to try to correct children who write $2 + \underline{8} = 6$ by writing 4 in
the blank. A few first graders become able to write the correct answer as a
result of this correction. This possibility of a few children to learn probably
explains why missing addends continue to be included in first grade
arithmetic. Arguments in favor of eliminating them would include the
following:

1. If some children can write correct answers, this is not a reason for
   imposing missing addends on the others (one-third to two-thirds) who
   cannot.

2. It is undesirable to impose something difficult on first graders if the same material becomes easy in the second or third grade.
3. It is undesirable for first graders to be corrected by the teacher, thereby losing confidence in their ability to figure things out and learning that math is a particularly hard subject.

The reader may have noticed my use of the term "equation" in the preceding discussion of missing addends, rather than "number sentence." The reason for my avoidance of number sentences is that we must be careful not to confuse equations with sentences. First graders have no difficulty filling in the missing parts in sentences such as the following:

I _____ an apple.
_____ hit Mary.
Cats and _____ are animals.

First graders' syntactic and semantic knowledge is sufficient to fill in the missing words. Equations, on the other hand, stand for relationships and not for (spoken) sentences, and first graders have trouble with such relationships. This statement will be clarified below with research conducted in the United States, Mexico, and Switzerland.

RESEARCH ON WHAT YOUNG CHILDREN READ INTO AN EQUATION

Three of my studies. The first study took place in a Chicago public school after the children had completed worksheets full of equations for five months. The children belonged to the highest group in a trichotomy of high-, middle-, and low-level first graders. Testing was done individually and had a "decoding" part and an "encoding" part.

In the "decoding" part, I asked each child to complete the following equation: $4 + 2 = $ ___. When he had written the answer, I asked him to give to a doll "what is written here" or "what the whole thing says." Two-thirds of the children gave six chips, but the others gave twelve chips! The latter read three juxtaposed quantities in the equation, rather than hierarchically related ones.

In the "encoding" part, I put out a handful of chips on the desk, pulled three of them toward me and hid them under the other hand saying, "See, I am hiding three under my hand." I then hid two more under the same hand saying, "I am hiding two more." After this demonstration, I gave a pencil and piece of paper to the child asking him to "Write what I just did. Remember (demonstrating again), I had three and added two more." The children had a tendency to write 5. Whenever this happened, I asked for "a different way" by asking the child to start with a 3 to show that "I had three first and then

TABLE 5.3.   The Encoding of

	N = 29
2 numerals are written (the initial collections)	
3 2 or 2 3	34.5%
3 + 2	10.5
3 numerals are written (the initial collections and the final whole)	
3 + 2 = 5 or 2 + 3 = 5	10.5
3 + 2 5	3.5
3 2 5	3.5
2 3 5	3.5
5 3 2	3.5
Other responses	
3 5 or 3 5 (the initial collection and the final whole)	10.5
5 ("I can't write 3 because the 3 are already in the 5.")	3.5
3 4 5	3.5
3 + 5 = 5	3.5
+3 2 - 5	3.5
3 = 2	3.5
2	3.5

added two more." The purpose of this task was to better understand what children read into equations. By finding out what came out of children when a blank sheet of paper was given, I felt that I might better understand what children read into equations.

The findings summarized in Table 5.3 proved this hunch to be correct.

The great variety of responses to such a simple request is striking. Only 10.5 percent wrote 3 + 2 = 5, which revealed how foreign equations are to the way first graders think. Almost half of the children (45 percent) represented only the two initial collections without the final whole (by writing 3 2, 2 3, or 3 + 2). Only 24.5 percent wrote three numerals. The (implicit) representation of a hierarchical relationship with three numerals is thus rare in first grade. This is not surprising, since children cannot express on paper ideas that are not in their heads! It can be observed, furthermore, that the operation (+) and relation (=) are represented with conventional signs only by 24.5 percent and 10.5 percent of the children, respectively. The representation of an action and the resultant part-whole relationship with explicit, conventional signs is thus also rare.

These tasks were later given in Geneva, Switzerland, and Glen Ellyn, Illinois. The percentages obtained were slightly different from place to place, but the pattern was the same everywhere. The findings suggested that equations involving addition are not mere "number sentences," but a highly unusual form of written representation in which the elements are ideographic (rather than phonetic), with the following characteristics:

1. In 3 + 2 = 5, each element is represented twice—once in 3 + 2 and again in 5.
2. 3 + 2 = 5 is atemporal. The 3 and 2 disappear into 5 when they are joined, but 3 + 2 = 5 is written as if the 3 and 2 continued to exist along with the 5. Moreover, 5 = 3 + 2 does not represent a temporal sequence opposite to 3 + 2 = 5.
3. 3 + 2 = 5 involves the following three levels of abstraction:

Level 1.	3 and 2	The numbers constructed by one's (mental) action on objects.
Level 2.	3 + 2	An operation on the numbers.
Level 3.	5	The result of the above operation.

In other words, the 3 + 2 on one side of the equation is at a lower level of abstraction than the 5 on the other side, and the " = " sign stands for the relationship between the two. These differences in levels of abstraction may explain the following observations:

I have seen children who wrote numerals without writing either the " + " or the " = " sign.

I have seen children who wrote the " + " sign without writing the " = " sign.

I have never seen a child who wrote the " = " sign correctly without writing the " + " sign correctly.

First graders' responses to the "encoding" task help us to understand what they read into the equation in the "decoding" task. The children (one-third of the sample) who gave 12 chips to the doll by reading $4 + 2 = \underline{6}$ were not only not reading a hierarchical relationship into the numerals, but also responding as if the " + " and " = " signs had not been there. They would probably have given twelve if they had seen 4 2 6. Quantities (numerals) are easier to read than the " + " and " = " signs because they are at a lower level of abstraction than the latter.

Associationist versus Piagetian views of representation. Representation is much more complicated than authors of first grade texts assume it is on the basis of associationist thinking. In associationism, signs such as 6 are believed to be learned by association. More specifically, the sign "6" is believed to be learned by association with six objects, the picture of six objects, and/or the spoken word "six." The " + " sign is likewise believed to be learned by association with the observable action of joining two sets, along with a verbal explanation that this action means "putting them together." Note that according to this empiricist belief, all knowledge comes from sources external to the child.

According to Piaget, the child learns conventional signs not through association with objects but through assimilation. Children assimilate signs into the ideas they have constructed through reflective abstraction. When the child cannot yet construct a hierarchical relationship, he assimilates 4 + 2 = 6 into the relationships that he can make, and reads the equation as three juxtaposed quantities at the same level.

When he writes 3 2 or 3 5 in the "encoding" task, he is representing (externalizing) his own idea about what happened. Both 3 2 and 3 5 are correct in the sense that they both correspond to elements of what took place in external reality. Children's production of signs reveals their way of thinking more accurately than their reading of signs, because when they produce signs, they externalize their own ideas (constructed through reflective abstraction). Hence the wide variety of graphic representations in the "encoding" task.

Four other studies. Four other studies involving "decoding" or "encoding" support the conclusion from my research. In a "decoding" task given in Mexico, Reyes and Vargas Suarez (1979) found that the hierarchical relationship is hard to read into an equation even in second grade for middle-class children. They asked each child to fill in the missing addend in ___ + 7 = 9 and to show what each numeral stood for by drawing circles around dots (see Figure 5.4a). In a second task, they showed a complete equation, 9 = 4 + 5, accompanied by 20 dots (see Figure 5.4b), and once again asked the child to draw circles to indicate what each numeral meant. Whether the child responded correctly or not, they followed the response with a countersuggestion. If the child responded incorrectly by drawing the circles shown in Figure 5.4c, they said, "I was talking to another little boy (or girl) this morning, and he said the 9 meant this (pointing in Figure 5.4d), the 4 meant this (pointing), and the 5 meant this (pointing). Who do you think is right, you or the other little boy (or girl)?" If, on the other hand, the child responded correctly as shown in Figure 5.4d, the solution shown in Figure 5.4c was suggested as a possible alternative to find out how sure the child was of his own reasoning.

None of the twenty-one second graders answered both questions correctly, and fifteen (71 percent) answered both questions incorrectly. The others were intermediary cases who responded to only one of the questions correctly. The hierarchical relationship among the three numerals in an equation thus does not seem to be easy even in second grade.

Conne (1981) investigated what first graders near Lausanne, Switzerland, read into an equation at the end of the year, after being taught to fill in the blanks in various forms such as a + ___ = c, ___ + b = c, ___ = a + b, c = ___ + b, and c = a + ___. I will summarize the highlights from part of his paper-and-pencil test. The tests were administered to the whole class (group administration) by the teacher in charge of each class. Five classes were involved, with a total of 93 children.

(a)   (b)

FIGURE 5.4.
The dots used to study what the
numerals meant in an equation.

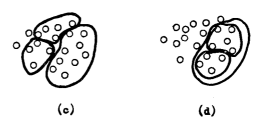

(c)   (d)

TABLE 5.4. First Graders' Ways of Completing Equations

	Children Who Responded Incorrectly (N = 93)	Children Who Added the Two Numbers	Children Who Took the "Difference" between Two Numbers
1. 2 + 6 = ___	10%	90%	3%
2. ___ = 5 + 2	30	70	6
3. 3 + ___ = 8	41	20	59
4. ___ + 3 = 9	42	24	58
5. 8 = ___ + 3	46	16	54
6. 7 = 2 + ___	56	41	44

Below is a list of some of the equations in which the child was asked to fill in the missing element:

$$1.\ 2 + 6 = \underline{\hspace{1cm}}$$
$$2.\ \underline{\hspace{1cm}} = 5 + 2$$
$$3.\ 3 + \underline{\hspace{1cm}} = 8$$
$$4.\ \underline{\hspace{1cm}} + 3 = 9$$
$$5.\ 8 = \underline{\hspace{1cm}} + 3$$
$$6.\ 7 = 2 + \underline{\hspace{1cm}}$$

The first two equations gave two parts, and the child was asked to deduce the whole. In the other four equations, the whole and one part were given, and the child had to deduce the other part. In some equations, the total was given at the end; in others, it was given at the beginning of the equation.

Table 5.4 gives the results. It can be observed from the second column that the first two equations were much easier than the others. The children made far fewer errors in deducing the whole when two parts were given, than when the whole and a part were given and they were asked to deduce the other part. The former does not require the hierarchical coordination of three quantities. When the children made errors in the latter situation, many of them did so by adding the two numbers ($3 + \underline{11} = 8$, for example). As can be seen in the third column of Table 5.4, the percentages of children who thus added the two numbers in Equations 3 to 6 were 20, 24, 16, and 41 respectively. This tendency was the strongest when the two numbers were at the beginning (Equation 6). The 7 and 2 appear where numerals are found in the basic form of a + b = ____.

The first grade curriculum in Lausanne requires the mastery of missing addends, and the children had devoted many hours to exercises such as 3 + ____ = 8. The last column of Table 5.4 shows the percentage of children who took the "difference" between the two numbers. We note that only about half of them took the differences in Equations 3 to 6 (percentages of 59, 58, 54, and 44 respectively). When half of a group makes errors after devoting hours over many weeks to similar exercises, there is something very wrong with this objective.

The following two studies involve "encoding." In an investigation mostly of middle-class children in and around Ithaca, New York, Allardice (1977) found that the writing of three quantities (two parts joined that make a whole) is rare among first graders, that the use of the " + " and " = " signs is also rare, and that the " = " sign appears less frequently than the " + " sign. Her sample of twenty first graders ranged in age from 6;4 to 7;3, with a mean of 6;10, and were all using "formal addition and subtraction symbolism in the classroom" (p. 108). In the part of her work that concerns us here, she placed a shallow cup on the table containing some toy owls and said, "See here we have two owls. Now I'm going to put two more in here. You put something on your paper to show Snoopy (the animal who was the recipient of the message, and whose back was turned to the child) that *first* we had two and *then* two more" (p. 41). If the child represented only the final whole, she asked him to, "Tell me everything I just did." Then she gave three similar tasks that involved the representation of addition.

Of the possible maximum of 60 responses, only 4 were the complete equation, and only 6 included both parts and the whole. The total number of " = " signs that appeared was 7, and the " + " sign was written only 19 of a possible 60 times. The 7 " = " signs were produced by 3 of the 20 children, and the 19 " + " signs were produced by 7 individuals.

The last study to be cited comes from a project in Geneva, Switzerland, designed to investigate the effects of social interaction on graphic representation. In the part that is relevant to the present discussion, Schubauer-Leoni and Perret-Clermont (1980) report that the conventional signs " + ," " − ," and " = " are rarely used even in the second grade. Their technique used a heap of candy and an opaque bag made of cloth. The experimenter first showed two pieces of candy to the child and put them into the bag. He then showed four pieces to the child and put them into the bag. Then he took one piece out of the bag and asked the child if it was possible to know how many pieces were left inside. The experimenter was careful not to comment on his actions and was especially careful not to use words such as "add" and "take out." He asked the child to describe what happened to the candy and, if necessary, helped the child reconstruct the event. When the child could recreate the event, he was given a pencil and sheet of paper with the request, "I want you to explain to a child who did not see what we did with the candy everything that happened and how many were left at the end. Try to make him understand what we did with the candy before getting five in the bag at the end."

Only 25 of the 89 second graders (28 percent) used the conventional mathematical signs " + ," " − ," and/or " = " to represent what happened. Less than half of the 25 (9 out of 25, or 10 percent of 89) used these signs correctly as can be seen in Table 5.5. The other 72 percent drew pictures or wrote

TABLE 5.5.   Second Graders' Ways of Representing $2 + 4 - 1 = 5$

Category	Frequency $N = 25$
I. Complete and correct formulation in one equation $2 + 4 - 1 = 5$	
II. Complete and correct formulation in two equations $2 + 4 = 6$ $6 - 1 = 5$	9
III. "Chaining" $2 + 4 = 6 - 1 = 5$	7
IV. The addition is implicit $6 - 1 = 5$	3
V. Partially correct formulation $2 + 4 = 6$ $2 + 3 = 5$	3
VI. The subtraction is implicit $2 + 4 = 5$	1
VII. Conventional signs are not consistently used. $2 + 4 = 6 \not= 5$	1

natural language ("I take 2 candies and then 4 candies, I take away 1 candy, 5 candies are left.") or a string of numerals ("2 4 1 5" or "2/4/1/5").

The results of this study are consistent with my "encoding" task results. It showed that in second grade children continue to use a surprisingly wide variety of ways to represent addition and subtraction, in spite of the instruction they receive that emphasizes equations. It also showed that second graders, too, rarely use the " + ," " − ," and " = " signs, and that the number who use these signs correctly is even smaller.

Reflecting on Conne's work and Schubauer-Leoni and Perret-Clermont's, Brun (1981), a collaborator of theirs, said that the use of mathematical signs cannot be viewed merely as a "passage to symbolism." Children learn mathematical signs not by association and absorption from the environment but by assimilation into the ideas they have constructed. The numerals are easiest to assimilate because quantities are constructed first. An operation (+) on these quantities is at a higher level of abstraction, and the resultant relationship (=) is at an even higher level. Only after the child has constructed a hierarchical relationship can he read it into an equation. Only then can he deal with equations that have missing addends.

The Vertical Addition of Two Digit Numbers

It is very easy to teach first graders how to write the correct answer to questions such as

$$\begin{array}{r} 21 \\ + 13 \\ \hline \end{array}$$

by adding each column. If we go on to ask them orally what 21 + 13 is, they usually count on, thereby adding 1 thirteen times to 21, and cannot make any relationship between the answer thus obtained and the one they wrote by adding each column. This is not surprising in view of the fact (discussed in Chapter 4) that first graders cannot understand place value. If they cannot understand place value, they can obviously not understand the horizontal addition of two digit numbers either.

First graders are still constructing the number series with the operation of + 1 and, therefore, repeat + 1 thirteen times. They cannot yet do the following thinking necessary to understand the addition of each column:

$$\begin{aligned} 21 + 13 &= (2 \times 10 + 1) + (1 \times 10 + 3) \\ &= (2 \times 10) + (1 \times 10) + (1 + 3) \\ &= 30 + 4 \\ &= 34 \end{aligned}$$

Needless to say, I am talking only about the child's thinking, and not about his ability to read or write these equations. The equations were written to remind the reader that place value involves the higher-order unit of 10 and multiplication, neither of which is possible at the age of six to seven.

The addition of two digit numbers is a dangerous objective because it gives to the child two different and unrelated ways of getting answers to the same question: with the trick learned at school (the algorithm) and with his own way of thinking. The danger of this kind of schizophrenic development has been documented especially well by Erlwanger (1975), who showed how children come to distrust their own thinking when they are taught to solve problems in ways that involve thinking that is foreign to them. (An excerpt from one of his interviews can be found in Chapter 11.)

STORY PROBLEMS

"Story" or "word" problems usually come after the teaching of sums as applications of the latter. However, there are two reasons why story problems ought to be introduced concurrently with sums. (1) Children construct arithmetic out of their own reality; and (2) research has shown that verbal problems are easily solved by first graders without formal instruction. These reasons are elaborated below.

The child constructs arithmetic as he logico-arithmetizes reality. "You have two sticks of gum and your sister gives you two more" is the kind of reality out of which children create the knowledge of $2 + 2$. Children live in the content-filled world of peers, bikes, library books, skates, and so forth, and structure numerical quantity as they navigate through it. Making them memorize $2 + 2$, and so forth, in the absence of content is contrary to how learning occurs outside the classroom.

When I say that story problems ought to be introduced concurrently with sums, I do not mean that these problems should come, as they usually do, out of books. They should come out of children's real life in the classroom. For example, in a game in which ten guesses are allowed, children spontaneously say, "Two more to go!" when the eighth guess is taken. The teacher who understands Piaget's theory will regard this remark as a highly valuable one and make the most of it. "How do you know that?" "Does everybody agree?" and "Does anybody have a different idea?" are examples of what the teacher might say to make the most out of this situation. In a similar situation, he might subsequently wait for the fifth or seventh guess[5] to ask

---

5. I say "the fifth or seventh guess" for the following reasons: The number left after the fifth guess is easy to deduce because $5 + 5$ is an easy sum. For children who can tell that there are two guesses left after the eighth one, the number left after the seventh guess is also an appropriate question to think about.

"How many more guesses do we have?" (Other examples of situations that the teacher can use are given in Chapter 7.) Story problems ought to be introduced from the beginning of first grade by making the most of naturally occurring events and not by giving stories parachuted out of the blue.

Research has shown verbal addition problems to be very easy in kindergarten and first grade, before children are instructed in how to deal with written computational problems. Carpenter, Hiebert, and Moser (1979) found that, before receiving instruction in how to write equations for verbal problems, most first graders correctly answered the following types of questions:[6]

> Wally had 3 pennies. His father gave him 8 more pennies. How many pennies does Wally have altogether?

> Some children were ice skating. 4 were girls and 7 were boys. How many children were skating altogether?

The numbers they used in these questions were 3 + 8, 3 + 9, 4 + 7, 4 + 8, 4 + 9, 5 + 7, 5 + 8, 5 + 9, 6 + 8, and 6 + 9, which were chosen because of the following characteristics:

1. The addends were greater than 2 and less than 10.
2. Their sum was greater than 10 and less than 16.
3. The difference between the two addends was greater than 1.

The numbers of children ($N = 43$) who gave the correct answers to the two questions were 34 and 37 (79 percent and 86 percent), respectively. I replicated their study with first graders in Geneva, Switzerland, and Glen Ellyn, Illinois, and obtained the same results. Ibarra and Lindvall (1982) conducted an analogous experiment with kindergarten children but limited the sums to 7. They found that about 60 percent of the children answered correctly.

Children are often asked to write an equation for a given problem before solving it. But verbal problems must first be thought about without pencils, just as the addition of numbers should be done in the head without pencils first. In my research on children's ability to solve verbal problems, I found

---

6. The authors also present what they consider to be a third type of addition. "Ralph has x pieces of gum. Jeff has y more pieces than Ralph. How many pieces of gum does Jeff have?" I do not agree that this is just an addition problem, because the part-whole relationship involved in this situation is very complicated. To answer this question, the child has to mentally transport Ralph's whole to Jeff's collection and think about Ralph's whole as part of Jeff's whole. This kind of part-whole relationship is much too hard in first grade.

that children answered the question first, and when I then asked them to show me with chips how they got the answer, they often said, "I just did it in my head" or "I don't know how I did it." (This point is discussed in more detail in Chapter 6.)

COMMENTS AND CONCLUSIONS

Math educators articulate their objectives in terms of children's learning of "addition facts" and writing of equations. In this chapter, I pointed out that these goals amount to putting the cart in front of the horse and hence blocking its forward movement. If children add numerical quantities repeatedly, actively, in the context of everyday classroom occurrences, games, and problems that they understand, they *will* remember the results of these mental actions and *will* become able to read and write conventional mathematical signs. The focus of the teacher's concern should be on children's *thinking* rather than on their ability to *write* correct answers. Children's thinking grows out of their natural intuition and logic, and educators should foster that development rather than seeking to define objectives foreign to that way of thinking.

CHAPTER 6

Subtraction as an Objective

From the point of view of mathematicians and other adults, subtraction is simply the inverse of addition. Children who can write answers to questions such as $3 + 2 =$ _____ are presumed to be ready for such questions as $5 - 2 =$ _____. While it is not hard for most first graders to learn to write answers to these questions, this is not in itself a valid reason for imposing written subtraction as an objective for them. In the first part of the chapter, we will see why written subtraction should be postponed until the second grade. In the second part I take up the issue of story problems and argue that problems with content, especially content that emanates from children's actual in- and out-of-class experiences, are the only form of subtraction exercises that seem desirable for first graders.

CRITIQUE OF A TYPICAL APPROACH

First let us examine objectives of a unit entitled "Subtraction I" taken from a typical first grade program, *Macmillan Mathematics* (Thoburn, Forbes, Bechtel, and Nelson, 1978). This critique will serve as a background for understanding why subtraction should be considered an undesirable objective for first grade arithmetic.

> The purpose of the unit [Subtraction I] is to establish the meaning of subtraction, to introduce some associated language and symbolism, and to develop a reliable technique for finding differences of two numbers. Subtraction facts with first numbers 5 or less are presented in vertical form. There is no pressure to memorize these 21 facts, but they are repeated often enough that some children should begin to retain them.
>
> In the first developmental phase, children take away objects from given sets of five or less objects and find how many are left. The children relate a subtraction fact to each take away situation and then they record the difference. For example: [see Figure 6.1a]. . . .
>
> In the second developmental phase, children look first at a subtraction exercise, then use objects or pictures of objects to aid them in finding the difference. For example: [see Figure 6.1b]. . . .

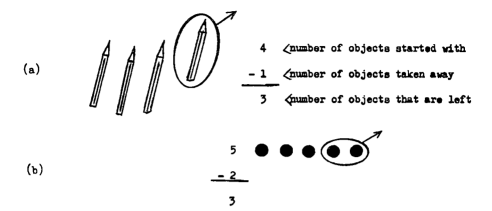

(a)

4   ⟨number of objects started with

− 1   ⟨number of objects taken away

3   ⟨number of objects that are left

(b)

5

− 2

3

FIGURE 6.1.   Learning to write answers (a) by associating the "concrete" with the written exercise and (b) by writing the answer with the aid of a picture.

NOTE: Reprinted, with permission of the publisher, from T. Thoburn, J. E. Forbes, R. D. Bechtel, and L. D. Nelson, *Macmillan Mathematics*, Level 1, Teacher's Edition (New York: Macmillan, 1978), p. 43A.

> The final developmental phase focuses again on interpreting take away situations. . . . This lesson may be thought of as readiness for solving take away story problems. (p. 43A)

I have two criticisms of the Macmillan approach, in addition to the authors' empiricist view of subtraction as a collection of "facts."[1] First, the objectives center on teaching *techniques* for becoming able to *write* correct answers. The teacher is thus directed to "the first developmental phase" of presenting objects for children to manipulate. The children are to "relate a subtraction fact to each take away situation and then [to] record the difference." The "second developmental phase" consists of the inverse procedure: Give them written problems and ask them to use objects and pictures to help them find solutions. In the course of going through such procedures, children presumably build linkages between "interpreting take away situations" and written arithmetic.

I believe that the objective in subtraction, as in addition, should be to encourage children to think and to remember the results of their own thinking. It should not be to teach children specific techniques for producing written answers. In Chapter 5, we saw that once children have constructed

---

1. As stated in Chapter 5, "=" is a relationship, and not a fact. Facts are observable and "out there" in external reality, but number, addition, and subtraction are not empirical knowledge.

sums and have committed them to memory, they are able to express this knowledge on paper. Those who can thus make additive relationships correspond to written numerals ought to be able to use this knowledge to express their thinking in subtraction. The teaching of techniques that can be used mechanically results in a very poor foundation for learning in the future.

My second criticism is related to the first and concerns the authors' final "developmental phase," which is to solve "take away story problems." Arithmetic should grow out of children's real lives, as beginning points rather than end points of a unit on any operation. By the time children enter first grade, they can already do take away problems. If a first grader were asked how many crayons he would have left if he gave the child next to him one or two of the five he had in his hand, he would undoubtedly figure out the answer by using his own natural ability to think. He might partition a collection or count on fingers, and in this sense he already knows the meaning of subtraction. This meaning does not need to be established for him, and from a Piagetian point of view, it cannot be established by anyone outside the individual.

The emphasis on techniques and conventional signs, instead of on children's own ability to think, is the greatest shortcoming of this kind of traditional instruction. The sequence of instruction (the first, second, and third "developmental" phases as articulated in *Macmillan Mathematics*) comes out of how adults think about subtraction rather than the way the child thinks about separating a whole into numerically smaller parts, comparing two collections for numerical differences, and so on.

If children invent a technique, such as the counting of dots and fingers, that method is their own, rooted in their way of thinking. When we give them the same procedure in ready-made form, we teach them tricks from the outside that they can use mechanically, for the purpose of producing answers to please adults.

WHY SUBTRACTION SEEMS INAPPROPRIATE IN FIRST GRADE

Two bodies of data suggest that subtraction may not be appropriate as an objective for first graders. The first consists of data collected in Georgia DeClark's class. The second comes from the research findings of Piaget (1974b) and his collaborators that demonstrated the extent to which young children's thinking focuses on the positive aspects of action, perception, and cognition. Inverse, reciprocal, or otherwise negative aspects are a later construction.

The Ease of Subtraction When Sums Are Solidly Known

Certain sums are much easier for children to remember than are others (see Chapter 5, Table 5.1). Combinations such as 2 + 2, 5 + 5, and 4 + 1 are better known than 2 + 3. In midyear Georgia and I tested the children individually on worksheets containing subtraction problems. Neither of us had taught subtraction, but to our surprise, answers to 4 − 2, 10 − 5, and 5 − 1 came immediately. The children simply did not need to take the time to think; nor did they use fingers or count backwards, two actions that all but the advanced children (who had known 2 + 3 = 5 and 4 + 2 = 6 for a long time) *did* employ for 5 − 3 and 6 − 2. We hypothesized that when the corresponding addition was well known and "second nature," problems asking for subtraction would pose little difficulty.

We reasoned that if strength in addition prefigured competence in subtraction, and if the children became able to do subtraction without formal instruction, then it would be best to continue encouraging children to engage in addition and to put subtraction on the shelf. Besides, the one simple subtraction game we had introduced (Subtraction Lotto, described in Chapter 7) gathered dust on the shelf, while at the same time the ones involving addition were in constant use. We concluded that these children did not like subtraction. (Even second grade teachers are greeted with a chorus of "Oh, no!" when they announce that the day's math lesson will consist of "take-aways.")

The research by Piaget and his collaborators had alerted me to this possibility. Their studies had shown that young children generally focus on the positive aspects of actions, thought, and perception, and that they later construct the negative aspects. The research that showed the initial primacy of these positive aspects will now be presented.

The Initial Primacy of Positive Aspects Over Negative Ones

In *Research on Contradictions, Volume 2, Relations Between Affirmations and Negations,* Piaget (1974b) pointed out that all actions, perception, and cognition first function positively. When a child picks up and places a block in a new location, he thinks about this action positively, rather than negatively as the removal of the object from its original spot. Likewise, when he drives a nail into a board, he thinks about the results of this action. He does not think about the object as "not a needle," and does not think about the action as "not pulling" or "not squeezing (as in squeezing a tube)." These are examples of what Piaget meant by the initial primacy of the positive aspects of perception, cognition, and action. When young children act, they usually act to satisfy a need, and they think about the positive aspects of objects and actions that satisfy these needs.

Later, however, as children put objects and actions into relationships, they construct negative aspects that are not readily observable. The small, unidirectional relationships they constructed before develop into systems of operations in which every direct operation has a corresponding reverse operation. I will describe two tasks in order to clarify this statement. The first one involves the transfer of objects from one set to another, and the second deals with children's descriptions of the complementary class.

The transfer of chips from one row to the other.   When two rows of eight chips each are made in one-to-one correspondence (Figure 6.2a), and then one chip is moved from one row to the other, this transfer has a negative as well as positive aspect. The negative aspect is the subtraction of a chip from one row, and the positive aspect is the addition of that same chip to the other. Young children focus only on the positive aspect of this action, and when asked to anticipate the difference between the two rows, they predict a difference of one, rather than of two. At first, they do not even accept the fact that there are two chips sticking out beyond the spatial frontier of the other row (Figure 6.2c). Later, at level II, they continue to predict a difference of 1 but quickly understand why the observed difference is 2. Still later, at level III, they become able to predict, before seeing the transfer of the chip, that the difference will be 2. The experiment was devised by Henriques-Christophides, a collaborator of Piaget's. Her method and findings were as follows (Piaget, 1974b, Chapter 9).

I. Method
  A. The experimenter began by making two rows of eight chips each in one-to-one correspondence (Figure 6.2a). One row was designated as the child's, and the other as the experimenter's. The experimenter then ascertained that the child thought he had "just as many" ("as much," "the same much," etc.) as the experimenter.
  B. A screen was then placed over the experimenter's row (Figure 6.2b), and the child was asked how many more he would have if 1 chip was moved from the experimenter's row to the child's. Observing the appearance of the additional chip, younger children usually predicted a difference of 1. The screen was then removed, and the child saw a difference of 2 (Figure 6.2c). He was then asked to explain why the difference was 2 rather than 1.
  C. The number transferred was varied to 2 and 3, and the transfer was sometimes made in the opposite direction, from the child's row to

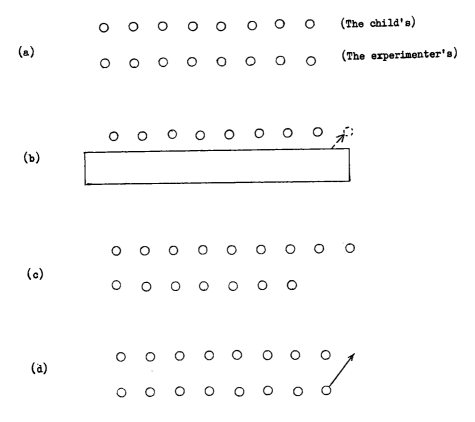

FIGURE 6.2.   The difference between the rows when one chip is transferred from one row to the other.

the experimenter's. A request for a prediction was always followed by an observation of the two rows and a request for an explanation of what happened.

D. The same procedures were repeated without the screen (Figure 6.2d). In this part of the task, the child could observe the action, which was simultaneously negative and positive.

II. Findings: The children's reactions were categorized into the following three levels.

Level I. The child anticipated a difference of *n*, and even when the transfer was made without the screen, he did not understand why the difference was 2*n*. Below is an example of such a child.

MAR (5;7) for a transfer of 1 (under the screen) does not want to believe the difference of 2: *"One is missing.—*Where?*—It is underneath* [under the last chip of the row from which 1 had been removed].—Then do I cheat?—*Yes, a little bit."* When he transfers 3 himself and observes a difference of 6 instead of 3, he puts the 3 back to their initial places (without the screen), one at a time, and explains the 6: *"I gave 3 to you and 3 to me,"* as if they counted positively for both sets at the same time. He gives 1 again and observes a difference of 2 [after predicting 1]: *"It's because the other one* [the second one from the end] *moved here, it went there"* [he thus believes that 2 had been transfered]. Without the screen: transfer of 2—"Why 4?—*Because these 2 were there, they were there."* He could thus be said to have understood, but for another transfer of 2 in the opposite direction, he again predicts a difference of 2. (p. 24)

Level II. Like the child at the previous level, the level II child anticipated a difference of *n,* but upon seeing the transfer of the chip, immediately noticed the negative aspect as can be seen in the example.

LIE (6;9). The usual errors, then, without the screen: *"Ah, I understood: it's because I took 1 from there"* [hence the difference of 2]. (p. 26)

Note that the empirical observation of the transfer did not help the level I child, but it did help this child, who was at a higher cognitive level. In other words, the level II child could "see" that the chip was subtracted from one row before being added to the other.

Level III. Many intermediary levels were found between the ages seven to eight and eleven to twelve. The following child anticipated a difference of 2*n* without seeing the movement of the chip from one row to the other.

PAN (10;11). *"He took away 1, that's 1 less. He gave me 1, that's 1 more;* [in all] *that makes 2."* (p. 27)

It is truly remarkable that the level I child does not notice the observable lacuna left by the chip that leaves a row. For the level I child, addition is a completely unidirectional, positive action, as if adding could take place without reducing the number of the other set. At level II, the child can empirically notice and understand that the difference between the rows consists of what is added *plus* what is taken away from the other row. The level II child is like the level I child in that he anticipates a difference of *n,* but he can quickly understand, *after* observing the result of the action, why the difference is 2*n.* At level III, the child can anticipate a difference of 2*n* because he can think of the single material action as two operations. For the level III child, the addition of *n* to one set *necessarily* implies the subtraction of *n* from the other set.

The initial primacy of the positive aspect can also be seen in the next example involving the child's description of the complementary class.

The description of the complementary class. When young children are asked to dichotomize a group of objects and to give a label to the complementary class, they give positive labels (e.g., "a mixture"). Older children give negative ones (e.g., "all the flowers that are *not* primulas"). The experimental method and highlights of the findings reported in Piaget (1974a) and Inhelder and Piaget (1959) are summarized below.

I. Method
   A. Materials: Two sets of cards were used, one of flowers and another one of fruit. The first set consisted of primulas of various colors and of other flowers, such as a rose, a pansy, a tulip, and a lily-of-the valley. The second set consisted of several apples and other fruit such as one or two pears, two cherries, a banana, a melon, a bunch of grapes, and an orange.
   B. Procedure
      1. Dichotomy: The child was asked to make two groups of flowers (or of fruit) by putting together the ones that belonged together.
      2. Giving a label to each group of cards: When the dichotomy was made, the child was asked to give a name for a label to put on each of two boxes into which the cards would be placed.
II. Findings (only the findings concerning flowers are given here): All the children said the first group should be called "primulas." For the second group, however, they had different ideas that could be categorized into the following three levels.
   Level I. "Rose(s), tulip(s), pansies," and so on. These children, below the age of five, named each flower *positively*, sometimes in the plural, without thinking about them as a group.
   Level II. "The others" or "a mixture." This type of label, which began to appear around the age of five, described the complementary class *positively* with a collective name, in loose relation to the first class. "The others" explicitly referred to the first group. "A mixture" implied that the first group was homogeneous while the second group was not.
   Level III. "All the flowers *except* the primulas" or "flowers that are *not* primulas." These children described the complementary class *negatively* by constructing a total class for all the objects and considering the complementary class in opposition to a positively defined subclass.

At level I, the child labeled the complementary class in terms of individual objects, such as "a rose, a pansy, and a lily-of-the-valley." Level II showed progress in two ways: The child put individual objects into relationship and considered them as a group, and he put this group loosely into a relationship with the other group. The term "the others" reflects the child's thinking about "primulas" at some level. While there was thus progress, the child's label was still *positive*.

When he became able to make a hierarchical relationship at level III, the child began to give a *negative* description, i.e., "all the flowers that are *not* primulas." This label designates the complementary class by clearly defining its upper and lower boundaries. "All the flowers" defines the upper boundary of the superordinate class by separating "flowers" from "all other objects that are *not* flowers." "The primulas" define the lower boundary of the complementary class by drawing a line of demarcation between "the primulas" and "all other flowers that are *not* primulas." Negative descriptions thus grow out of the child's increasing ability to make relationships, which culminates in reversibility.

The initial primacy of positive aspects has also been observed by teachers in classrooms. For example, when we present two unequal sets of objects to four-year-olds, we are much more likely to get the correct answer by asking where are there *more* than by asking where are there *less* (fewer).

When presented with a pageful of addition problems, first graders hardly ever slip into subtraction. When a worksheet contains subtraction problems, on the other hand, first graders often make "addition for subtraction" errors. Addition, a positive action, is thus natural in first grade, and subtraction is a secondary construction that is both harder and unnatural when young children are still constructing sums.

Because children tend to think positively, and because they construct subtraction *after* and *out of* addition, I advocate the postponement of subtraction until the second grade. Just as they notice the subtraction of one chip *after* noticing its addition and view the complementary class negatively *after* considering it positively, children become able to substract *after* they become able to do addition in their heads.

This does not imply that first graders cannot do any subtraction or that those who show interest should be prevented from using techniques of counting. My objection is to teaching them mindless techniques that serve only as tricks. Furthermore, subtraction comes easily anyway once the corresponding sum is solidly known.

Set partitioning, on the other hand, is an excellent approach to subtraction through addition. Set partitioning refers to knowing, for example, that "10" can be made with $9 + 1$, $8 + 2$, $7 + 3$, and so on (see Chapter 5). In set partitioning, the child looks for two numbers that combine to make a certain total. This is a positive mental action, which is much more natural for them than the negative action of subtraction. Once a child knows that $9 + 1 = 10$, $8 + 2 = 10$, $7 + 3 = 10$, and so on, he will soon know, without any instruction or effort, that $10 - 1 = 9$, $10 - 9 = 1$, $10 - 2 = 8$, $10 - 8 = 2$, and so on.

STORY PROBLEMS

"Story" problems involving subtraction can and ought to be emphasized from the beginning of first grade in real-life situations. In fact, story problems in real life, such as knowing how many cards to look for when only 38 of a deck of 40 can be found, are the only kinds of subtraction problems I advocate in first grade.

I will discuss story problems in three parts. In the first part, I will elaborate my reasons for advocating story problems. In the second part, I suggest that children should become able to logico-arithmetize their reality by making part-whole relationships rather than to solve specific subtraction problems such as "separating," "comparing," and "equalizing," or writing equations. The last part gives further evidence from research that led me to these conclusions.

Why Advocate Story Problems?

I advocate story problems in subtraction for the same reasons I recommend them in addition: First, children construct arithmetic by logico-arithmetizing reality; and, second, research has shown these problems to be relatively easy for first graders, in the absence of instruction.

Most math educators think about verbal problems as applications of computational "skills," rather than as the beginning point that eventually leads to generalized computation, without content, context, or practical purpose. But in subtraction, as in addition, children construct contentless numerical relationships such as $5 - 2 = 3$ out of their ideas about contents in everyday life. Having to eat two more pieces of carrots before being allowed to leave the table, receiving one more present than one's sibling, and wondering how many pieces of gum will be left after consuming a piece and giving one to a friend, are examples of such situations. Children construct arithmetic by logico-arithmetizing these contents (through reflective abstraction). Whether the objects involved are gum, presents, cards, or sea shells is unimportant.

The teaching of computational "skills" first, before the presentation of verbal problems, out of books rather than children's own lives, is a manifestation of the belief that skills are "put into" the child from books that are the repositories of knowledge, and that without these skills, children are not capable of thinking arithmetically. Children *do* have the capacity to think logically, and arithmetic develops out of this natural ability.

The research reported by Carpenter, Hiebert, and Moser (1979) and Carpenter and Moser (1982) shows how easy verbal problems are for first graders not only in addition but also in subtraction. Examples of the subtraction problems the latter gave are the following:

> *Separating:* Fred had 11 pieces of candy. He gave 7 pieces to Linda. How many pieces of candy did Fred have left?
> *Part-Part-Whole:* Brian has 14 flowers. Eight of them are red and the rest are yellow. How many yellow flowers does Brian have?
> *Comparison:* There are 6 boys and 8 girls on the soccer team. How many more girls than boys are there on the team? (p. 17)

The number triples used in these questions were the same as those used in the second category of their research on addition cited in Chapter 5: $3 + 8 = 11, 3 + 9 = 12, 4 + 7 = 11, 4 + 8 = 12, 4 + 9 = 13, 5 + 7 = 12, 5 + 8 = 13, 5 + 9 = 14, 6 + 8 = 14$, and $6 + 9 = 15$. The interviews were conducted in September, before the first graders received any formal instruction.

The percentages of children who gave correct answers to each of the three categories of questions were 42, 35, and 38 respectively (Carpenter and Moser, 1982, p. 19). The part-part-whole problems, the hardest of the three categories of questions (answered correctly by only 35 percent), involves class inclusion, which is cognitively difficult before the age of seven or eight (Chapter 1).

Ibarra and Lindvall (1982) obtained similar results with kindergarten children. With small numbers up to 7, they found that 37 percent of the children's answers were correct to questions such as "I have seven flowers. I give you three of my flowers. How many flowers do I have left?"

Logical Thinking as the Objective in Story Problems

Math educators and researchers such as Gibb (1956) and Schell and Burns (1962) have long viewed story problems in subtraction as consisting of "separating," "comparing," and "equalizing." Instead of thinking about verbal problems as addition or subtraction problems, we should view them as questions that children try to answer by thinking in their own ways. For example, the child does not necessarily have to use subtraction to answer an "equalizing" question that asks how many more children are needed to make a team of twelve. The logic of one-to-one correspondence or addition is adequate to solve this problem, and in fact Gibb noted that three-fourths of the second graders in her sample did use addition. Yet, she continued to interpret the problem as being one of the three applications of subtraction.

In real life, it is often impossible to draw clear lines of demarcation among addition, subtraction, multiplication, and division. I will illustrate with an example from Georgia DeClark's class. The children played a special game on Friday afternoon in which the class tried to guess what was in the paper bag brought by one of its members to school. There were thirteen children who had not had a turn to bring an object, and only three Fridays remained before the end of the year. The class had to decide how many children should have a turn on each subsequent Friday—a moral question of fairness as well as an intellectual question of arithmetic.

Some of the children proceeded to think about the problem by trying $3 + 3 + 3 = 9$ first, and then $4 + 4 + 4 = 12$. Others suggested a process of subtraction, that is, $13 - 3 = 10$ (ten left after the first Friday), $10 - 3 = 7$ (seven left after the second Friday), and $7 - 3 = 4$ (four left after the last Friday). There were two different ways of approaching the question, and a solution did not depend on whether the children proceeded by addition or by subtraction.

The problem could have been considered a division problem and, therefore, too hard for first graders. But if first graders are allowed to use their own ability to think, and the numbers involved are not too big, they are often capable of finding solutions. They knew that neither $1 + 1 + 1$ nor $2 + 2 + 2$ would come close to 13. This is why they tried $3 + 3 + 3$, and then $4 + 4 + 4$, by putting up the same number of fingers on each of three hands and counting the total.

The use of fingers in situations such as these is highly significant, and it attests to the undesirability of making first graders solve story problems by means of writing equations. While written equations help adults to think logically, first graders think better by using movable personal symbols such as fingers and chips. Equations should be tools for thinking, and not the ends that "prove" the acquisition of mathematical knowledge. In first grade, the imposition of writing, especially in the form of equations, can only interfere with children's thinking.

Our objective in story problems should be neither for children to become able to solve specific "subtraction" problems such as "separating," "comparing," and "equalizing," nor for them to become able to write equations. Rather, the objective should be for children to become able to logico-arithmetize their reality by making part-whole relationships.

In the rest of the chapter, I would like to discuss the research that led me to this conclusion. In essence, research has shown that in story problems the difficulty children have is, first, in the logic of part-whole relationships and, second, in arithmetic. Furthermore, thinking is one thing for first graders, and writing equations is quite another. Research has also shown that children articulate their confusion about which operation to use ("Is it a plus or a take-away?") only after being instructed in school.

The Research That Suggested Logical Thinking as the Objective

The importance of part-whole relationships. The verbs to "logicize" and to "logico-arithmetize" are helpful for understanding both the nature of arithmetic and story problems. In the class-inclusion task (in Chapter 1) children logicize, or make logical variables out of, the beads, flowers, fruit, or animals that are put in front of them. All the objects used in the task are observable, and all the words are understood by the child. Yet, young children in the preoperational period say that there are more dogs than animals, and more apples than fruit. They do this because they logicize reality in terms of a *succession* of part-whole relationships rather than *simultaneously* thinking about parts (dogs and cats) and wholes (animals). Only after making this logical relationship can they be expected to deduce the exact number of cats when the numbers of animals and dogs are given in a story problem. Piaget showed that children have to logicize reality before logico-arithmetizing it, and that arithmetic develops out of logic. Note that "logicize" and "logico-arithmetize" are verbs describing (mental) actions, that is, what the child *does*. This is a very different view of arithmetic from the notion that it is a body of knowledge consisting of "concepts," "facts," and "skills" to be learned.

Carpenter and Moser showed "part-part-whole" to be harder for first graders than "separating" as discussed above. Other researchers (Gibb, 1956, and Schell and Burns, 1962) have consistently found "comparing" to be harder than "separating" for second graders.

I suspected in light of Piaget's theory that if one kind of problem was more difficult than another, this might be because of differences in the difficulty of making correct part-whole relationships. For example, "separating" seemed easy because it involved only the (mental) removal of one part from a whole. The child could get the answer by thinking first about the whole and then about each part, and this could be done as successive rather than simultaneous acts. "Comparing" seemed much harder than "separating" because it involves two wholes, one of which must be mentally "transported" to the other and considered a part of the bigger whole. For example, if Mark has five balloons and Connie has twelve, and the child wants to know how many more Connie has, he mentally has to "transport" Mark's five to Connie's twelve and consider the five as part of the twelve. The logic of this part-whole relationship seems extremely difficult before the age of seven or eight because the difference between the two sets cannot be known without thinking simultaneously about the parts and the whole.

Based on the above considerations, I individually interviewed children in grades 1 to 5 in a Geneva public school[2] and later replicated this research in Glen Ellyn, Illinois. Among the questions I asked were the following:

> *Separating:* You have seven pieces of candy. You give me three of them. How many pieces do you have left?
>
> *Comparing:* You have seven pieces of candy. I have only three pieces. How many more do you have than I do?
>
> *Equalizing:* I have three little candles. I need seven of them for a birthday cake. How many more do I need? (The total number of candles needed was changed to eight for second graders, to nine for third graders, and so on, to make the question fit the reality of each age group.)

Inasmuch as I was interested in children's logic of part-whole relationships rather than in their arithmetic, I purposely kept the numbers small. I also provided the children with twenty to thirty chips and suggested that they use them if they wanted to. The interviews were conducted in May, at the end of the school year. The official curriculum of the Geneva public schools requires sums in first grade, but not subtraction and story problems. Story problems were sometimes given by individual teachers as supplements.

As expected, the first question (separating) turned out to be the easiest. One hundred percent of the children answered it correctly by the second grade (Table 6.1). In first grade, half of the children got the correct answer, and the other half could be divided into four categories. The first group (16 percent) gave 7 as the answer by taking seven chips out for themselves, giving three others to me, and explaining that there were seven left for themselves! The instruction they had "heard" was apparently "You have seven pieces of candy. You give me three pieces of candy." Eight percent gave 10 as the answer by adding 7 and 3. While these two groups made errors in part-whole relationships, the other two groups made errors of numerical precision. By counting out eight or six at the beginning instead of seven, one of these groups gave answers to 8 − 3 or to 6 − 3. The other group explained that they guessed to arrive at their wrong answer.

Of these findings, the most illuminating was the children's reason for

---

2. The assistance of Christiane Chabot, a teacher in the Geneva public schools, is gratefully acknowledged.

TABLE 6.1. Proportion of Children's Responses to Three "Subtraction" Problems

| | | Grade Level | | | | |
		1 N=50	2 N=51	3 N=20	4 N=44	5 N=18
Separating	The correct answer (Ans. 4)	52%	100%	100%	100%	100%
	Incorrect answers The child's whole (Ans. 7)	16				
	2 independent wholes added (Ans. 10)	8				
	Miscounting the initial whole (Ans. 5 or 3)	12				
	Guessing the answer (Ans. 5)	12				
Comparing	The correct answer (Ans. 4)	10	53	80	91	100
	Incorrect answers The child's whole (Ans. 7)	60	14	5		
	The 2 wholes added (Ans. 10)	4	10	5	2	
	Correction (to Ans. 4) when a justification of answering 7 or 10 was requested	26	12			
	Errors in numerical precision (e.g., Ans. 5)		12	10	7	
Equalizing	The correct answer (Ans. 4)	46	57	95	93	100
	Incorrect answers The whole (Ans. 7)	14	8	5	2	
	Correction (to Ans. 4) when a justification of answering 7 was requested	30	20			
	Others (e.g., answering 10 followed by 7 and errors in numerical precision)	10	14		5	

giving 7 as the answer. I had known from previous research that children often used one of the numbers given in the problem as the answer. But the reason for this behavior had never been explained. I could now see that the statement, "You give me three of them" could easily be related not to *his* collection but to the real or imaginary pool of candy. My respect for children's intelligence was reinforced again. They indeed make mistakes *because* they think, and the teacher cannot react to these errors without understanding how the child is thinking.

Once I understood the first category of error, the second one became easier to interpret. Since young children tend to think positively in all kinds of situations, it is not surprising that a few added the two sets. When children become able to make more relationships, they interpret words such as "of them" and "have left" in a different way ("You give me three *of them*" and "How many pieces do you *have left?*")

While the first two categories of errors can be accounted for as faulty logic, the other two categories were the results of numerical imprecision. The children who took out eight chips instead of seven, and said that $8 - 3 = 5$ had made the correct part-whole relationship. Those who gave 5 as the answer by guessing it were likewise correct in their logic, but not in arithmetic. Table 6.1 thus suggested that to become able to solve story problems, children must first develop their logic. Once their logic is developed, they can (with care) deduce the right number.

As expected from previous research, the "comparing" question turned out to be the most difficult one for first graders. Only 10 percent of the first graders answered this question correctly (Table 6.1). Sixty percent replied, "seven," as if the question had been, "How many do you have?" rather than "How many *more* do you have?"[3] When asked to use the chips to explain how they got seven as the answer, these children gave seven to themselves and three to me before saying, "See? I have seven." Their difficulty was indeed in the logic of the part-whole relationship. By assimilating my question to their logic, they "heard" a question that was different from the one I asked.

Four percent of the first graders added the two wholes and gave ten as the answer. Twenty-six percent corrected themselves when asked to explain, using chips, how they had arrived at seven or ten. In other words, 90 percent of the first graders gave wrong answers, but about a third of them corrected themselves when asked for an explanation. This illustrates that children sometimes correct themselves when they try to explain their reasoning to someone else. In the context of trying to make sense to another person, children often make relationships at a higher level than before.

These error patterns confirm the theory that at age seven or eight there is

---

3. Gibb (1956) reported the same phenomenon.

a major turning point in children's development of logic. The percentages of children who answered the question correctly increased from 10 in first grade to 53, 80, 91, and 100 respectively in the subsequent grades (Table 6.1). Those who gave seven as the answer decreased from 60 percent in first grade to 14 percent in second and 0 percent in fourth grade.

Table 6.1 suggests once again the importance of children's development of logic. Answers resulting from numerical errors are almost completely absent from this table; it can be said that children's difficulty in this type of situation is because of incorrect part-whole relationships.

The "equalizing" question (How many more . . .?") was easier than the previous one for first graders but about the same in difficulty for those in second grade and beyond. The part-whole relationship is easier for first graders to make because only one set is involved, with the positive action of addition. While being a little easier than the previous question, the data in Table 6.1 also support the idea that second grade is a special time in children's development of logic. The percentages of correct answers rose from 46 in first grade to 57, 95, 93, and 100 respectively in the subsequent grades.

At this point, a comment can be made about the role of instruction in the preceding discussion. In my view, especially with respect to arithmetic, children learn from instruction only what they can learn with the knowledge they have already constructed. This is the same argument that undergirded the discussions of place value (Chapter 4) and equations (Chapter 5). Place value is taught in first grade, but first graders cannot understand it and, therefore, do not learn it. The reading and writing of equations are also taught in first grade, but children learn these differently according to their levels of development. If correct answers were attributable to instruction, furthermore, Carpenter and others would have obtained percentages of correct answers near 0 prior to instruction instead of near 40. The effects of instruction can thus be inferred to be minimal.

The discussion of Table 6.1 highlights the difference between Piaget's theory of logico-arithmetical knowledge and math educators and other researchers' empiricist views. For them, relationships exist *inside* story problems, outside the child's head, and are not constructions that have to be made by each child. For Gibb (1956), for example, problems are simply "understood" or "not understood" by the child:

> The lack of understanding for comparative problems was observed in particular during the interviews. For example, when a child was presented with eight forks and five knives and the question, "How many more forks do you have than knives?" the response was commonly "Eight forks." (p. 74)

For Carpenter, Hiebert, and Moser (1979), what is "out there" is "the structure of the problem" and the child's (mental) actions consist only of "strategies." Examples of the strategies they give for addition problems are "counting-all," "counting-on from first number," "counting-on from larger number," "known fact," and "heuristics." For subtraction, they delineate the strategies of "separating," "separating to," "adding on," "matching," "counting back," "counting back to," "counting up from smaller," "known fact," and "heuristic." In this conception of verbal problems, children use a variety of "strategies" rather than logico-arithmetizing (structuring) reality.

There can be no "structure of the problem" for a child until *he* makes this structure in his head! In a school that encourages each child to think actively in his own way in all kinds of situations, I fully expect the part-whole structure (or relationship) to be made earlier by more children.

The undesirability of making children write equations. The writing of equations helps adults solve story problems in two steps, first by putting the numbers into the correct logical relationship, and then by computing the answer. Math educators teach children to write equations because they assume that children, too, solve these problems in the same way. Piaget's theory and research suggest that the reasoning implicit in this writing is about three levels beyond the way children think to solve story problems. This premature writing amounts to forcing the child to think in ways that are alien to him.

Children first think, or mentally act, to get the answer. Having done this, they can think about what they did and conceptualize how they produced the desired answer. Once they know how they produced the answer, they become able to represent, or externalize, this knowledge. This representation is done first in their own words with personal symbols (such as counters and fingers). The writing of equations is the next level that involves conventional signs and rules. The research by Piaget and his collaborators clarifies the difference between the first two levels mentioned above. It shows, in essence, that children cannot think about their own thinking, if they do not think first!

When children are given a story problem, they think to get the answer (reflective abstraction). Once they get the answer, they often do not know how they reasoned to arrive at it. In the research reported in Table 6.1, for example, children often gave the correct answer, but when I asked them how they got it, they replied, "I don't know," "I just did it in my head," or "I just know it."

This phenomenon reminded me of the many studies reported in *The*

Grasp of Consciousness (Piaget, 1974c).[4] These studies demonstrated that children first become able to produce a desired effect, and only later become able to think about their own actions and to construct ideas about how they produced the desired effect. He further showed that this construction takes place very slowly, through a number of "wrong" levels.

For example, children become able to crawl at a very early age. Henriques-Christophides asked children between the ages of four and ten how they crawled on all fours and found three levels among their descriptions— the "Z" pattern, the "N" pattern, and the "X" pattern. In the "Z" pattern, typically given around age four, children say that the left hand advances first and then the right hand, followed by the left leg and right leg. In the "N" pattern, given around the ages of five to six, the explanation is that the left hand and left leg advance simultaneously first, followed by the simultaneous movement of the right hand and leg. The "X" pattern, the correct one, is given around the ages of seven to eight. At this level, the child says he makes the left hand and right leg advance first, and then the right hand and left leg. In other words, when children think about how they produced the desired effect, they do one thing and think they are doing something else, before becoming able to conceptualize their own actions accurately.

Walking on all fours involves external actions. Solving story problems, by contrast, involves mental actions that are not observable. While these actions may seem different from external ones, one is really an extension of the other. Mental and material actions are both involved when the child figures out how to walk on all fours. Mental and physical actions are likewise indissociably involved when the child takes out three candles, and makes a separate group of four as he counts, "4-5-6-7." The external actions that are necessary for the younger child later become unnecessary, and as they do, mental action becomes independent of physical actions.

Children who finally become aware of how they produce an answer are better able to express their ideas with everyday language and movable symbols than with equations. When children show how they got the answer by putting out three chips (or fingers), and counting out four more while saying, "4-5-6-7," they are simply externalizing the action they went through to get the answer.

Equations, by contrast, involve conventional rules that may be in conflict with the way the child thinks and talks. Children's writing "3 − 7= 4"

---

4. The original title of this book was *La Prise de Conscience (Taking Cognizance* or *Becoming Aware)*, and its English translation is unfortunate. I say "unfortunate" because it is one more example of an empiricist assimilation of Piaget's theory, implying that consciousness can be grasped, as if it existed somewhere to be grasped.

illustrates this point. This sequence of numbers corresponds to the way the child talks when he says, "If I have three but want seven, I need four more." Chances are, however, that the way the child really thinks is $3 + 1 + 1 + 1 + 1 = 7$.

In Chapter 5, I stated with evidence from research that equations are not "number sentences," but a highly unusual form of writing that is different from the representation of ordinary speech. In an ordinary sentence, for example, we do not say the same thing twice, but in $7 - 3 = 4$, as well as in $4 + 3 = 7$, each element is represented twice. Many studies were cited in Chapter 5 to show that being able to add numbers is one thing (reflective abstraction), and that being able to read and write equations is quite another thing (representation of the reflective abstraction with conventional signs).

Carpenter and his collaborators retested the first graders in May, after instruction in how to read and write equations. The instruction these children received in the DMP program (*Developing Mathematical Processes*, Romberg, Harvey, Moser, Montgomery, and Dana, 1974) single-mindedly emphasized the reading and writing of equations. In presenting the findings, Carpenter made the following observations that pointed up the difference between thinking and writing equations for first graders:

> Once they had written a sentence (equation) most children appeared to ignore it and used the verbal problem to decide on a solution strategy. (Carpenter, 1980, p. 27)
>
> Only a third of the children wrote valid sentences for the Comparison subtraction or Equalizing problems while over three-fourths generated appropriate solutions. (p. 24) . . . In cases where children wrote an incorrect sentence but computed the correct answer, they would often complete the open sentence with their answer. (pp. 27–28)
>
> In spite of the fact that children were consistently given directions to write the sentence before they solved the problem, about a fourth of the children generally solved the problem before they wrote the sentence. In many cases it appeared that they were unable to write the sentence before they knew the complete number triple (the answer). (p. 22)

In their earlier report, Carpenter and his collaborators (1979, p. 59) noted that very few children used the wrong operation before instruction. Referring to older children's asking, "Is this a plus or take-away?" they also speculated that this problem may be "a result of learning symbolic representation." In my opinion, these authors should have gone further in pointing out the harm done by traditional instruction.

In schools that use other programs, teachers often give tricks by saying to children that if the problem includes the expression "in all" or "altogether," it is a "plus," and that if it says, "How many are *left?*" it is a "take-away."

Children begin to ask absurd questions such as "Is this a plus or take-away?" only after being instructed in school.

COMMENTS AND CONCLUSION

Story problems in real life situations can and ought to be the focus of children's activity. The emphasis should be on the child's own thinking in his own way to logico-arithmetize his reality. This objective is very different both from those quoted at the beginning of this chapter *(Macmillan Mathematics)* and from those of such forward-looking programs as DMP. These series emphasize techniques for children to use to become able to *write* correct answers.

Piaget's theory of logico-mathematical knowledge leads to very different objectives. Since logico-mathematical knowledge consists of relationships made by the child, what is important is what happens in the child's head. By eliminating mindless techniques and arbitrary rules to produce correct, written answers, and by encouraging children to think in their own honest ways, we can turn out students who can think and trust their own thinking. Students who can think have a solid foundation for further learning. Those who can only apply ready-made techniques may get good grades and high test scores for a few years, but they will not have the foundation necessary for higher mathematics.

Part III

ACTIVITIES AND PRINCIPLES OF TEACHING

CHAPTER 7

Activities to Stimulate
Numerical Thinking

Written with Georgia DeClark

Having discussed the parts of Piaget's theory that are particularly important for first grade arithmetic (Part I), and having conceptualized its objectives (Part II), we are now ready to consider the activities that will foster their attainment. We have developed two kinds of activities described by Piaget: problem solving in daily living (Piaget, 1936) and group games (Piaget, 1932). In this chapter, we will give many examples from both categories. But first we will set out in general terms what we think are the advantages of such activities over traditional instructional methods. Teachers' use of worksheets and their reliance on them will be singled out for special criticism.

ADVANTAGES OF USING ARITHMETIC-RELATED ACTIVITIES

Situations in Daily Living

   Situations in everyday life in the classroom can be mined for the opportunities they present for arithmetic in action. The use of these situations (1) encourages children to logico-arithmetize reality and (2) provokes the development of their autonomy. The first point focuses on children's construction of arithmetic, while the second emphasizes the broader context in which arithmetic (as well as other subjects) is meaningfully learned.
   Arithmetic comes not from books, teachers' explanations, or computer programs, but from each child's thinking as he logico-arithmetizes his reality. Situations in daily living stimulate this natural process. For example, recall the situation described in Chapter 2 in which 13 out of 24 first graders voted for the first of two alternatives. Then one child announced that it was not necessary to continue the voting because the outcome was obvious to him. Most children were unable to follow this reasoning, but *did* know that by counting the votes for the other alternative, they would come to a "fair"

decision. These first graders thus logico-arithmetized this situation, either by thinking that 13 + 13 is greater than 24 (a part-whole relationship), or by reasoning that 13 is greater than 11 (a comparison of parts).

In traditional elementary math programs, computation is introduced prior to word or "story" problems. These verbal problems are conceived of as problem-solving exercises to which well-known computational "skills" should be applied. We think otherwise. We believe that the contents of, and situations in, children's lives should serve as the context for their constructing (inventing) formal arithmetic.[1] It is contrary to what we know about the way children think to begin with contentless computation and only afterwards move on to applications of that know-how in the real world. Parenthetically, if one of the purposes of teaching arithmetic is to enable children to solve real-life problems, it behooves us to encourage them to deal with real problems from the very first day of grade one.

Let us proceed to the second point. A teacher who fosters the development of children's autonomy is one who encourages them to think and to make decisions for themselves. Voting cannot occur without alternatives to vote on, and children have to think in order to create these alternatives. Hence democratic decision making fosters children's social, moral, and political development as well as their intellectual development in general and their learning of arithmetic.

Decisions are made by individuals as well as groups. When a child is asked to go to the office and return with one book for each person in the class, he has to think not only about how many children are present but also about those who are absent and about the teacher. Autonomous children are more likely to develop the initiative to think about all the factors relevant to a decision. Heteronomous children rely on being told.

Situations in daily living present opportunities for children to structure and define problems out of the ambiguities of the real world. These opportunities are lost when problems are structured for them. Worksheets present ready-made problems, neatly organized and presented in a purified form. The teacher tells the pupils what the problems are and considers it his responsibility to teach them how to solve them. Worksheets encourage obedience, passivity, and the mechanical application of techniques. Hence their use reinforces children's natural heteronomy, thereby slowing down their development of autonomy.

In everyday living, children formulate their own problems out of the ambiguities of reality, and figure out how to solve these problems in their

---

1. Those who say, "Arithmetic is all around us," do not understand the nature of arithmetic. Arithmetic is made by each individual out of his interaction with the environment. It is not "out there" in external reality, around us.

own ways. Autonomous children are more likely to take the initiative in posing questions about the things *they* notice. These children are more likely to think hard about *their* questions, in the course of which inventions or novel approaches to problems are made. This mental activity is what lies at the heart of intellectual or cognitive development.

Group Games

While problems encountered in day-to-day life encourage logico-arithmetical reasoning, they do not lend themselves to repetitive acts of addition. It is in the context of play that children can practice addition. Group games provide an avenue for structured play, in which they are intrinsically motivated to think about and remember numerical combinations. Group games also allow children to decide which specific game they want to play, when, and with whom. Finally, they encourage social interaction and feedback from peers.

Work and play.   Most adults, including educators, make a sharp dichotomy between "work" and "play." In this common-sense view, worksheets are included in "work," and games are included in "play." Proponents of this view say that children have to learn to live and work in the world of adults, and classroom experiences therefore have to prepare them for work. These people grant that children *do* need to play but relegate this need to recess, gym, and playground activities. When group games are allowed in the serious atmosphere of the classroom, they are generally reserved for "after the children have finished their work."

There is no differentiation between work and play during infancy, and babies learn an enormous amount during the first two years. They learn about objects both physically and logico-mathematically (Sinclair, Stambak, Lézine, Rayna and Verba, 1982) and about people in all sorts of ways. They also learn to walk, talk, and otherwise make their presence very well known.

Work and play become differentiated as the child grows older, but this differentiation is never complete, even in adulthood. "Pure work" stands for the unpleasant tasks we engage in for extrinsic rewards. "Pure play" represents the things we do for our own pleasure, for intrinsic rather than extrinsic reasons. But some play involves hard work, and some hard work is intrinsically rewarding. Adults' hobbies and vacation activities (sports, cooking, making pottery, playing musical instruments, climbing up mountains, skiing down slopes, and visiting ancient ruins) often require a great deal of concerted effort. Work and play can share common elements (intrinsic motivation, enjoyment, learning, and a sense of accomplishment).

The argument that children have to learn to do unpleasant, hard work because they will eventually have to earn a living is misplaced. Adults get paid for the unpleasant work they do. They work for things they choose to have (family, house, car, etc.), and that is different from working under compulsory attendance laws and adult expectations. Finally, hard work and unpleasant work are not one and the same.

Moreover, children are in school supposedly to learn. But not all school-work is conducive to learning. Work that does not necessarily result in learning includes busywork (especially in the form of worksheets), activities intended to teach contents that are, in reality, too hard for children (place value in first grade), and memorizing words for the sole purpose of passing a test.

While some play does not lead to learning, it is amazing how children learn as they play. Some of their knowledge remains intuitive for a long time (e.g., the physics learned from flying kites, the zoology learned from visiting caged animals, and the sociology picked up from watching appalling hours of television). When play becomes too easy or too passive (e.g., the card game of War at age eight), children indeed cease to learn. It must be pointed out, however, that there are many levels of "knowing." As will be discussed in Chapter 10, our children continued to count the dots on the dice for months to obtain results that they already "knew." When they finally *really* knew a sum, this behavior stopped. It is thus not easy to tell exactly when play ceases to have educational value.

The point we are trying to make is that many adults, including educators, fail to be cognizant of the importance of play. Early childhood educators have long been convinced of its educational value, and its continuation into the first grade is what we are advocating here. Teachers can often be heard asking a child, "Have you finished your work?" This question usually means "Have you produced observable results?" But results of what? Thinking? Learning? The question we should be asking is not whether children are working and producing results, but whether they are thinking about and learning what we want them to learn in an optimal way.

Social interaction.   Group games necessitate interaction among the players. We will not repeat here what was said elsewhere (Kamii and DeVries, 1980, Chapter 2) about the advantages of group games in general for the development of autonomy. Suffice it to say that group games involve rules and social interaction, and the possibility of making rules and decisions together is essential for the development of autonomy. When children are allowed to make decisions for themselves, they negotiate rules and see the consequences of their own decisions. When they are not allowed to make decisions, they become passive and heteronomous.

The social interaction involved in math games provides an alternative to the teacher as the source of right answers. When peers debate which answers are correct, they become sources of truth, and children develop confidence in their own ability to figure things out. Furthermore, since the challenges are immediate, children have the possibility of defending and/or correcting their own processes of thinking rather than waiting for worksheet answers to be returned the following day.

It is true that worksheets sometimes produce some learning. Some children do learn the result of 4 + 2 after they have written the answer often enough. But in games, children are mentally more active. They constantly supervise each other. Furthermore, they often notice more intelligent ways of dealing with numbers than mechanically adding them. In Double War, for example, when 4 + 2 and 3 + 2 turn up, they notice that it is stupid to add the numbers because all they have to do is compare the 4 and the 3. They also notice that 6 + 3 is the same thing as 3 + 6, and that adding-on is easier if they change 3 + 6 to 6 + 3.

Games are a natural form of human activity that begin to emerge around age five (e.g., in games such as Musical Chairs and board games) and continue to be of interest throughout the life span (e.g., football and bridge). Children are mentally more active while playing games that they choose and that interest them than while filling out worksheets. Many children like to fill out worksheets, but what they learn from them is that truth comes from the teacher's head and that math is a mysterious set of rules that come from sources external to their own thinking.

Worksheets and group games are direct expressions of different theories about how children learn arithmetic. Worksheets are based on the notion of facilitating the individual's internalization (rather than reconstruction or personal reinvention) of society's knowledge, and this without the interference of a group. Social interaction is valued in a Piagetian approach because of its importance for the construction of logico-mathematical knowledge. According to Piaget, the confrontation of points of view causes children to decenter and often results in a higher-level coordination *(équilibration majorante)*.

DEVELOPING ARITHMETIC ACTIVITIES
FROM DAILY LIVING SITUATIONS

First, we will see how situations in daily living provide occasions for numerical thinking. For our purposes, these situations will be described as they arise in the classroom and range, for example, from voting to planning a party. All of these activities are presented from the perspective of the teacher (Georgia DeClark).

Voting

Choosing a name for one's reading group. I divided the class into four reading groups and told them that I wanted each group to choose a name for itself. The only stipulation I made was that everyone in the group had to agree on the name.

Marty's group had six children in it. As the children discussed and argued about names, Marty shook his head and said, "If we only get three people who like my idea, it won't win 'cause that means that three people don't like it." When I reminded him that everyone in the group had to be in agreement, he laughed and said, "Oh, that's got to be six for it and 0 against it. We'll *never* be able to agree on that!"

The group eventually agreed on the name "Red Devils."

Deciding how many times to practice. The children usually protested against having to fill in the entire line with the letter they were working on in their handwriting books each day. I asked how many times they thought they should practice writing the letter "M" on each line. As they offered their suggestions and votes, I wrote them on the board as follows:

6 times: 20 votes
9 times: 5 votes

One of the five who had voted for the second alternative then announced that he wanted to change his vote. I asked, "What do I have to do to what I wrote on the board?" Some children replied, "Change the 20 to 21, and the 5 to 4." One child said, "You don't need to change anything because the 20 still win."

Settling a dispute. A dispute had developed over the pickup sticks, and the children were screaming and shouting. I decided to intervene and asked the children to let me hold the sticks, so that they could decide what to do without screaming and shouting. As usual, I told them that they could have the pickup sticks when they decided on a fair way to resolve the conflict.

The next thing I noticed was a vote in which Ann was asking, "Who thinks the boys should have them?" All the boys were, of course, voting for the boys. All the girls likewise voted for themselves.

Marty and Ed then came to me to say that the vote was unfair because there were fifteen girls and only ten boys in the class. I told them that they had to talk to the other children, and not to me, because I was not involved in the dispute and was not even voting.

Nobody understood the two boys' argument, and the girls did not even pay attention (either because they were emotionally unwilling to listen or because they were cognitively unable to understand).

Marty and Ed decided to go out in the hallway looking for boys to come in and vote! They said they needed five more boys to make the vote fair—not a bad solution to a hard problem of proportionality. (Thankfully, it didn't occur to them to exclude five girls!)

Electing the president. During the time of the 1980 presidential election, the class and I discussed different aspects of voting, such as secret ballots, voting only once, election officials, and so on. On November 2, we visited the polling place in our school, noticing the workers, voting booths, and the locked box for completed ballots. The children then decided to have their own election in the classroom.

During the discussion that followed, someone suggested passing a sheet of paper around the room for each person to sign. The list would then be given to the "worker" at the booth. When each pupil came up to vote, the "worker" would cross his or her name off the list and give one ballot, thus making sure that each person voted only once. I made mimeographed ballots and the children proceeded to make a voting booth with things from around the room. They chose Steve to be the "worker," found a box for the ballots, and began the voting.

When Steve said that everyone had voted, we counted the ballots. I began by writing "Reagan" and "Carter" on the board. I then proceeded to open each ballot and write a numeral under each name. As the total changed, I erased the old numeral and wrote the next number. The totals increased fairly evenly, that is, 6 votes each for Carter and Reagan, followed by 6 versus 7, 7 versus 7, 8 versus 7, and so on.

When the votes totaled 11 for Reagan and 9 for Carter, Ed commented that we were getting close to the end, since 11 + 9 was 20, and we had 25 children in the class. Someone else pointed out that one person was absent and we would have only 24 votes. The next vote was for Carter, and we now had 10 for him and 11 for Reagan. The children commented that there must be only three ballots left to count. Marty quickly pointed out that if it ended up with 12 and 12, I would have to vote to break the tie. When the last ballot was found to be for Reagan, making the totals 13 for him and 11 for Carter, the Reagan "fans" cheered. As the noise subsided, I heard someone say, "What about Evan? He's not here today. We will have to wait till he comes back and votes to see who won." Brad was quick to disagree, saying, "Evan's vote doesn't matter because if he votes for Carter, it'll be 13 to 12, and Reagan will still win."

Taking Attendance

Class attendance was an important topic, particularly since we did so much voting and needed to know the total number of children present each day. The children were responsible for "checking in" every morning and afternoon by putting their cards in their pockets on an attendance chart. The person whose job it was to report the attendance would then look at the chart to know whose cards were left in the big pocket for the entire class, write those names on an attendance slip, and take it to the office.

I often asked about the number of children present. I found that if I said, "I see that only twenty-one people have checked in today. How many people are absent?" almost all the children could figure it out. However, if I reversed the question by saying, "Wow, there are four people out today. How many are here?" it was more difficult to figure out the answer.

Making Sure Things Don't Get Lost

Scissors. I found only two pairs of scissors in the can that should have contained twenty-five pairs. I communicated this dissatisfaction to the class and asked how many more had to be found.

This was a hard question, like deducing the number present from the small number absent. I did not insist on getting the answer. We collected some, counted the total, and looked for more . . . until we found twenty-five pairs.

Knowing how many cards to look for. The children used many decks of cards for the various card games they played in the classroom. Because most decks were "customized" for a particular game, it was necessary to keep track of which deck was to be used for which game. The children suggested adding a piece of paper to each deck, noting the game and the number of cards. They also discussed the importance of counting the cards at the end of the game to be sure that no cards were lost. For example, if at the end of a game of Double War, the children found only thirty-eight cards from a deck of forty, they knew they needed to look for the two that were missing.

Taking a card game to the lunchroom. Just before we adjourned for lunch, Geraldine and Kristina asked me if they could take a game to the lunchroom. "Like *Piggy Bank?*" I asked. This was *exactly* the game I wanted them to play to learn the set partitioning of 5. The children answered, "Yes."

I told them that it was OK with me as long as they did not lose any cards. "What can you do to make sure you won't lose any?" I asked.

Kristina said, "Count them now, and count them before coming back." I asked them to write the number on a piece of paper before leaving the room, just to make sure they would not forget how many would have to be found.

Pieces of a game. When we finished a game of *Tens* a little too early for the lunch break, I decided to call the kids' attention to the fact that it said "72 playing pieces" at the corner of the box. "Could we check to make sure we have seventy-two pieces?" I asked. The children each started counting and got mixed up about which pieces they had counted.

"We could make little piles," Ed suggested. "How many should there be in each pile?" I asked. Skip said, "Eight," and Brad suggested, "Ten."

The children agreed on ten after the usual amount of argument and found seventy-four pieces altogether (seven piles, which they counted by 10's, and four loose ones). They immediately knew that there was something wrong. Ed said, "I think some piles have less than ten" (an astute hypothesis). Skip suggested comparing the height of the piles (a more intelligent method than what *I* had thought of). They quickly found two piles that were lower than the others and had the satisfaction of having found the right number of pieces.

Distributing Things

Letters to go home. A messenger from the office brought copies of a letter to all the parents. Brad wanted to distribute them in all the mailboxes. (We had two rows of 2-lb coffee cans in front of the room to serve as the children's mailboxes.)

When he finished distributing the letters, Brad had three copies left over and asked me what he should do with them. "I think we can use them as scratch paper," I told him, and went on to ask, "How many copies do you think Mrs. X sent from the office?"

Brad pondered the question, looked at the mailboxes, and announced "twenty-eight." When I asked the class if everybody agreed, some children had no idea what we were talking about. Brad explained that there were twenty-five mailboxes and three letters left over. As usual, some children insisted on an empirical approach: counting.

Letters to go home on another occasion. Kristina and Carol were distributing notes in the mailboxes, having agreed that Kristina would fill the thirteen mailboxes on the top row and Carol would fill the 12 on the bottom row. Carol gave Kristina the thirteen notes she needed and proceeded to put the rest into the cans on the bottom row.

As Carol worked, she realized that she did not have enough notes to fill all twelve cans. Her first idea was to ask Kristina to give four notes back to her. "No," Kristina refused, "you gave me thirteen, and I need all of them." "But I don't have enough, and I need four more," Carol insisted. When the girls told me of their problem, I said, "I guess you'll need to get some more. How many notes did Mrs. X give us?" Carol's approach was to run back to the mailboxes and count each note. Kristina looked confused and chose to let

Carol figure out the answer. And Ed, who had been listening to us, casually remarked "21 'cause it's 22-23-24-25, the four notes you're missing."

Buttons to return.   A nearby school had been closed, and the children who used to attend it began to come to Lincoln School. To promote a school spirit, the P.T.A. decided to give a "button" to every child saying, "I go to Lincoln School."

The office said it was sending "a few extra" to make sure no one is left out, with the request that the leftover buttons be returned.

"How can we decide how many to return?" I asked the class. Mary said, "Count twenty-five and return the rest." Kristina said, "No, give one to everybody, and *then* return the rest."

Counting was apparently not a dependable technique for Kristina for such an important distribution, and she wanted to see a button in every hand before returning the leftover ones. We tried Mary's way, predicted how many will have to be returned according to her way (three), and ended up doing what Kristina had suggested. The result was the same.

Construction paper with which to make books.   I announced to the class that I had just enough contruction paper for each person to have two pieces, one for the cover and one for the back of the book that everybody was about to make.

Marty asked if I had enough for Jane, the only child absent that day. When I assured him that I did, he announced, "That means you have fifty." When I asked him how he figured that out, he said it was like two quarters that made 50 cents.

Collecting Permission Slips

The children had taken permission slips home to have their parents sign them to authorize the taking of pictures at school. The official class list given by the office was divided into boys and girls, and I had no say in this practice. I usually did not like to see competition between the boys and girls either, but had noticed that this was a situation in which *everybody* worked hard to determine which team won. So I decided to write the following on the board after checking off in my list the names of those who had brought their slips back:

Boys: 3 in
Girls: 6 in

I asked how many more boys and how many more girls needed to bring their slips back. The children asked how many boys and girls there were in the class, and I asked them, as usual, "How can you figure it out?" They suggested having the boys stand up to count them, having the girls stand up afterwards, and looking at the attendance chart. After thus finding ten boys and fifteen girls, they counted on their fingers and managed to agree on seven as the answer for the boys.

When the children tried to figure out how many more girls needed to bring their slips back, Marty (one of the most advanced children) remarked that it was much harder to work with (a total of) fifteen than (a total of) twenty-five! When I asked the class if they agreed, most of them said "Yes!" Some children paired up to have fifteen fingers altogether and some began to say, "Nine more."

Kate announced, "Four more," and explained her answer by putting up ten fingers and taking six away. She had forgotten that she had meant to use one hand twice to get fifteen! I suggested she pair up with someone else to have fifteen fingers available. She was *very* surprised to find nine as the answer.

Everybody finally agreed on the answers and I put the following on the board:

Boys (10):   3 in, 7 more
Girls (15):   6 in, 9 more

The boys declared themselves ahead because only seven more had to bring their slips back! Some girls retorted that *they* won because more girls had turned theirs in. I decided not to pursue this argument because proportionality was much too hard for them.

Later, I figured out why a total of twenty-five was easier for the children than fifteen. There were usually no more than 5 absent. Not having to deal with a change in "decades" must have made 20 + 5, for example, easier than 15 − 6.

Returning Library Books

The class went to the school library once a week to hear a story and check books out. Although it was the children's responsibility to return the books on time, I became involved from time to time, when the librarian brought me a list of names of the people who had overdue books. In order to help the children remember to return the books, I wrote their names on the board, followed by the number of books that needed to be returned, as follows:

Overdue Books

Skip	8
Jackie	1
Kristina	6
Roger	1
Bob	3

(I began by asking the *child* to write his own name on the board. I had to abandon this practice when I found that kids began not to return books because of the attraction of writing on the board!) When a child had eight overdue books, for example, and brought back three of them, I posed the following question to the entire class: "Skip had eight overdue books, but he has brought back three of them. Now he needs to erase the eight after his name. What number does he need to write in?"

On March 17, Geraldine told me she had a book due that day and another one that was due on the nineteenth. "How many more days do you have until that one is due?" I asked her. After a moment of reflection, she said, "One, if you count only tomorrow; two, if you count today and tomorrow; and three, if you count today and tomorrow and the day after."

Opening Books

I noticed that when I told the children to open their books at page 43, for example, some had no idea whether to search in front or in back of page 56, if they happened to have opened their book there. Those who did not know how to look for the numeral 43 looked around to see what picture was on page 43 and looked for the same picture.

I did not want to discourage this intelligent behavior but nevertheless wanted children to figure out whether page 43 came before or after page 56. Soliciting the more advanced children's help had to be ruled out, since these children tended to do the work for others. I decided, therefore, to ask the children individually, if they were still engaged in trial-and-error, "Now, let's think. Should 43 come before or after 56?"

It is easy for children to know which number is *bigger*. The before-after and left-right convention of a book introduces a small element of difficulty that encourages trial-and-error. My question was enough to encourage these children to think about the possibility of thinking.

Planning a Party

While planning a farewell party for a student observer from a nearby college, the children were trying to decide what kinds and amounts of food to bring. When someone suggested bringing apples, I posed the question, "If everyone agrees to apples, how many apples do you think we will need, since you have also decided we will have carrots, celery, peanuts, and raisins?"

Mary thought for a moment and said, "If five people bring five apples and someone else brings one, there will be enough for everybody." (There were twenty-six children in the class at that time.) I was astounded by her quick thinking and asked, "How did you figure that out so quickly?" Her response: "I counted by 5's. See? 5-10-15-20-25, and then 1 more is 26."

Marty pointed out to her, however, that 26 apples would be enough only for the children, and that the teacher and guest would not get any. Mary accepted this idea and said, "Okay, then, the last person will have to bring three instead of one." It was very clear to her what needed to be changed, and Marty also understood Mary's thinking. The majority of the class, however, did not follow this exchange and did not care.

Limiting the Number in a Group

I made a cozy reading corner, which was carpeted, sectioned off with a divider, and meant for the kids to sit up or lie down to look at or read books. There were so many children in this corner at the beginning that the class voted, with my assistance, to limit the number that could be there at any given time to seven.

The children would then go to this corner, count the number of children already there, and say, for example, "Four. Three more can go, you, you, and me, but not you!"

Knowing How Many Guesses Are Left and Making a Schedule

The children played a guessing game on Friday afternoons in which the class tried to guess what was in the paper bag brought to school by one of its members. Ten guesses were allowed.

Until today (October 13, 1980), somebody began to say "Two more!" after the eighth guess. Today, however, a few started saying, "Three more!" after the seventh guess. They, of course, continued to announce, "two more" and "only one left" after the eighth and ninth guesses.

Toward the end of the year, there were thirteen children in the final round who had not had a turn to bring an object in a bag, and three Fridays left before the end of the year. The class had to decide how many children should have a turn on each subsequent Friday. Some of the children proceeded by addition and tried 3 + 3 + 3 and then 4 + 4 + 4. Others suggested a process of subtraction, that is, 13 − 3 = 10, 10 − 3 = 7, 7 − 3 = 4; and then 13 − 4 = 9 and 9 − 4 = 5. In the end, the class agreed to schedule four people on the first two Fridays and five on the last one.

Making a Calendar as a Christmas Present

In previous years, I had always had each child make a calendar as a Christmas present for his parents. This year, however, I was more conscious of the educational value of this activity, since the children were not writing numerals in workbooks. Making calendars seemed to be an excellent activity because, in making them, children write numerals for a personally meaningful purpose rather than practicing writing just to obey the teacher.

I made ditto sheets with seven columns for each day of the week and six rows. With the children, I made a model on the board for each month so that they could copy it later. After writing "January, 1981," for example, I told them that the first fell on a Thursday. I was particularly careful when we got to the teens because some children still wanted to "spell" "thirteen, fourteen, fifteen," for example, by writing "31, 41, 51."

When we got to twenty-eight, one child volunteered the information that if it had been written with an 8 and a 2, that would have been eighty-two.

When we got to September, another child remarked that there were three months left.

By that time, I decided not to fill in every single day of the month, and told the kids to figure out what to write in between and to check with the Saturdays filled in (5, 12, 19, 26) to know whether or not they made any mistake.

The kids had trouble, and when they came to a vote as to whether they preferred copying everything from the board or filling in the blanks on their own, everybody except two or three voted for copying.

The reversed 3, 4, 5, 7, and 9 posed no problem, but some 6's looked like 2's, and vice versa. I decided not to correct any of the reversals, since these problems take care of themselves in the long run. I asked the children to check their own work, and to trade with someone else to check each other's work. "You need to make sure the numbers are all readable and no number has been skipped," I told them.

Talking About Time

Skip had been very interested in time. For example, he asked me one day, "How many hours are we here from morning to lunchtime?" "About 3 hours," I told him. "THREE HOURS!?!? It takes 3 hours to get to my grandmother's house," he exclaimed with astonishment.

"How much more time do we stay here after gym, before lunch?" he asked me with this awkward sentence that reflected the difficulty of coordinating a sequence with an interval. "About 30 minutes," I told him. "Is that more or less than half an hour?" was his next question. "Thirty minutes *is* half of an hour; so 30 minutes *is* the same thing as half an hour," I explained.

Skip went on, "Forty-five minutes, is that more than an hour?" "It's more than half an hour because it is more than 30 minutes," I answered when we were interrupted by someone. I was sure he would be back with similar questions within a day or two.

At 11:15 one morning, Steve asked me, "How much longer do we have before it's lunchtime?" "A half hour," I answered. "How many minutes in a half hour?" he went on. "Thirty," I said. "Then there's 60 minutes in an hour, right?" he asked. "That's right," I told him.

Skip had been listening and inquired, "You mean that show my mom watches, '60 Minutes,' goes for an hour?" "Yeah," Steve said, " 'cause 60 minutes is the same as an hour."

Carl was moving to another state, and today was his last day with us. During our usual meeting in the morning, I asked how many children will be left tomorrow (twenty-four), how many boys will be left (nine), and how many girls will be left (fifteen).

Later that afternoon we expected Carl's mother to bring ice cream at 3:00 P.M. for a farewell party. Skip asked, "How long will it be until 3:00?" "Seventeen minutes," I told him. Bob then asked, "How many minutes do we have until it's time to go home?" "Let's see, it's 17 minutes and 30 minutes," I responded, wondering whether or not the child would be satisfied with this answer. Sure enough, Skip asked, "How long will that be?"

Brad piped up: "That's easy. I'll show you," and wrote the following on the board:

$$\begin{array}{r} 17 \\ \underline{30} \\ 47 \end{array}$$

Brad was the only child in the room who was instructed at home. When I asked him why he added the 7 and the 0, and then the 1 and the 3, his only explanation was " 'Cause that's what my mom told me."

Throughout the year, both Connie and I tried in various ways to get the children interested in learning how to tell time. When they asked how much time was left before lunchtime, for example, we tried to get them to accept our offer of instruction. They always reacted with total indifference, and continued to ask if they had enough time to do this or that.

Skip was the only child who came up with frequent questions about time. Even he had absolutely no desire to learn to read the clock.

First grade math books include many pages on this aspect. This year's experience convinced both Connie and me that telling time is a totally inappropriate objective for first graders. Some children already know how, and those who do not will learn quickly when they become interested.

Just Chatting

$7 + 7 = 14$ *out of the blue.* Carol told me, out of the blue, "You know what? $7 + 7 = 14$." "How do you know that?" I inquired. " 'Cause there's 14 days in two weeks," she answered.

Who is older?   One day, upon returning from lunch, Alma asked me point blank, "How old are you?" "Twenty-eight," I told her. "My mom is thirty," she said with the same nonchalance as before.

"Who is older?" I decided to ask. "My mom," Alma replied. "How many years older is she?" I continued. "I think two," answered Alma.

Needless to say some others who were listening started to tell me their parents' ages.

Valentines.   In early February, we prepared for Valentine's Day by making Valentine bags and hanging them along the edges of the children's desks. As the children made their Valentines at home, they brought them to school and distributed them into the bags. Each morning and afternoon before school started, the children enjoyed counting their Valentines and comparing their totals with their neighbors'.

When Marty approached me and asked me to guess how many he had in his bag, I said I would agree to try, if he gave me clues of "more" or "less" to help me. He agreed, and I began by guessing two. He laughed and said, "More." My next guess was twenty. He said, "Less." I continued with, "six?" "More." "Seven?" "More." "Twelve?" "Less." "Nine?" "More." "Ten?" "You got it!"

All the while, Jane, a lower-level pupil, was standing by watching us. She asked if I would play with her, and when I agreed, she said she had to go back to her desk to count her Valentines. Meanwhile, Marty came back to my desk and asked me to guess again. I smiled and said, "I bet it's eleven." He said, "You're right!" When I asked him if he knew why I guessed eleven, he said, "Sure, because just before this, it was ten, and somebody just put one more in my bag."

When Jane returned, I guessed five, thinking that she had more and would give me the clue "More." Instead, she thought about it for a short while and said, "No, it's twelve." The rule of the game that she had apparently assimilated while watching Marty and me was that one person takes one guess. If the guesser is lucky, he is correct. If not, he is told the correct number!

On the next day, Kate wanted me to play the same game, but it turned out to be different and at a very low level of development.

"Twenty?" I asked. "No," she replied and waited for me to take the next guess. "You have to tell me if it's more or less than twenty," I told her. "More," she answered with a big grin.

"Thirty-five?" was my second guess. "No," she said again. We waited for each other to say something, and I finally told her again that she had to tell me whether it was more or less than thirty-five. "Less," she obliged, still beaming.

"Twenty-five?" was my third guess. "No" was all Kate said. I decided simply to ask "Is it more or less?" "More," she informed me.

When I guessed thirty-one, she again said, "No," and nothing else. I found out by asking her that the number was less than thirty-one.

"Twenty-seven?" I guessed, and she said no more than "no." In answer to my question, she told me "more."

"Twenty-nine?" "No," we continued. "More or less than twenty-nine?" "More." "Then it must be thirty," I said, and Kate was delighted.

She apparently had no seriated system of numbers in her head. For her, there seemed to be only two categories of judgment—"yes" and "no." The game was, therefore, to take random guesses. For her, there was no relationship among the relationships of "more" and "less" (than the numbers guessed). This is why she continued to say only "no" in spite of my attempts to get her to say "more" or "less."

A sister's birthday.   Cathy came up to my desk after lunch one day and told me, "My sister's gonna have a birthday this month." She asked me to guess which day that was. "The sixteenth?" I guessed. "More," she responded. "The twenty-sixth?" I continued. "Less," she said. . . .

My father-in-law's age.   My father-in-law had his fifty-fifth birthday one day, and I asked the class if they wanted to guess how old he was. The first guess was "ninety." "Less," I responded. The second guess was "twenty." Let us conclude this section with a sigh. Age twenty must be a ripe, old age for first graders.

GROUP GAMES TO USE AS ARITHMETIC ACTIVITIES

Games cannot be classified neatly when addition is involved because the child's very construction of the number series involves the addition of one to each successive number. Therefore, it is impossible to say, for example, that "addition" is a category separate from "comparing numbers" and "set partitioning." While the following categories thus have many overlaps, we present them to show the kinds of thinking each game promotes.

The games are grouped into the five categories of those that are popular in kindergarten, addition, set partitioning, subtraction, and comparing numbers. While those in a later category generally tend to be more difficult than those in an earlier group, this is not always the case. For example, the group for doubles up to 10 + 10 appears earlier, but is more difficult than the group on comparing two numbers. (A game is considered easy when a large proportion of children can give correct answers immediately.) Within each category, the easier games also tend to appear at the beginning of the list but not always. For each game the directions will be given first followed by an analysis of its educational value. Principles of teaching with games are discussed in Chapter 8, and a month-by-month account of the games played by a first grade class during one school year can be found in Chapter 10.

Games That Are Popular in Kindergarten

Not all the games in this category deal with number. They are discussed here because many of our first graders enjoyed them, especially at the beginning of the school year (see Chapter 10), and some are appropriate for low-level first graders. Other easy games involving number and arithmetic can be found in *Number in Preschool and Kindergarten* (Kamii, 1982) and in *Group Games in Early Education* (Kamii and DeVries, 1980, Chapter 3).

CARD GAMES

War

All fifty-two cards are dealt to two players. (The teacher may want to eliminate all the face cards at first.) Without looking at the cards, each player puts his pile face down in front of himself. The two players then simultaneously turn up the top card of their respective piles. The person who turned up the card having the larger number takes both.

If there is a tie, this situation is called "War." Each player in this situation places the next card, face down, on the card that made the tie. Each player then turns over another card from his pile and places it on the one he just put on the first card. The person who turns up the bigger number takes all six cards.

The player who collects more cards than the other at the end is the winner.

When children play War, they judge which of two numbers is the bigger. While judgments can be made perceptually when the numbers are very different (2 versus 9, for example), small differences between two large numbers such as "8" and "9" cannot be judged perceptually.

In first grade arithmetic, children are usually required to write "$<$," "$>$," or "$=$" in exercises such as 7 $\Box$ 5. War involves only the thinking part of this exercise, namely the comparison of two numbers. Learning to write "$<$" and "$>$," and to say "greater than" and "smaller than," does not contribute to the development of thinking. In fact, having to think about confusing conventional signs can interfere with children's logico-mathematical thinking.

In the game of War, each card stands for the number represented by the symbols and signs. At the end of the game, however, when the children try to determine who won, the cards become objects to be counted.

Go Fish

If there are two players, each is dealt seven cards. If there are three or four players, each receives five cards. The rest are spread out on the table, face down, and are called the "fish pond." Each player first makes all the pairs he can find in his own hand and puts them down in front of himself, face up. (If he has three that are the same, he can put down only a pair and must keep the third card.) The dealer then begins the game by asking someone for a card to make a pair. For example, if Mary thinks John has a "5," she may say, "John, do you have a '5'?" If John has one, he must give it to her. If he does not, he says, "Go fish." Mary then takes a card from the fish pond and puts a pair down if she can. If she cannot, she simply keeps that card, and the turn passes to the player on Mary's left.[2] Each player can keep asking for a card as long as he gets one that enables him to make a pair. Play continues until all the cards have been put down in pairs. The person who makes the most pairs is the winner.

Go Fish contributes to the development of logical thinking rather than arithmetic. For example, if a person asks for a 5 and does not get one, he is very likely to have a 5. If no one has put down a pair of 5's, the probability of that person's having a 5 is even greater.

Concentration

The teacher selects ten to fifteen pairs of cards that are easily distinguishable (such as those showing dogs, cats, elephants, cars, flowers, and so on). The players arrange them face down in neat rows. They take turns turning up two cards, trying to make pairs. When a player succeeds in making the second card match the first one, he can keep the pair and continue playing. When he fails, he must turn the two cards over so that they are face down again, and the turn passes to the person on his left. The winner is the person who makes more pairs than anybody else.

Concentration can be played with regular playing cards. However, it is better to use cards with pictures on them because it is easier to look for two flowers or monkeys, for example, than to look for two 6's or 7's.

A BOARD GAME

Tic Tac Toe

The *Tic Tac Toe* shown in Photograph 7.1 is commercially made. A piece of heavy cardboard, 12 inches square, is divided by lines into a 3 × 3 matrix. Included with the game are ten plastic pieces, five of which are X's and five

---

2. This is an adaptation of the usual way of playing Go Fish. In the standard version, the turn passes to the person who did not have the card requested. For young children, however, this rule seems more confusing than simply taking turns by going around the circle.

are O's. One player uses the X's and the other uses the O's. In turn, each player puts one of his pieces in a space as shown in the picture. The object of the game is to get three of one's pieces in a line, vertically, horizontally, or diagonally. The girl in the photograph would win if she puts her O down in a diagonal line.

Tic Tac Toe does not involve arithmetic either, but we introduced it early in the year (see Chapter 10) because it is a game that encourages decentering. Children have to take the opponent's point of view to win, while simultaneously preventing the other person from winning.

Children can, of course, use paper and pencil, or chalk and a chalkboard, to play this game. By January, the popularity of this game declined. Some played with two boards simultaneously side by side to make the game more difficult.

Addition

TWO ADDENDS UP TO 4, 6 (WITH DICE), AND THEN 10

Double War

Double War is a modification of War played by two children as shown in Photograph 7.2. Thirty-two cards, eight each from "1" through "4" from two decks, are used. All cards are dealt, face down, so that each player will have

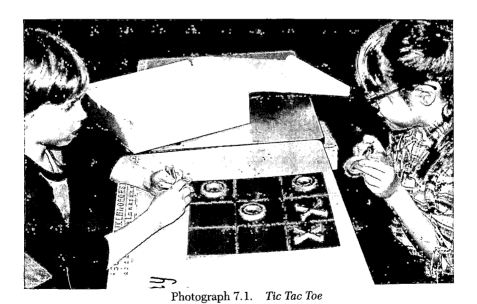

Photograph 7.1.   *Tic Tac Toe*

Photograph 7.2.   Double War

two stacks. Without looking at the cards, each player simultaneously turns up the top cards. The person whose total is more takes all four cards. The player who has more cards at the end is the winner.

If there is a tie, each player takes the top card of each of his piles and places it, face down, on the cards that made the tie. Each player then turns over a third card from each of his piles and places it on the ones he just put down. The player whose new total is greater takes all twelve cards. (Later in the year, children sometimes decide to add up the total of six cards to determine who would take all twelve cards.)

The first objective in addition given in Chapter 5 is adding addends up to 4. Double War is the only game in this chapter that presents addends only up to 4. (Another way of getting addends only up to 4 is to use two dice with 1, 2, 2, 3, 3, and 4 dots respectively on the six sides.)

When the game becomes too easy with numbers up to 4, the teacher can introduce the 5's as shown in Photograph 7.2. A detailed account of children playing this game can be found in Chapter 8.

In deciding when to add the addends above 5, the teacher needs to consider the sequence of objectives discussed in Chapter 5. She may also want to reduce the total number of cards if the game becomes too long.

Fifty Chips

Each player uses one of the eight boards divided into fifty squares (see Photograph 7.3), with five rows of ten squares, 1¼ inches in size. In turn, each player rolls two dice, adds the two numbers, and puts that many chips on his board. The winner is the first player to fill his card.

Fifty Chips and the four games that follow (Hop to It, *Benji*, Dinosaurs, and XYZ) are board games involving the addition of two numbers turned up by two dice. Fifty Chips is different from the other four games in that the players put objects on the board. In the other four games, they take the number of steps indicated by the dice.

As recommended in *Number in Preschool and Kindergarten* (Kamii, 1982, p. 60), Fifty Chips can be played by four-year-olds with one die and boards

Photograph 7.3.   Fifty Chips

having only twelve squares on them. In other words, any number between twelve and fifty squares is possible for this game.

Hop to It

The board shown in Photograph 7.4 is a homemade game with a path along which the players move their pieces. Two dice and a marker for each of four players are used. Each player takes a turn throwing the dice. He then adds the two numbers and moves the total number of spaces along the path. The winner is the first player to get his marker to the end of the path.

Benji

The board, which used to be commercially made (Mulberry Square Productions, 1976), has a circular path, with most of the spaces numbered from 1 to 63. Two dice and a marker for each of six players are used. Each player takes a turn throwing the two dice. He adds the numbers indicated by the dice and moves that many spaces along the path. If he lands on a space with a picture, he draws a card and follows the directions written on it. (Examples of directions are "Run forward 4 spaces," "Run back 5 spaces," "Run to stoplight and miss one turn," and "Run to bone at 59.") The winner is the first player to get his marker to the end of the path.

Dinosaurs

The homemade board shown in Photograph 7.5 has a circular path with spaces numbered from 1 to 60. The TILE die shown in Figure 7.1a and a marker

Photograph 7.4.   Hop to It

Photograph 7.5.   Dinosaurs

for each of four players are used. Each player takes a turn throwing the die and moving that many spaces along the path. If he lands on a space that has a picture, he draws an instruction card and follows the directions written on it. The winner is the first player to get his marker to the end of the path.

XYZ

The name of this game stands for the idea that the content can be anything that appeals to first graders. As can be seen in Photograph 7.6, this game uses a homemade board. The numbers begin with 1 in the lower left corner and go from 9 to 10 in the lower right corner. To move one's marker through the sequence, a player must move to the right on one row, to the left on the next row, to the right on the third row, and so on. Two dice and a marker for each of six players are used. One die has a 5 on each side. The other has the numeral 1, 2, 3, 3, 4, or 5 on each of its sides. Each player takes a turn throwing the two dice. He adds the numbers indicated by the dice and moves that many spaces along the path. If he lands on a space with a picture, he draws an instruction card and follows the directions written on it. (The cards are similar to those in *Benji* and Dinosaurs.) The winner is the first player to get his marker to the end of the path.

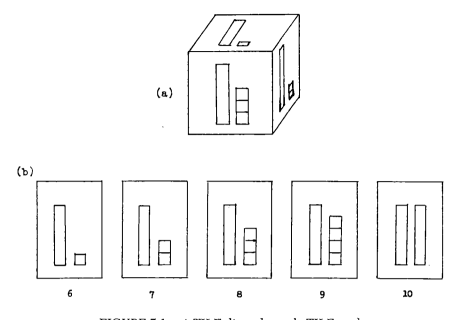

FIGURE 7.1.   A TILE die and sample TILE cards.

Photograph 7.6.   XYZ

Hop to It has a much shorter path than the other three similar games. *Benji* and Dinosaurs have circular paths that are easier to follow than XYZ.

Hop to It can be played with one die. When two dice are used, children suggest the choice of using either one or two dice when they get close to the goal. Some children propose the rule that a player cannot move unless there are enough spaces left to take the required number of steps forward. Others say that one should always be allowed to move, but must take steps backwards, away from the goal, when a larger number comes up. These ideas are excellent for the negotiation of a rule that all the players will have to follow.

Benji is one of the most popular games, probably because there are many interesting things for children to do with the instruction cards. The card that says, "Move any player back or forward to 18 (or 28, 38, or 48)" provokes disagreement and interesting negotiations. Some children say "any player" means "any player" including themselves, but others say it means "any player except the one who drew the card." The card saying "Move any player back or forward to 18 (or to 41)" introduces another interesting problem because the space for 18 has only a picture and no numeral. In fact, the spaces for 18 and 19, and for 41 and 42 have only pictures, and children have to infer the places for 18 and 41 from "16, 17, □, □ 20, 21" and from "39, 40 □, □ 43, 44."

While commercial games like *Benji* are generally well made, they usually have shortcomings that can be corrected with a bit of research. The following list shows examples of instructions that came in the box and the modifications we made on our homemade cards:

Printed instructions	*Our modification*
Run forward 4 spaces	Run forward four spaces →
Walk forward 1 space	Go forward one space →
Run back 4 spaces	Run back 4 spaces ←
Walk back 2 spaces	Go back 2 spaces ←
Move any player back to 18	Move any player back ← or forward → to 18
Visit Louise the cat at 5	Go to see the cat at five
Have dinner at 45	Run to the dog food dish

We changed the word "walk" to "go" because the former is well known to be hard for beginning readers. Our spelling out "one," "four," "five," and "six" was a concession to the school curriculum, which requires the reading not only of numerals but also of these words. This is one more example of the overemphasis placed on social (conventional) knowledge in traditional math, and this concession was unwise in light of Ferreiro and Teberosky's (1982, Chapter 2) findings. We present it in this description in hopes that other people will avoid this pitfall.

"Move any player back to (a certain number)" seemed to be an unfortunately limited instruction. To increase the fun of this card, we changed it to "Move any player back or forward to (a certain number)."

The addition of pictures and simplification of the language were for the benefit of the children who were not able to read the instructions. "Have dinner at" was changed to "Run to the dog food dish (with a picture of dog food in a dish)."

Dinosaurs is the same game as *Benji* except for the TILE die that is used (refer to Figure 7.1a). TILE (Hatano, 1980, 1982) cards (see Figure 7.1b) are like Dienes blocks except that they are flat instead of being three dimensional. Another, more important difference is that TILEs use 5 as an intermediary higher-order unit. As stated in Chapter 5, we wanted children to think about 6, 7, 8, 9, and 10 as 5 + 1, 5 + 2, 5 + 3, 5 + 4, and 5 + 5 in adding these addends larger than 5. By playing with this die, we thought that children would come to think of a stick and a "1" instantly as "6," a stick and a "2" instantly as "7," and so forth.

We were attracted by TILEs not only because they used 5 as an intermediary higher-order unit, but also because they used spatial configurations effectively. The research in Geneva by Ackermann-Valladaō (1982) was beginning to suggest that in their early numerical quantification, young children use space and time (spatial patterns and rhythm) in dealing with larger quantities by breaking them down into small groups. Since bigger numbers from 6 to 9 cannot be visualized mentally like perceptual numbers (small numbers up to 4 or 5), we felt the TILEs would help children picture them spatially, thereby becoming better able to think about them.

TILEs thus fitted into Piagetian ideas, but not the didactic ways of using them advocated by Tohyama (1965). For example, Tohyama had children do 4 + 3 by putting out four and three "1's," moving one of the three with the four, and exchange the five "1's" for a 5-cm stick. It seemed to us that this regrouping should be done mentally by children, on their own initiative, without being told to go through these physical motions. Hence the idea of using TILEs in games.

XYZ is very similar to Dinosaurs but uses two dice—one with the numeral 5 on all sides, and another with the numerals 1 through 5 on it. By looking at the 1, 2, 3, and so forth, on the latter, we thought, children would come to know immediately that they had a 6, 7, or 8, for example.

MANY NUMBERS

Concentration with *Huckleberry Hound* Cards

The deck consists of the following thirty-four cards shown in Photograph 7.7 (Ed-U-Cards, 1961):
>   eight cards with a 1-point value (two different sets)
>   eight cards with a 2-point value (two different sets)
>   eight cards with a 3-point value (two different sets)
>   four cards with a 4-point value
>   four cards with a 5-point value
>   two cards with a 10-point value

The players arrange all the cards face down in neat rows. They take turns turning up two cards, trying to make pairs of the same picture. When a player succeeds in making a pair, he can keep it and continue playing. When he fails, he must turn the two cards over so that they are face down again, and the turn passes to the person on his left. The winner can be determined in one of two ways: (1) by deciding who made more pairs than anyone else or (2) by finding out who got the highest total number of points.

The *Huckleberry Hound* cards were put out from the first day of school, and the children played Concentration by trying to make as many pairs as possible. By November, however, some children discovered the numerals in the corners of the cards and began to use them to determine who won.

Concentration with *Huckleberry Hound* cards highlights many advantages

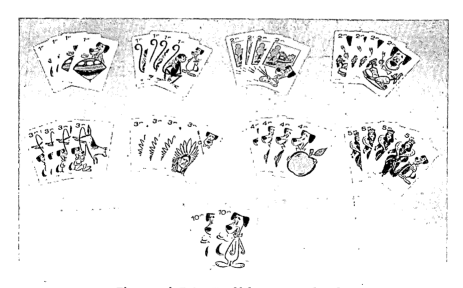

Photograph 7.7.   *Huckleberry Hound* cards

of card games over worksheets. First, children argue about how to count the points made with two cards. Some children say that two "3" cards count for 3 points. Others insist that they are worth 6 points. If the latter view prevails, which is usually the case, children get a great deal of practice with certain "doubles."

First graders often like big numbers. Concentration with *Huckleberry Hound* cards appeals to this interest. While workbooks control the difficulty level (with sums up to 5 first and then up to 10, for example), this card game yields much greater sums. We believe that there is a place for both kinds of addition in beginning arithmetic. Children should be encouraged to add lots of numbers if they want to. They *will* find ways of adding them if the desire to do so comes from them.

Another point concerns the place of writing in first grade arithmetic. We had been looking for situations in which writing might serve as a useful tool for children, rather than being another order to carry out to please the teacher. When children added their points in Concentration as they found pairs of cards, and could not remember their previous total, we suggested writing as a useful tool. The children obliged us while we were present, but preferred redoing the addition once we were gone. There thus seemed to be something unnatural about writing totals in this game. The children were busy trying to remember where specific cards were located, and writing totals seemed to interfere with their mental activity in the game. (We will see later that the idea of writing was accepted immediately in another game called Guess My Number.)

Another interesting phenomenon was observed when the children began to notice the advantage of finding cards with larger point values. After realizing that $10 + 10$ yielded a much greater total than many other pairs that produced only $(1 + 1) + (1 + 1) + (2 + 2) + (2 + 2) = 12$ points, for example, some children tried too single-mindedly to get higher-value cards and ended up losing the game. They then constructed higher-level strategies that took into account the fact that cards with lower point values were easier to find. Worksheets do not present such possibilities.

Put and Take

This commercially made game (Schaper Manufacturing Co., 1977) is played by 2, 3, or 4 players. Sixty-two yellow, twenty-two red, and twenty-two blue chips with the respective value of 1, 2, and 10 points are used, along with a top and a cup called a "kitty." To begin play, each player takes ten yellow, five red, and two blue chips (a total of 40 points) and contributes 3 points to the "kitty." In turn, each player spins the top and follows the directions written on the side of the top that came up. If "TAKE 2" comes up, for example, the player takes chips worth 2 points from the "kitty." If "PUT 3" comes up, he puts some of his chips into the "kitty." The first player to get 60 points is the winner.

Put and Take offers many possibilities for many kinds of thinking. The one that can be observed immediately involves how to make 3 points. When a player puts a red chip and a yellow one in the kitty, for example, another sometimes says, "No, you have to put three yellow ones in."

Another advantage can be observed when children have to trade a blue chip in for smaller units. Some children know that a blue one is worth five red ones. But most count the red ones by saying, "1-2, 3-4, 5-6, 7-8, 9-10" and a few by saying, "2, 4, 6, 8, 10." Some children trade a blue chip in for some red ones and some yellow ones, while others get to this result in two steps—by taking five red ones first and then exchanging some red ones for yellow ones.

Finally, children have to count their totals to know when they have won. Many children do not bother to do this because, for them, the point of the game is only the process of playing. Others make stacks of each color and use a process that resembles multiplication. Pointing at two blue chips, they say "20," for example, and say "10 more" as they look at five red chips. Most children, however, count their points by 1's, with their chips scattered all over the floor.

We have made two modifications in the rules printed on the box. One was to say that the total required to win should be 60 points, rather than 100 points (if four or more people are playing) or 75 points (if only three are playing). Children are more likely to count their totals if the criterion for winning is closer to the 40 points they had at the beginning.

The other modification we made was to write 1, 2, or 10 on each chip to make playing easier when the game is first introduced. The fact that a yellow chip is worth 1 point and a red one, 2 points, or vice versa, is arbitrary. Children learn nothing of value by having to memorize arbitrary associations.

The spinner gives only the following small numbers:

PUT 1   TAKE 1
PUT 2   TAKE 2
PUT 3   TAKE 3
PUT 4   TAKE ALL

The teacher can change them as well as the value of the chips.

DOUBLES UP TO 10 + 10

Double *Parcheesi*

Double *Parcheesi* uses the board shown in Photograph 7.8, which is commercially made for the well-known game of *Parcheesi* (Selchow and Righter, 1975). Each player selects one of the four colors (green, blue, red, and yellow) and

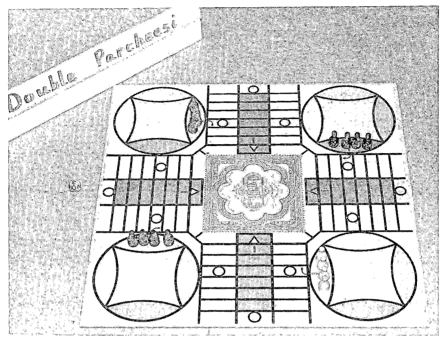

Photograph 7.8. Double *Parcheesi*

begins by placing four markers of that color in the corresponding circle (as shown in Photograph 7.8). The object of the game is to move all four of one's markers around the board to Home. Double *Parcheesi* is different from *Parcheesi* in that the players double the number shown by the die. A ten-sided die with the numerals 1 to 10 on each side is used. If two markers land on the same space, the one already there is sent back to its starting point. There are twelve safety spaces (indicated by circles) where a marker is safe from being sent back.

Doubles are generally easier for children to remember than sums of two different numbers. We invented Double *Parcheesi* to provide opportunities for children to double all the numbers from 1 to 10. The commercially made *Parcheesi* board has a long path, and children like the idea of moving fast. It also uses four markers that increases the attractiveness of moving fast.

Double *Parcheesi* has the added advantage of requiring anticipation forward (to try to send someone else back to "start" and backward (to avoid being sent back). The way to send someone else back is to maintain a relatively short distance to one of his markers. The way to avoid being sent back is to keep a distance of twenty spaces between one's marker and someone else's that is behind.

Photograph 7.9. *Sorry*

Sorry

Sorry is a modification of the commercially made game (Parker Brothers, 1972) shown in Photograph 7.9. Each player selects one of the four colors (green, blue, red, and yellow) and begins by placing the four pieces of that color in the corresponding circle. The object of the game is to move all four of one's markers around the board to Home. The players take turns rolling a ten-sided die with the numerals 1 to 10 on each side, and move their markers double the number shown on the die. If a player lands on a space already occupied by an opponent's piece, that piece is sent back to its starting point. Once a player has one of his pieces in his safety zone close to Home, he can choose to move either the number shown on the die, or double the number. The first player to get all four pieces to Home is the winner.

Sorry is very similar to Double *Parcheesi* but offers an additional advantage. There are arrows printed on the path, and if a marker lands on the end of an arrow, it can advance four more spaces to its head. This rule makes children think about odd and even numbers in relation to the doubles. In Photograph 7.9, for example, the boy holding his marker has a chance of landing on an arrow (by rolling a "1"). If he were in the space to the left, however, he would have absolutely no chance of landing on the end of the arrow. There would, therefore, be no point in waiting for the possibility of getting a certain number on the die. In *Sorry,* children land in spaces close to the end of an arrow, sometimes with an odd number of spaces in between, and sometimes with an even number.

Set Partitioning

Piggy Bank

The commercially made deck (Ed-U-Cards, 1965) consists of the following thirty cards having pictures of coins:

> seven cards showing 1 penny
> six cards showing 2 pennies
> six cards showing 3 pennies
> seven cards showing 4 pennies
> two cards showing 5 pennies
> two cards showing 1 nickel

The players put money in the bank, but they can do this only by depositing 5 cents at a time. All the cards are dealt. Each player puts all his cards in a pile in front of himself, face down. When his turn comes, he turns up the top card of his pile. If it shows either 5 pennies or a nickel, he can put it in his "bank." If it shows any other number, he must discard the card in the middle of the table, face up. The next player who turns up a card that does not show 5 pennies or a nickel looks among the discarded cards trying to find one that gives a total of 5 cents. (If, for example, he is holding a 3 and finds a 2, he can pick up the 2 and deposit 5 cents in his bank.) The winner is the person who saves the most money.

Piggy Bank involves the set partitioning of 5. For lower-level children it is better to use only the cards with 1 to 4 pennies. The rule of the game can then be simplified from "find one or two cards that make a total of 5" to "find two cards that make a total of 5." The only possible combinations in this game are 4 + 1 and 3 + 2, but low-level children cannot remember them for a long time.

The cards can be made at home with self-adhesive circles that can be bought at stationery stores, pictures of coins (found in workbooks), or a rubber stamp of a penny that can be ordered through a catalog. The cards can also be made with numerals for use later in the year.

Tens with Playing Cards

This game is usually played by two or three children and uses thirty-six cards, four each of ace through 9. One player turns up the top nine cards from the pile, and arranges them into a 3 × 3 matrix. The remaining pile of cards is left face down, near the playing area. The players take turns looking for pairs of cards that make a total of 10. When a player succeeds in making a pair, he can keep it and continue playing. When he cannot find any more, he fills in the empty places with cards from the pile, and the turn passes to the next player. The person who finds the most pairs is the winner.

Tens with Playing Cards can be played at many levels. Some children know the various combinations by heart. Others play by trial-and-error and by resorting to counting.

Tens Concentration is the same game except that the cards are turned face down. It is a much harder game because children have to know which combinations to look for. In other words, trial-and-error and counting do not work when the cards are turned down. Children often decide to count by 10's at the end of this game to determine who won.

Tens

Tens is a commercially made game (House of Games, 1975) shown in Photograph 7.10. It is played by two to five people. All 72 triangular pieces are placed face down in the box. (Each piece is divided into three segments, as can be seen in Figure 7.2. Each segment has one of six colors and a number from 0 to 10.) Each player takes six pieces, turning them up, and the extra pieces remain in the box.

Photograph 7.10. *Tens*

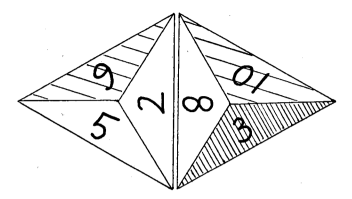

FIGURE 7.2.   How two pieces can go together in *Tens*.

Play begins with one piece from the box turned up and placed in the center of the table. In turn, each player tries to put down one of his pieces by looking for a segment that has the same color and a number that makes a total of 10 (refer to Figure 7.2). If he does not have a piece that can be put down, he takes a piece from the box and tries again. If he still cannot add a piece to those in the middle of the table, the turn passes to the next player. The winner is the first to get rid of all his pieces.

Tens is harder than Tens with Playing Cards, partly because it provides nothing to count, and partly because the possibilities to consider increase enormously as the game progresses.

Sevens

Twenty-four cards from 1 through 6 are used ($6 \times 4 = 24$). All the cards are stacked as a drawing pile except the top three cards which are turned up and placed on the table in a row. The object of the game is to find two cards that make a total of 7 ($6 + 1$, $5 + 2$, or $4 + 3$). When his turn comes, each player picks up two cards, if possible, and replaces them with two from the top of the drawing pile. If he cannot make a total of 7 from the cards turned up, he passes. Each time a player cannot pick up two cards that make a total of 7, the next player takes the top card of the drawing pile and tries to make 7 with it. If he cannot, he starts a discard pile. As soon as a player can take two cards, the discard pile is put back in the drawing pile at the bottom. The winner is the person who ends up with the most cards.

Sevens turned out not to be popular because $4 + 3$ is one of the harder combinations to remember, and $5 + 2$ is not easy either (see Table 5.1). It is presented here to illustrate a principle for inventing other games involving set partitioning. The principle is to use cards with numbers up to 1 less than the set to be partitioned, and to turn up three cards as in Sevens, nine cards as in Tens with Playing Cards, or any other number in between. For example, if 8 is to be partitioned, cards up to 7 are used, and five cards can be turned up.

This game did not work well with first graders, but it was excellent for some "slow" inner city third graders who were seemingly unable to remember sums. Their teacher corrected the same errors on worksheets day after day, and one day she decided to introduce Sevens. To her amazement, a few children came back the next day remembering all the combinations. The children who were not willing to memorize sums to please the teacher were willing to do so to be able to play intelligently with their friends. Those who did not know the combinations by heart became motivated to emulate the smart players.

Uncover

This is a homemade game[3] using the board shown in Figure 7.3. Two dice, each with numerals 0 to 5, and 20 poker chips are used. The game begins with all the numerals covered by these chips. The players, sitting across from each

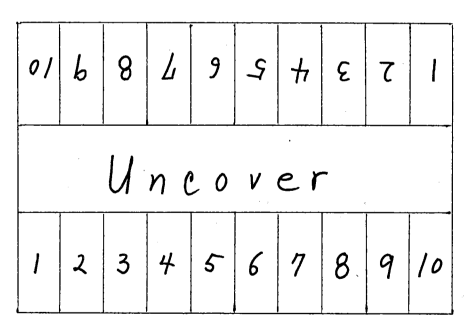

FIGURE 7.3.   The board used for Uncover.

---

3. Credit goes to Marjorie Cole, of the Glen Ellyn (Illinois) Public Schools, for the invention of this game.

other, alternately take turns rolling the dice. Each player determines the sum of the two numbers rolled and uncovers that numeral on his side of the board. The first player to uncover all the numerals on his side is the winner.

Punta

This homemade card game is played with two to six people. The deck consists of sixty cards, ten each of the numbers 1 to 6. The game begins with all these cards dealt. A set of TILE cards, shown in Figure 7.4, is also used. These cards are placed face down in the middle of the playing area in a pile.

One player flips over the top TILE card. The players then look at their cards and try to use as many cards as possible to make the total indicated on the TILE card. For example, a 9 (on the TILE card) can be made with a 6 + 2 + 1, 6 + 3, 5 + 4, 1 + 1 + 1 + 2 + 4, and so on. The first player to get rid of all his cards is the winner.

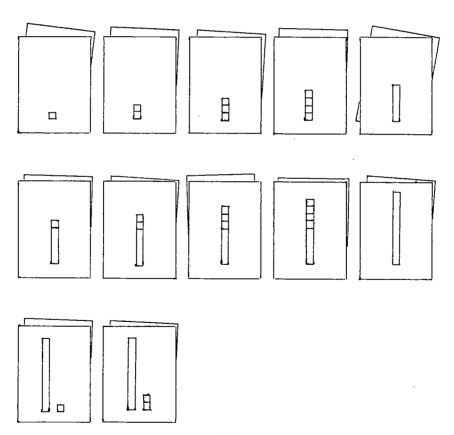

FIGURE 7.4.   TILE cards used in Punta.

Punta is an excellent game that can involve the manipulation of numbers in a rich variety of ways. For example, 12 can be made with 6 + 6, which can be broken down to (3 + 3) + (3 + 3), (4 + 2) + (4 + 2), or (5 + 1) + (5 + 1). It can also be made with three "4's".

It is desirable to play Punta by trying to use up the big numbers first, because the "1's" and "2's" are more versatile than bigger numbers: "1's" and "2's" can be used to make a 6, but a 6 cannot be used to make a 2. Young children do not think of this strategy and are glad to find any cards that make the desired total.

The TILE cards used in Punta encourage children to think about larger numbers such as 7 as 5 + 2, and 12 as 10 + 2. The use of a short stick (5 cm) and a long one (10 cm) reinforces the mental regrouping that happens naturally as children use their fingers to add numbers.

Subtraction

In Chapter 6, we explained that subtraction is not an appropriate objective for first graders except insofar as it is involved in problems that come up in daily living. A few subtraction games are presented below for the reader to know what we have tried. Teachers might want to experiment with their advanced first graders who are not challenged by the other games.

In addition, some of the games discussed earlier can be adapted to subtraction. Double War with Subtraction is a modification of Double War. Each player simultaneously turns up the top cards of his stacks, and the person who gets a larger difference between his cards takes all four of them. In a game like *Benji* two green dice and also a red one can be used. Each player adds the numbers turned up by the green dice and subtracts the number turned up by the red one.

Subtraction Lotto

Each player's board is different and contains numbers such as 0, 1, 1, 3, 4, 6, 7, and 9. A caller has a stack of cards with one subtraction problem on each. As he turns them up one at a time and reads each one, the players who have the answer put a chip on that number. The first to cover all the numerals on his board is the winner.

The problems given on the cards are given here. They consist of easy ones corresponding to the easiest sums to remember. (Refer to Table 5.1 to recall that the easiest sums to remember are the doubles, the "+1's," and those involving very small addends.)

Doubles	− 1's		−2's with a difference of 0 or 1
4 − 2	10 − 1		3 − 2
6 − 3	9 − 1	(2 cards	2 − 2
8 − 4	8 − 1	of each)	
10 − 5	7 − 1		
	6 − 1		
	5 − 1		
	4 − 1		
	3 − 1		
	2 − 1		

Football

This is a homemade game using the board shown in Figure 7.5. Thirty-three cards, three each of the numerals 0 to 10, are also used. The game begins with the football on the 50-yard line, on the X. All the cards are dealt, face down, to the two players. The one who turns up the higher number wins, as in War, and moves the football one line toward the goal his opponent is defending. If his opponent draws the higher number the next turn, the ball goes back to the 50-yard line, and so on. The first player to move the ball into the touchdown area is the winner.

The game can be made more difficult by using cards with numbers going up to 50.

Another modification, more appropriate for second grade, is to include subtraction. In this version, a difference of 3 or more means an instant touchdown (when cards up to 10 are used). For example, if a 5 and a 2 are drawn,

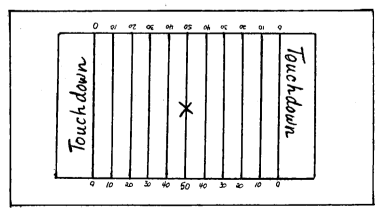

FIGURE 7.5.   The board made for Football.

the player with the 5 scores a touchdown. If a 5 and a 3 are turned up, on the other hand, the player with the 5 can advance only to the next line.

Football with subtraction was impossible even for Steve, one of the most advanced children (also discussed in Chapter 10). This game was, therefore, presented to the rest of the class as a game like War. The cards up to 50 turned out to be very easy for all the children and increased the popularity of this game.

Comparing Numbers

TWO NUMBERS

Coin War

This homemade card game is played just like War with two children as shown in Photograph 7.11. The only difference is that forty-four cards are used, composed of the following variety:

   1 through 10 cents with pennies only (twenty cards, two of each)
   5 cents, with only a nickel (four cards)
   6 through 10 cents, with a nickel and one or more pennies (twenty cards,
       four of each)

The cards that can be seen in Photograph 7.11 are an improved, second-year version. The coins on these cards are arranged in columns with a maximum of 5 (see Figure 7.6a). In other words, the numbers 1, 2, 3, 4, and

Photograph 7.11.   Coin War

(a)   (b)

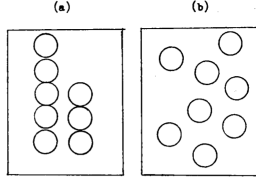

FIGURE 7.6. Two different
ways of arranging pennies on
cards for Coin War.

5 were represented with a column of one, two, three, four, or five pennies, or with a nickel. The numbers from 6 through 10 were represented with either a nickel or five pennies in the left-hand column, and one, two, three, four, or five pennies in the right-hand column. The cards the two girls are comparing in Photograph 7.11 represent 7 cents and 9 cents, both with a nickel in the left-hand column.

The cards made during the first year were similar except that the coins were randomly placed over the surface of each card, as can be seen in Figure 7.6b. This arrangement encouraged the most mechanical, eternal counting imaginable! When the spatial arrangement of the coins was changed to columns during the second year, the counting did not appear.

Make the Biggest Number

This game is played by two to four children. Fifty cards, 5 each of the numerals 0 to 9, are used. The game begins with all the cards in the box, face down. Each player draws two cards and tries to make the biggest number possible. The person who made the biggest number takes all four cards. Play continues until the box is empty. The winner is the one with the most cards.

Both Make the Biggest Number and Football with numbers up to 50 illustrate the enormous difference between being able to read and "spell" two digit numbers, and being able to understand place value. Make the Biggest Number is very easy for first graders, but place value is impossible for them to understand as stated in Chapter 4.

The "spelling" of two-digit numbers can be learned merely by knowing how to repeat a cyclical order. This order consists of beginning with a 1 on the left-hand side and repeating it in combination with another number on the right-hand side that goes from 0 to 9. When the 9 is reached, the number on the left is changed to 2. The sequence is then repeated with the numbers from 0 to 9 on the right, and so on. This sequence is social (conventional) knowledge, which is very different in nature from the logico-mathematical knowledge involved in place value.

MANY NUMBERS (TWO AT A TIME)

Guess My Number

One person thinks of a number, and the rest of the group tries to guess it in this game. As one person after another takes a guess, the leader responds by saying, "It is more" or "It is less." For example, if the number in the leader's head is 50, and the first guess is 100, the leader says, "No, it's less." The person who guesses the number correctly is the leader of the next round.

This game can be played by the entire class, a small group, or two people.

Guess My Number involves the comparison of many numbers, two at a time. As pointed out by Piaget, Grize, Szeminska, and Bäng (1968), young children can put two elements into a relationship, but a third element is often too much for them. After being told that the number in question is less than 98 and more than 45, for example, some children ask "Is it 13?" When this happens, other children laugh out loud and say this guess is dumb. When children can put "X < 98" and "X > 45" into a single relationship, it is obvious to them that X cannot possibly be 13. When they can remember only one relationship at a time, "X < 98," on the other hand, nothing can convince them that "Is it 13?" is a bad question. The nature of logico-mathematical knowledge and constructivism can be understood best by observing children over and over in such situations.

The children were happy to play this game orally, when we suggested that it might be helpful to write the guesses on the board. Unlike what happened in Concentration with *Huckleberry Hound* cards, the children accepted this suggestion immediately. This game turned out to be excellent for children to learn how to write numbers. For example, the "spelling" of "sixteen" suggests "61," and our children asked each other whether to write "61" or "16."

How the children decided to write "more than" and "less than" was also very instructive. One child suggested, and the rest accepted, the idea of writing "m" for "more" and "l" for "less." "More than 45" was thus written

$$45$$
$$m$$

and "less than 98" was written

$$98$$
$$l$$

The children were learning a phonological system, and this convention made much better sense to us than the ">" and "<" signs, which are as dear to math educators as they are useless and frustrating to teachers and children.

CHAPTER 8

Principles
of Teaching

Written with Georgia DeClark

It is easy to misuse games and other activities. For teachers trained in pre-Piagetian pedagogy, heteronomously directing games and making children follow rules seem both natural and necessary. When arithmetic is taught in the context of autonomy as the broader aim, however, traditional practices have to change. This is the hardest part of constructivist teaching. We begin this chapter with the general principles of teaching that flow from the conviction that autonomy is the aim of education. We then discuss principles that are particularly important in situations in daily living and in group games. A detailed account of Georgia DeClark playing Double War with two children will then be presented to illustrate these principles in practice. The chapter will conclude with some do's and don'ts concerning some of the specific games described in Chapter 7.

PRINCIPLES FLOWING FROM AUTONOMY AS THE BROAD GOAL

Principles of teaching related to the development of autonomy will be discussed with respect to three areas: children's relationships with adults, their relationships with peers, and their relationship to learning.

Autonomy in Children's Relationships with Adults

The most general principle for the teacher to keep in mind is to *reduce adult power as much as possible and to exchange points of view with children*. This means that reward and punishment should be avoided as much as possible because it is through them that power is most often exercised. By telling people that we will reward them for doing X, or punish them for doing Y, we can influence them and keep them under control. When we keep children under our control, we prevent them from making autonomous decisions based on what *they* think is right. (We will not repeat here the principles of teaching already given in Chapter 3. Refer again especially to those related to sanctions by reciprocity and to the importance of exchanging points of view and negotiating rules with children.)

Adult power is pervasive in most classrooms even when reward and punishment are eliminated. For example, children often ask if they can be first in starting a game. It is very natural for the teacher to say "Yes" to a child who asks, "Can I be first?" Most teachers are not aware that they are exercising power in such a situation. It is a rare teacher who responds by saying, "It's not up to *me* to decide," or "You'll have to ask the other players what *they* think."

The degree of adult power that exists in a classroom can be judged by certain indices. If the children seem free to speak their minds, to disagree with the teacher, and/or to discuss problems with him, this environment can be said to foster the development of autonomy. In a kindergarten room one day, a child raised his hand during group time saying, "Teacher, you have to wait just a minute because we have a problem here we have to settle before we can go on." This is a sign of autonomy on the child's part and of a good relationship with the teacher. It is very rare that a child takes the initiative to make such a request. Usually, the teacher goes on with the group activity, and children sneak to continue their dispute.

Reducing adult power *as much as possible* does not mean that the teacher becomes completely powerless and lets children do everything they want. The result of such a situation would, of course, be chaos. Since the teacher is responsible for the peace and safety of the classroom, there are times when he has to use his influence. Most teachers, however, use more power than is necessary and do not trust children to govern themselves. Many think that the only way to run an orderly classroom is to keep children on short leashes.

After an all-day outing of an entire school in Switzerland one day, many teachers of older children remarked that the group who behaved the best on the bus and elsewhere throughout the day was the youngest group of preschoolers. The older children pushed and shoved each other, yelled, and at times screamed like wild animals out of their cages. The preschool teachers were the only ones who had heard about autonomy. All the other teachers had unwittingly been reinforcing children's heteronomy by keeping them under control. The result was that once out of the classroom, the older children were much less able to govern themselves than the preschoolers.

As stated in Chapter 3, the more children have developed autonomy, the more they have the possibility of becoming even more autonomous. Some children come to first grade much more heteronomous than others because certain cultural, historic, and family backgrounds reinforce heteronomy. With these children, the teacher needs to be more patient and judicious about letting children gradually make their own decisions. The tragedy now is that heteronomous children tend to be in schools that are more controlling, punitive, and coercive than middle-class, suburban schools. Heteronomous adults thus beget heteronomy, and more autonomous adults beget more autonomy.

Autonomy in Children's Relationships with Peers

It must be obvious from Chapters 2 and 3 that the general principle to remember under this heading is to *encourage the exchange and coordination of points of view among peers*. The coordination of viewpoints is essential for the development of moral autonomy as well as of logico-mathematical knowledge. We will briefly discuss how to do this in situations of interpersonal conflict and in those involving arithmetic.

When children become frustrated by their inability to settle a dispute, they naturally turn to the teacher to solve the problem. Although the quickest and easiest reaction is to tell them what to do, it is better for the development of autonomy to ask them to work out a solution. Frequently, all they need is a question such as "What can you do to come to an agreement?" It did not take the children in our class long to realize that it was up to them to settle their own disputes, whenever possible. On one occasion, two girls were arguing about who was going to play a particular game next. When Jackie threatened to come to one of us, Alma replied, "Don't ask Mrs. DeClark. She'll just say, 'What do *you* think you should do?' " Those who are used to exchanging ideas honestly all day will do the same thing in arithmetic.

Autonomy in Relation to Learning

The principle we advocate in relation to learning is this: *Encourage children to think in their own ways (rather than to recite "right" answers) and to engage in activities with intrinsic motivation*.

As stated in Chapter 3, when a child makes an arithmetical error such as 8 + 5 = 12, it is much better to ask if everybody agrees than to correct the answer or to tell him that his answer is wrong. Since there is absolutely nothing arbitrary in logico-mathematical knowledge, children are bound to find the truth if they argue long enough. Similarly, in reading in class when children confuse "Jason" with "Jesse," and "Nicky" with "Nathan," it is best for the teacher not to correct them, since the children whose names are involved are likely to do the correcting. Reading involves social knowledge, which requires input from people, but it is important even in this realm to be mindful of children's own construction of knowledge. In the teaching of writing, "invented spelling" (such as "MOM AND DOD") has quickly become accepted by language specialists and some first grade teachers. This is evidence of recognition that spelling, too, develops through a number of "wrong" levels, and that it is best not to demand perfection from the beginning.

We are not saying that all direct transmission is bad and should be avoided at all times, but there are generally better ways than trying to stuff right answers bit by bit into children's heads. When teachers consider the teaching of the three R's in view of constructivism and autonomy as the broader aim, they try to encourage children's initiative. Answering children's questions about how to read a word they want to know is very different from imposing the same information in a list of words to be learned.

All the children in our class played games voluntarily. We never had to tell them that they could not go out to recess unless they first finished their work. On the contrary, some asked if they could take cards to the lunchroom as we saw in Chapter 7. In Geneva, Switzerland, where children sometimes spend most of the afternoon in a park in June, some asked if they could take playing cards with them.

Some children, however, especially the lower-level ones who particularly needed to play, did not touch games for a long time. When this happened, we sometimes tried to use children's desire to play with adults and asked them if they wanted to play with us. They *really* felt free to accept or refuse, and we respected their wishes. Later in the year, when their logico-mathematical knowledge was more developed, many of these children began to take the initiative to play games and blossomed. They thus taught us to have faith in them. Children who are pushed into the mold learn to do only the minimum necessary to satisfy the teacher.

We conclude this discussion of children's intrinsic motivation by saying that it is very important for the teacher to be enthusiastic about what children are doing. Children like games, but they become even more enthusiastic when adults value and participate in their play.

PRINCIPLES CONCERNING SITUATIONS IN DAILY LIVING

We now come to the activities used to "teach" arithmetic in the context of autonomy as the aim of education, and the first of these concerns situations in everyday living. We will discuss four approaches to fostering children's thinking in these situations.

Be constantly on the lookout for appropriate situations. The examples given in Chapter 7 should convince the reader that these situations came up frequently, and that all the teacher had to do was to recognize them and use them. The distribution of materials, the taking of attendance, and cleanup are part of life in any classroom. Furthermore, when children know that the teacher is interested in talking about numbers, they initiate conversations about numerical quantities as we saw in Chapter 7 ("Just Chatting").

Situations in daily living come up in a wide variety of ways and can usually not be planned. Specific principles of teaching can, therefore, be understood best by reviewing the examples in Chapter 7. The only points we will add here concern voting and taking attendance.

In voting, the teacher begins by clarifying the problem and the possible solutions (or choices) by leading a conversation with all the children who will be voting. The problem has to be clear to everybody, and the proposed solutions must be realistic and acceptable to all concerned. As the alternatives are formulated, the teacher writes them on the board (an occasion for using reading and writing). When the alternatives are thus publicly on the board and accepted by all the members, the teacher asks children to vote and writes the number supporting each alternative. The expression of all relevant ideas is encouraged throughout this procedure, and some of those ideas will deal with numerical aspects of the situation. Children should also be encouraged to go through this procedure without the teacher.

One way to have children take attendance is by preparing an attendance chart. We made one with a small pocket for each child's card and a big pocket for all the cards. As each person arrived every morning and afternoon, he was asked to "check in" by finding his card in the big pocket and putting it in his individual pocket. The person in charge of taking attendance looked in the big pocket, copied on an official slip the names of those who were absent, and took the slip to the office.

(The collection of money for milk, lunch, and field trips also is usually an excellent occasion for numerical thinking. In our class, however, this was not possible because parents paid an annual fee directly to the office with checks.)

The way to recognize usable situations is to review the teacher's day, looking for everything that involves numerical reasoning. Taking attendance is usually done by the teacher, without the children's awareness. This is a real and natural task that can be changed into one that first graders can manage with pleasure. The numbers of children absent and present are highly relevant to many activities, such as voting and the distribution of materials. The attendance pocket chart is only one of the possible ways of adapting the task to first graders' intellectual level and motivation.

Don't be afraid of difficult problems.   Many teachers believe that 25 to 30 (the number of children in a classroom) is too big a number for first graders to deal with. This may be true, but not always. If children are truly interested in solving a problem, they are motivated to find the answer for themselves. As we saw in Chapter 2 in the example of 13 out of 24 children who voted for one alternative, different children approach the same question at different levels. It is, in fact, good for children to work at hard problems like this one, thereby becoming confident about their own ability to figure things out.

Another example of a difficult problem is the dispute over pickup sticks we saw in Chapter 7 between the boys and the girls. The problem was one of proportionality, inasmuch as there were ten boys and fifteen girls in the class. The children solved the problem in a way we had not expected: The boys imported boys from the hallway! Numerical problems can basically be solved with the operation of + 1. If a problem is important for children to solve, they often come up with a solution such as this one that is based on the operation of + 1.

Don't be afraid of wasting time. Teachers often say that they cannot afford to take time to organize a group discussion to deal with problems that come up because the curriculum is so heavy that there is already too little time. Our response is that the curriculum contains a great deal that is useless to teach. As stated in Chapters 4 and 5, for example, place value and missing addends are useless and even harmful to teach in first grade. If place value is impossible for first graders to understand, double-column addition is also pointless to teach.

Wastes can be found not only in objectives (curriculum contents) but also in means (types of activities used to reach the objectives). For example, many children who already know how to do 2 + 2 and 6 + 2 may spend time mindlessly writing answers they have known for a long time if that is the prescribed activity. The time children spend earnestly thinking is hardly ever wasted. If children think, they usually do so because the question involved is meaningful to them and appropriate for their level of development. The child who writes the answer to 6 + 2 that he already knows is neither thinking nor learning anything new. The one who is trying to win in a dispute between ten boys and fifteen girls, on the other hand, is thinking hard and constructing logico-mathematical knowledge.

Encourage children to think in other subjects and activities as well. It is important to encourage numerical reasoning in daily living, but the ability to reason numerically does not grow only out of numerical thinking. It is rooted in the child's general ability to think, that is, to put things into relationships. This means that it is important to encourage children to think in all kinds of situations. Below are three examples of activities. What is new is not the activities per se but the theoretical rationale that shows that logico-mathematical knowledge grows out of children's ability to put all kinds of things into all kinds of relationships and that social interaction is important for children's thinking.

The first example is a modification of "Show and Tell." We started having "Show and Tell," which the children seemed to like. We noticed, however, that the activity was enjoyed mainly by the child who was egocentrically talking in front of the group, and that the others were by and large not even listening. When we tried to discontinue the activity by pointing this problem out, however, the class refused to drop it.

We, therefore, suggested a modified version: We suggested that four or five children would have a turn every Friday to bring something from home in a paper bag for the rest of the class to guess by asking up to ten questions. The children accepted this idea and suggested that the guessers should be allowed to ask for clues. The activity went well every Friday afternoon for the rest of the year, and below is an example of what happened when Jane brought a toy sea horse.

Jane	*The rest of the class*
It's bumpy.	Is it a camel? (Marty)
No. (She wrote 1 on the board.)	
The bumps are hard.	A dinosaur (Marty).
No. (She wrote 2 on the board).	
It's got a curled tail.	A cat (Ann).
No. (She wrote 3 on the board.)	
I don't have any more clues.	It can't be big (Rod).
	A paper doll (Alma).
No. (She wrote 4 on the board.)	Paper dolls don't have tails (Skip).
	A pig (Nancy).
No. (She wrote 5 on the board.)	Pigs don't have bumps (Rod).
	A porcupine (Steve).
No. (She wrote 6 on the board.)	Porcupines don't have tails (Rod). (A big discussion followed about how big porcupines are and whether they have tails.) We have only four more guesses (Skip).
They used to live in the sea.	A scorpion (Ed).
No. (She wrote 7 on the board.)	A sea horse (Alma).
Yes. I didn't want to say, "It looks like a horse" because everybody would know.	

This example is particularly rich because it uses children's knowledge of animals in an intelligent way. Rather than reciting the descriptions of porcupines, scorpions, and so on, the children were talking about these characteristics for a purpose. The context of the guessing game made it important to know whether or not porcupines had tails, for example. Nobody knew for sure, and the children critically evaluated each other's evidence and degree of certitude. Skip's saying "Paper dolls don't have tails" and Rod's saying "Pigs don't have bumps" are other examples of children's critical evaluation of each other's ideas.

For the child who is in front of the class with the paper bag, this is an activity that requires decentering. Jane gave only four clues, but they were good ones in the sense that they contained just the right amount of information. Her announcing that she did not have any more clues was both intelligent and cute, and the class was willing to accept this announcement. In addition, the game was run without the teacher and was, therefore, good for Jane's development of leadership.

The game also included math. After the sixth guess, Skip said there were only four more left. In this kind of game, writing is helpful to remember the number of guesses taken. Writing should thus take place not because the teacher demands it, but because the children want to record something that is useful to them.

Our second example is an activity in reading. The teacher makes a transparency of any text to project on the screen with an overhead projector but puts masking tape on every tenth word. This paragraph would then look like the following:

> Our second example is an activity in reading. The   makes a
> transparency of any text to project on   screen with an overhead
> projector but puts masking tape   every tenth word.

The children offer ideas about what word could have been masked and critically evaluate each other's ideas. The discussion encourages them to mobilize the totality of their knowledge, including that of syntax and the length of each word. Only a noun can go into the first space, and the only words that can go into the second space are "a" and "the" (O'Brien, 1980).

This group activity stimulates much more thinking than taking turns reading to the teacher. In the latter, children are told to be quiet unless it is their turn to read. This practice encourages them not to pay attention to what is going on. This is why teachers have to keep reminding children to pay attention!

Our third example involves the teacher's reading aloud from certain kinds of books that offer the possibility of thinking and group discussion. *The King*

Who Rained (Gwynne, 1970) is an example of such a book. As this title suggests, the book gives a collection of expressions that children assimilate incorrectly and humorously into what they already know. "The king who rained" is what they "hear" when they are told about "the king who reigned."

One of the pictures in the book shows a church wedding in which the couple is standing at the altar in front of a minister. The curious thing about this picture is that it shows a huge locomotive held up by a little girl standing in front of all the guests. The text says, "My big sister's getting married and she says I can hold up her train." When we asked the children if they found anything funny, they came up with the following remarks:

> Susie: She means flowers.
> Kate: No, it means the back of her long dress.
> Cathy: She can mean a toy train.
> Jane: You wouldn't bring a toy train to a wedding.

This is an example of thinking and putting all kinds of things into all kinds of relationships by exchanging viewpoints; each child comes up with an interpretation in such a situation by mobilizing everything he knows. The children in our example were listening to each other and critically evaluating each other's ideas. Children who are encouraged in this way develop logico-mathematical knowledge in general, and the ability to think in arithmetic grows out of that general ability.

PRINCIPLES CONCERNING GROUP GAMES

Games must be selected, introduced, played, and talked about. For each of these aspects, we will discuss the principle of teaching involved.

Choosing Games

The first task for the teacher is to choose appropriate games. This is part of a larger consideration concerning the materials available in the classroom. Other related questions are what kinds of dice to provide, how to make games accessible to children, and how to retire the ones that are no longer of interest.

Choose games that are neither too difficult nor too easy, but don't worry too much about this point. At the beginning of the school year, we chose simple games like Hop to It (see Chapter 7 for descriptions of all the games referred to in this chapter). This is a straightforward and short board game, which was played fairly often. The card game War was also appropriate, and children enjoyed playing it often.

A little later, we invented a modified version of War called Double War, which was an instant success. We also introduced Football, another game requiring the comparison of two numbers, with numbers only up to 10. When these numbers became too easy, larger ones up to 50 were added to the game.

As the school year progressed, the games we provided became more difficult. For example, in Double *Parcheesi,* the children rolled a ten-sided die and had to double the number that came up on it to know how many spaces to move along the board. In this activity, the addends went up to 10.

Another point, which may seem contradictory to our discussion, is the following: Don't worry about the appropriateness of a game. By and large, children know what games they like and play them frequently. If they do not like one, they will not play it, and its inappropriateness will quickly become obvious. For example, we saw that Sevens was rarely touched by human hands. We later understood that it was unpopular because most of the combinations that total 7 were difficult at that time.

We also found that children modified games according to their developmental levels. In *Huckleberry Hound* Concentration, for example, children only matched pictures in September as can be seen in Chapter 10. By November, however, they counted their cards to determine who won, and in January, when the criterion for winning became the total number of points, they discussed strategies for finding cards with the highest point value. The attractiveness of Double War over War also confirmed the statement that children move on to more difficult games without needing to be pushed by the teacher.

In the same way, it is easy to see when children outgrow easy games because those, too, remain on the shelves. We found by midyear that it became necessary to sort through all the games and remove the ones that were never played. I (G.D.) discussed with the class the problem of the cluttered shelves and invited the kids' suggestions about the easy games to put away. They voted on which ones to keep and suggested I store the others "for next year's first graders."

Provide dice with dots and with numerals, as well as others such as TILE dice. Just as children select games that are appropriate for their developmental levels, they choose well between dice with dots and those with numerals. We observed that many became frustrated when they were forced to use dice with numerals and their interest in the activity quickly diminished. Moreover, if the dice with dots were removed from a box and replaced with those with numerals, some children looked for a pair of conventional dice anyway. Our solution was to include a pair of each kind in the box so that the children could choose the ones they liked. (Some children decided to use all four dice at times.)

However, when we wanted the children to have the experience of using the TILE dice or the ones with 5's on all sides, we did not offer any alternatives. Instead, we presented those dice as part of the new game. (Refer to Chapter 7 for descriptions of these dice.) We hasten to add that TILE dice are undesirable for very low-level children who see the 5-cm stick as 1. A stick is indeed one object, and it is harmful to be told that it is a 5 when one can only see it as a 1.

A small pointer here concerns the desirability of making dice with foam rubber. These do not make noise when they are thrown and do not shake up the board, thereby moving the pieces on it.

Make a box for each game. We found that it was best to make a box for each game for the following reason: When the children could simply grab a box from a shelf, rather than having to dig around to find the necessary pieces, cards, and so on, they were more likely to play many different games at one sitting.

Since most of our card games used decks that were "customized," we organized them with rubber bands and a piece of paper labeling the game ("Double War," for example) and noting the number of cards in the deck ("40 cards," for example). In this way, the children needed only to grab the special deck, rather than having to sort through and separate the cards when they wanted to play a particular game.

After a teacher chooses a game, he has to introduce it to the class. We now proceed to a discussion of various ways in which a teacher can introduce a game.

Introducing Games

Different games should be introduced in different ways. Four ways of introduction that we tried out in the class are described here.

1. *Playing the game with a few children in front of the entire class to demonstrate how it goes.* This type of introduction tends to be more successful with board games than card games. Since a board game is big and takes up a lot of floor space, it is best for the spectators to watch by standing around the players seated on the floor. This type of demonstration also fosters interaction among the spectators and players. Onlookers have the opportunity to exchange ideas about strategies, offer unsolicited advice, and speculate on the outcome of the game.

This type of introduction would obviously not be desirable for games involving complicated rules. (See Chapter 10, September section, for an unsuccessful introduction of Card Dominoes.)

2. *Playing the game with several children and telling the rest of the class they can learn it from them.* Games with simple rules such as Double War are best suited for this type of introduction. An important consideration, however, involves the personalities and abilities of the children who first play with the teacher. These children need to be articulate and decentered enough to explain the rules to their peers effectively. It is advisable for the teacher to play the game enough times with the children to be sure that they understand how it goes. Sometimes, I (G.D.) have watched the children introducing a game to be sure that their explanation was understood.

3. *Playing the game with many small groups until all the children have played with the teacher.* Although this is a time-consuming way of introducing a game, it is necessary for the more complicated ones such as Punta. When the rules are complicated, children need to be reminded often and shown examples until they "catch on." The exchange of opinions and strategies can be facilitated more easily in small groups as well. (See Chapter 10, March section, for Ann's involvement in Punta.) We would also like to point out that parents are often glad to come once a week to play games with children. A father in Selma, Alabama, for example, gave up his lunch hour once a week to play games with his child and her classmates. He had fun in the process and readily talked about the pleasure he had.

4. *Showing a game to the children and asking if it needs to be explained.* Many games, particularly board games such as *Benji*, have similar formats which are easily recognizable. Thus, if children have had some experience playing games, they may know at a glance what to do with a similar one.

We found that children usually did not want to be told what to do with a game they thought they could figure out by themselves. We were pleased to see this autonomy for several reasons. First, it enabled us to decrease our adult power. Second, the responsibility they felt about settling their own disputes concerning rules became greater when the children thus invented their own rules.

This type of introduction would obviously not be appropriate for unfamiliar games or those with complicated rules. It is not advisable either with modified commercial games. For example, when the children saw the game *Sorry*, some said they did not need an introduction because they played it at home and knew what to do with it. However, since we wanted the children to make doubles and had no need for the cards that came in the box with arbitrary rules, we modified the game and pre-sented it as a "new" game.

Playing Games

Playing games with children is an experience not to be missed. It is wonderful to see the enthusiasm, interest, and hard work that go into their play. However, Piaget's theory makes us realize the need to intervene in ways that are different from the way adults usually play with children. Those ways will be explained as we discuss the principles that apply here.

Go along with children's ideas and their way of thinking, even if these seem very peculiar. Young children have ways of playing games that seem very peculiar to adults (see Kamii and DeVries, 1980, for an elaboration of this statement). Constructivism enables us to understand why it is best to encourage children to play in their own way, rather than imposing a foreign, adult way of taking turns, dealing cards, not "cheating," and so forth.

From an adult's point of view, for example, it makes sense to have the players' turns go clockwise around the table. However, children often choose turns by saying, "I'm first," "I'm second," and so on, until each player has spoken. The resulting order appears confusing to us, but each child usually takes his turn in the agreed-upon order, evidently remembering whom to follow. There is no reason to stifle their initiative in such a situation by imposing what seems to us to be a better way.

Our second example concerns choosing the first player. Because children like to be first, they often choose this privilege unintelligently. For example, it is to a player's advantage not to be first in *Piggy Bank,* where the probability of making 5 cents is small for the first player. However, children usually choose to be first, and it is best to say nothing and let the child figure out for himself the undesirability of this behavior.

Our third example is related to dealing cards. Children know that the cards have to be distributed before a game can begin. But many children do not see any need for all the players to start with the same number. We often saw the dealer pick up what appeared to be half of the deck and hand it to his opponent, keeping the other "half" for himself. It is useless to make children deal cards in the "correct" way. Requiring them to do it the "right" way is an imposition of an idea that is foreign to them. The "right" way will appear when their logic develops.

We often observed dealing which resulted in unequal numbers of cards for the players. The extent of our intervention was to ask, "Do you think you need to count your cards?" The children often said, "No." When they did count them and found unequal numbers, we continued with "What do you think you should do?" At first, they often said that it was OK not to have the same number. If they were satisfied with that, we did not impose our idea. In time, however, they solved the problem (if and when this became a problem *for them*) by giving some to those who had fewer.

To participate effectively in games requires a great deal of self-restraint on the part of the teacher. This statement applies particularly to "pecking," a term we used to describe the mechanical, eternal counting of dots on a die or card. It was very difficult for us to refrain from intervening. In Double War, for example, children endlessly pecked at the dots on the cards. We became impatient and tried unobtrusively to intervene by saying, for example, "I know a way of telling who has more without counting. Do you want me to tell you?" They usually wanted to know. We showed them with a 2 + 2 and a 2 + 5 combination that since the two 2's of the two players were the same, we needed only to compare the other 2 with the 5. With a 1 + 1 and a 3 + 4 combination, we pointed out that since 1 + 1 was less than 3, it did not matter what the other number was. The interesting thing about this teaching was its effect: Some children responded with blank faces. Others imitated us for several subsequent turns but soon reverted back to pecking. The lesson we learned was that it does not do any good to push children beyond the method that is best for them. In time, they gave up the pecking of their own accord, but it was *very* hard to sit back and wait for that glorious moment to come!

Because children enjoy playing games, it is not uncommon to see them do whatever is necessary to keep one going. For example, when two children were playing War and one of them ran out of cards, the other child grabbed a handful of his own and gave them to the first one saying, "Here, you take these and let's keep playing."

In a game of Concentration, one player had flipped two cards. Unsuccessful in her attempt to find a matching pair, she returned the second card to its face-down position and proceeded to turn over a third, fourth, and fifth card, trying to make a match. Most adults would term this action "cheating" and feel the necessity of stopping this behavior. It is better for the development of autonomy to say to the opponent, "Is it OK with you that so-and-so keeps looking for a match?" In this way, the decision about the rules rests with the players, and adult authority is minimized. (The opponent's response was, "Yeah, let's both turn over five cards.")

When children's autonomy is valued, it is important that *they* make and change rules. Adults are tempted to enforce the conventional, ready-made rules *they* think are "right." However, this enforcement increases adult power and results in heteronomous obedience on the part of the children. In contrast, when children set the rules, they are required to think about what is fair. They must also interact, decenter, and come to an agreement acceptable to all players. When they then have an argument about rules, they feel responsible about settling it. When I (G.D.) participated as a player, I felt free to participate in changing the rules. But when children came to me as the teacher complaining about unfair rules, my reply was, "I guess you need to make a new rule that everyone thinks is fair if you want the game to go on." That was usually all I needed to say to get them to discuss the problem and work toward a solution.

Finally, when first graders play games, especially at the beginning of the school year, they are often not even interested in knowing who won. (See Kamii and DeVries, 1980, Chapters 11 and 12, for a discussion of the development of children's ability to compete in games.) In Concentration, for example, one player had turned over one card. As she was about to turn over another, her opponent said, "Wait! That's not gonna match. Flip this one." In *Tens*, likewise, players often help each other by pointing out a possible move. It is difficult for a teacher to remain quiet in such situations, but to intervene would only force an issue which is of no interest to them at the time.

Give the children plenty of time to think. This principle seems obvious, but is not always easy to put into practice. When we participated in a game as a player, we occasionally saw one player take a very long time for his turn. This resulted in the other players' losing interest or patience. It seemed only natural to "act like an adult," taking charge and saying, "Okay, finish your turn. So-and-so is next." However, when children are actively involved in games and are working hard at playing, they need and deserve as much time as necessary. This need for patience occurs more often when a lower-level child plays with a more advanced player. We have tried to get the idea across to those waiting that everybody's time to think should be respected. One way of doing this is by saying, "I'm going to get a quick drink of water while so-and-so is finishing her turn."

Do not correct wrong answers or low-level play, and intervene indirectly instead. In games, it is best for the teacher to interact as another player. If, for example, the teacher sees one of the children move along the board incorrectly, it is better not to correct the child. Instead, an appropriate comment might be, "Wait, I don't understand. I thought you were supposed to move six spaces."

When we played games with the children and wanted to show them higher-level play, we kept the attempt in the context of the play. That is to say, we avoided making a lesson out of the game and gave the children a chance to respond (or not to respond) to our ideas. For example, during a game of Double War, a lower-level child named Kate turned over a 3 and a

2. I (G.D.) had a 2 and a 5, but turned over only the 5. As I paused and teasingly smiled, she said, "C'mon, Mrs. DeClark, turn over your other card!" When I asked her if it was necessary for me to do that to know who will take all four cards, she replied, "Yeah, that's the rules." It was clear to me that she had no idea what I was doing. I, therefore, went no further with the point I was trying to make. Marty, by contrast, understood my intention immediately. After he turned over his ace and 2 combination, I turned over a 4. He laughed as he pushed his cards toward me and said, "Forget it. You win." When I asked him if he wanted me to show him my other card, he said, "It doesn't matter what it is. 4 is already more than 3." I later noticed him using the same idea while playing with other children.

Encourage peer interaction. As stated in Chapter 2, it is good for children to exchange points of view among themselves. In *Put and Take*, for example, they discussed the different combinations of chips that made the same total. When one child put out a red chip and a yellow one (2 + 1), another insisted that that was wrong because he had to put out three yellow ones (1 + 1 + 1). Children are encouraged to think about 3 from different points of view when such a disagreement comes up.

Ending Games

Deemphasize competition and simply ask the children what they want to do next. The fact of winning should be no more than just that. A good rule of thumb for the teacher is to ask, "Who won?" and then immediately go on to ask, "What would you like to do next (choose another game or play the same one again)?"

The reader may be wondering about the desirability of asking "Who won?" We recommend raising this question casually because it stimulates numerical thinking and discussion about criteria of winning. In Concentration with *Huckleberry Hound* cards, for example, some children say that a pair of "3's" is worth three points, while others say it is worth six points. In *Piggy Bank*, some count cards, while others count money. To count money, some proceed by counting from 1, but others group all the 1's together, all the 2's together, all the 3's together, and so on, and try to count by 2's, 3's, 4's, and 5's.

As stated earlier, the reader is urged to read about the issue of competition in *Group Games in Early Education* (Kamii and DeVries, 1980, Chapter 11). In our classroom, competition was never a problem. In fact, being the winner often does not matter to first graders. We frequently saw children continuing to play a game even after the winner had been determined. When we asked about it, they said they liked to play, and wanted to see who would be the "second winner," "third winner," and so on.

Follow-Up after Games

From time to time, children come up with gems from which others can benefit. Because children are more open to discussion when they are not busy playing, *it is important after a game to provide an opportunity for them to talk with each other about what they did.* For example, I (G.D.) observed Cathy, a higher-level child, playing Guess My Number with another child one day. She had found out that the number in question was more than 19 and less than 40. She then thought for a moment and said, "I'm gonna guess 29, 'cause then I'll know if the number is in the 20's or the 30's." I was delighted with her astute thinking. After all the children were finished playing games, I organized a class discussion and began by saying, "I saw Cathy doing something interesting while she was playing Guess My Number. Would you like to tell us what you did when you knew the number was more than 19 and less than 40?" She repeated to the class what she had said, and I continued with, "Does that kind of guess make it easier to figure out the number?" Only a few of the advanced children followed Cathy's line of thinking, but the discussion provided all the children with the general idea that there were clever ways of asking better questions than others. These ideas are "gems" because they come from the children and not from adults.

This type of discussion can usually be conducted only spontaneously and when the moment "feels right." It is well worth the time it takes to organize such a discussion. Different ways of using fingers to do 6 + 6 can also be the topic of a useful conversation, since children often have trouble when an addend is greater than 5 and/or a total is greater than 10. Some children put up six fingers and say, "First, I put these six in my head" and then demonstrate counting-on with the same fingers.

AN EXAMPLE OF THE PRECEDING PRINCIPLES IN PRACTICE

How the principles discussed in the preceding section are put into practice is demonstrated in the following account of the moment-to-moment interaction and thinking involved as two children play Double War with their teacher (G.D.). The material is taken from a videotape made of the session.

I began by saying to Ann and Susie, "The question is who wants to play first?" "Why can't we play all together?" Ann suggested. "Shall we play all together?" I asked Susie. Susie agreed. "I've never played like that before. How shall we deal the cards if we are all going to play together?" I inquired. Ann pointed to the space in front of me as she said, "Somebody deals like two here, two here (in front of Susie), and two here (in front of her)." I responded with an "Oh," as Susie announced, "*Some*body but not me."

I shuffled the cards and asked, "Shall I deal, or does somebody else want to deal?" The girls looked at each other shrugging. "What do you think?" I pressed for an answer. The girls exchanged an impish look. "Do you want me to deal?" I asked, and the girls responded with big nods. "I thought so," I told them.

> NOTE: I was gently trying to get the children to express their ideas. Children naturally look to adults to run the show, and I pushed them gently into knowing their minds, taking a stand, and saying what they thought.

Game I

After dealing five cards per pile, I stopped and asked, "Is it important in this game that we all start with the same number of cards?" Instantly and emphatically, Susie answered, "Yes." "Shall we count how many we have after I deal one more?" I suggested. (We had forty cards up to 5 from two decks.)

Ann counted her cards and announced, "I got six."

Susie announced, "I got twelve."

I asked, "Twelve in each pile?" "No, twelve altogether," Susie replied and went on to count each pile. She found seven in one and six in the other.

> NOTE: This was very interesting from the point of view of young children's thinking, which goes only in one direction. Susie knew that 6 + 6 = 12. Yet, she had to count her twelve cards empirically to find out how many she had in each pile. Furthermore, when she found seven and six, she did not suspect any error on her part.

I said, "When you counted there, I'm not sure I saw seven. Let's count them again." Susie found six this time. "So we all have six," I remarked.

> NOTE: I could have left this error alone to let Susie find a solution for herself. At any rate, I was careful not to present myself as an all-knowing adult by saying it was logically impossible to get 7 + 6 = 12. I acted like another player who was not sure she *had seen* seven cards.

"And here we have four cards left," I remarked, and Susie lost no time in suggesting, "We should keep them out." "So we'll all have the same number of cards?" I asked, and Susie nodded with certainty.

The cards first turned up can be seen in Figure 8.1a.

Susie announced, "I got 5."

I also announced, "I got 5."

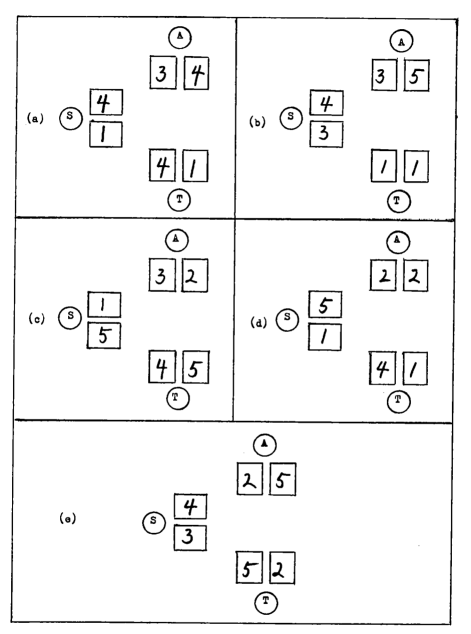

FIGURE 8.1.   Double War with three players.

Ann "pecked" on her card as she counted: "I got . . . 4/5–6–7." Susie immediately pushed her cards toward Ann as Ann declared, "I get them all."

> NOTE: "Pecking" is a term we used to refer to children's counting symbols on a card (or dots on a die) by touching each of them. As the reader will see in Chapter 10, we spent many weeks in anguish while the children continued to peck, even after committing a sum to memory.

The cards then turned up can be seen in Figure 8.1b. "I know I didn't do very well," I said as soon as I saw my cards.

Susie pecked, "4/5–6–7."

Ann, too, pecked and found "5/6–7–8." Stopping Susie from pushing her cards toward Ann, I remarked, "Look at these: 3 and 4 (pointing at each of Susie's cards), and 3 and 5 (pointing at each of Ann's cards)." Ann did not hear anything and busily collected all the cards saying, "I got 8."

> NOTE: I was trying to suggest subtly that addition was unnecessary to compare 3 + 4 with 3 + 5. Neither girl got the idea, and I decided not to impose my wisdom on them.

Figure 8.1c shows the cards turned up next.

Susie exclaimed, "6" as soon as she saw her cards.

Ann pecked, "3/4–5."

I pointed to my 5 saying "five." Both girls counted-on, "6–7–8–9," and immediately pushed their cards toward me. "Thank you, everyone," I said happily.

> NOTE: I tried again, without success, to encourage the children to reason logically rather than counting mechanically. I tried to get them to see that Ann's total was smaller than Susie's 5, and that since I also had a 5, all that needed to be compared was Susie's "1" with my "4". The children did not make any of the relationships I tried to suggest subtly.

The cards that came up then can be seen in Figure 8.1d.

Susie was the first to announce. "6." I said, "5," and Ann lost no time in saying, "4," without pecking.

Laughing with delight, Susie motioned with her hands for everybody to send all the cards toward her. Ann and I complied.

> NOTE: The children again added numbers instead of reasoning that 5 + 1 > 4 + 1, and that 4 + 1 > 2 + 2. I decided that it was useless to give "hints," inasmuch as the children were deaf to the relationships I had tried to suggest.

The cards that turned up next are shown in Figure 8.1e. No one said anything, and no one seemed about to do anything. I broke the silence by saying , "Oo-oo! Look at what Ann and I have." No one reacted for some reason.

"What do you have, Ann?" I asked. "2 and 5," Ann answered.

"And what do I have?" I continued. "2 and 5," Ann said.

To the next question, "And Susie has?" both girls responded "3 and 4."

Faced with this sudden reluctance even to add numbers, I posed the only question I could think of: "What is 5 and 2?" Both replied "7," without pecking.

"And 4 and 3?" I continued.

Ann pecked as she counted-all: "1–2–3/4–5–6–7. DOUBLE WAR!" Without a word, the two girls laid cards across, face down. Realizing that there were no more cards left in the piles, Susie suggested, "Then we take cards from what we've got."

> NOTE: I was pleased with Susie's initiative. Autonomous children do not wait for the teacher to point out that a new rule has to be made.

"Can we look? Can we pick the cards we want?" I asked. Both girls turned up a 5 and a 1, not hearing me. "I got 6," they both said.

"Can we pick the cards we want?" I repeated my question. Ann nodded half-heartedly as if she did not know too well what she was saying yes to. Susie, however, emphatically decreed, "No!" "No? I know what I'd do if I could peek," I remarked teasingly. "Yeah, take the highest one," Susie grunted, implying that that was obvious. I showed the 5 and 2 that I got without peeking, and the two girls immediately pushed their cards toward me.

> NOTE: Notice the intellectual-social-emotional-political nature of Susie's autonomy. She reasoned sharply, thought solutions up quickly, and had the emotional strength to be an assertive leader.

"Let's count the cards to see who the winner is," I suggested. Susie announced, "I got four." Ann counted hers and said, "I got ten." The two girls helped count my cards. When they reached eleven, I stopped and asked. "Do I need to go on counting?" Both girls nodded emphatically and continued counting to twenty-two in unison.

> NOTE: Game I was played at a very low level. The children did not have transitivity and, therefore, always had to look for the highest total instead of reasoning logically. *Transitivity* refers to the ability to put into

relationship a number of relationships between two elements. An example of transitivity is the ability to deduce that if Ann's total is greater than Susie's total (a relationship between two elements), and Susie's total equals my total (another relationship between two elements), then Ann's total is the highest of the three totals. Because their thought was not yet transitive, it did not occur to the children in the situation shown in Figure 8.1a that since the two (4 + 1)'s were the same, and since the two 4's in (4 + 3) and (4 + 1) were the same, all they had to compare were the 3 and the 1.

Both girls also pecked a great deal. The only sums they used from memory were the + 1's and (2 + 2).

"Thank you . . . Shall we play this Triple War again?" I said, and both girls answered, "No." I went on to point out, "I didn't have a chance to play regular Double War with either of you guys," and Susie offered, "You can play me." Ann lost no time to say, "You can play me, too."

"Shall we take turns?" I asked, and the girls nodded. "Who shall I play first?" I asked, and both children reacted with a "Me-me!" Laughing, I said, "Oh, no, I don't want to decide . . . I know, so that I won't have to decide! You can pick a number." Susie interrupted with a suggestion: "I know a way! We keep our eyes closed and put up fingers." "OK, how will I know who's the winner then?" I asked. "Whoever has the highest number," Susie replied. "So you guys close your eyes, and I keep mine open?" I inquired. When Susie answered in the affirmative, I said, "OK, close your eyes . . . Put up your numbers."

> NOTE: The children would have been perfectly happy to let me decide who would be first. However, I put the responsibility of making a fair decision on the children's shoulders. Susie showed a great deal of initiative in this situation. The more children are encouraged to exercise initiative and responsibility, the more they develop these qualities.

Susie put up ten fingers as she closed her eyes. Ann shut her eyes tightly but did not put up any fingers. "Ann, you have to put up a number," I told her. Ann put up six fingers with gusto. I said, "OK, open your eyes. Who has the higher number?"

> NOTE: By asking the children to open their eyes, I encouraged them to come to their own conclusion based on information obtained directly from its source.

"That means I play with Susie first. Ann, will you deal the cards?" I asked.

Game II

When Ann was through dealing, I asked, "How many do we get when we play regular Double War?" Both girls answered, "Ten." Ann and I found ten cards each in my piles, but Susie found eleven in her first pile. She took the last card out saying. "Maybe I have nine in here (the other stack)."

> NOTE: Susie's counting was often inaccurate, but her reasoning by compensation was excellent.

Susie found ten in the second pile and gave the "extra" card to the teacher. "You have an extra one?" I asked. Susie nodded yes, but Ann was not convinced. Ann counted Susie's first pile and found only nine in it. She added the "extra" card to Susie's pile with a tinge of contempt.

> NOTE: This is an example of the benefit of encouraging the exchange of points of view among peers. When Ann was intellectually sure of what was going on, she had initiative. In this situation, she was sure that she had dealt the cards with a dependable method. Social competence thus often goes hand in hand with intellectual competence.

When play began, Susie turned up a 3 and a 2. I looked at my cards, put down only a 5 (Figure 8.2a), and asked, "What do you know?" "You won," Susie replied immediately. "How do you know, without even looking at the other card?" I asked. " 'Cause you have 5," was Susie's explanation. "So whatever I have in the other hand, I'm the winner?" I went on to ask, and Susie nodded. I showed my other card, a 3, and collected all four cards, saying, "Thank you."

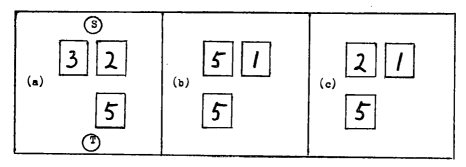

FIGURE 8.2.   Double War with two players.

NOTE: As soon as there were only two players and only two sums to compare, Susie started to play at a higher level. She reasoned logically rather than mechanically adding numbers.

Immediately after turning her next cards over (Figure 8.2b), Susie announced, "6." I studied my cards, hiding them from Susie's view, and showed only one of them, a 5 (Figure 8.2b). I then let my other card down, which was a 3. Without a word, Susie immediately pushed her cards toward me.

For the next round, Susie turned up a 1 and a 2, and I again held up my cards vertically, trying to decide which card(s) to show. (I had two 5's.) I showed only one of them (Figure 8.2c), asking, "What do you think?" "You get them," Susie answered. "What do you think I have back here?" I asked teasingly. Susie grinned without a word. "Does it matter?" I continued, and Susie replied, "No, you get them anyway."[1]

SOME DO'S AND DON'TS ABOUT SPECIFIC GAMES

Many suggestions were already made in Chapter 7 regarding what a teacher can do in specific games. Although a teacher who has understood the preceding discussion can invent what we have to say in the rest of this chapter, we add this section for those who would further like to benefit from our experience. The games are arranged in the order in which they appeared in Chapter 7, and we include only those about which we have some do's and don'ts.

War

A modification called Open War can be suggested when children "cheat" by looking at their cards. When children go through their cards looking for one to put down in War (rather than putting down the one turned up by chance), they are using their intelligence. When they thus "cheat," we prefer to go along with them and change the rule to their way of playing when we are the opponent. For example, if a child looks at all his cards, we

---

1. This account is taken from only one portion of the videotape showing Georgia DeClark and her students playing Double War, Punta, and Tens with Playing Cards. Another tape shows a low-level child completing worksheets before playing Double War and *Piggy Bank* with C. Kamii. A third tape shows two "slow" second graders with their teacher who is unaware that her "teaching" is preventing the children from thinking and constructing sums. Anyone interested in viewing these videotapes or reading the accounts transcribed from the tapes is urged to contact C. Kamii.

would simply say, "If *you* can look at *your* cards, *I* am going to look at mine, too, OK?" This is how we stumbled upon a new game called Open War.

One way to play Open War is by using twenty cards going up to five. After the cards are dealt, the players take turns putting down the first one. When I (C. K.) played with Marty, for example, he looked for all his 5's first and then for all his 4's, rather than saving them when possible. The play went as follows:

Marty put down a 5, and I put down a 1. He took them with glee.
I then put down a 1, and Marty put down a 1 to make "war."
Since it was "war," Marty said I had to put down the first card again; so I put down a 1 again. Marty took all 4 cards by using a 5.

NOTE: His move was not smart. Instead, he should have used a 2 and saved his 5.

Marty then put down a 5, and I used a 2, since I did not have any more 1's. He collected his cards with great pleasure.

I then put down a 5, and Marty used a 4, the strongest of the cards he had left.

NOTE: Marty did not think of using a 2, which he had. The tendency to use the strongest card in one's possession is common in first grade. However, by the second round, Marty had characteristically figured out the advantage of saving his 5's, and began at times to look for the smallest number necessary to win.

Go Fish

The reader may want to refer to Chapter 10 of *Group Games* (Kamii and DeVries, 1980) for the game Making Families. This game is very similar to Go Fish, and the kindergarten children in this moment-to-moment account are very interesting.

Double War

We will not repeat here the points already made earlier in this chapter regarding children's pecking and their low-level play. However, we would like to make the following suggestions:

Add higher-number cards gradually to the existing deck. At the beginning of the year, the set contains only cards going up to 4, from two original decks (8 × 4 = 32 cards). We suggest adding the 5's next, and letting the kids play with 40 cards for a while. The 6's and 7's from one deck might later be added (a total of 48 cards), and, later still, the 8's and 9's, also from one deck (a total of 56 cards). In this way, the addition of new cards will not be overwhelming. Some aces can be eliminated along the way if a smaller set is desired.

Try flipping one card at a time occasionally while playing with a child. As stated earlier in this chapter, when a child turns up a 1 + 1 or a 2 + 1 combination, for example, and the teacher has a 3 and a 4, she can show only the 3 and ask if it is necessary for her to turn the other card face up. This type of play can encourage rich discussions. It also yields valuable diagnostic information about the child's logic.

Fifty Chips

Encourage but don't push children into knowing how many chips are on their boards, or how many more they need. When kids are asked how many chips are already on the board or how many more they need, they sometimes think in terms of 5's and 10's (for the columns and rows on the boards). A question such as "Can you tell, just by looking, how many chips you need to fill up your board?" can be appropriate. This question involves grouping by 10's or by 5's and premultiplication. The next question might be: "Do you think you *could* fill up your board on this turn?" (This would be impossible if the two dice went from 0 to 5, and there were twelve more spaces to fill.)

Hop to It and *Benji*

Let children decide how to end the game. Kids have definite ideas about how to end board games, and they can and should make their own rules. For example, one child may insist on having the exact number, while another may suggest "getting in" on any number equal to or greater than the number of steps to reach the goal. This discussion may initiate a conversation about the desirability of using one die instead of two. Needless to say, these decisions should rest with the players.

Don't impose addition when children avoid it. We were horrified to see kids rolling a 4 and a 3, for example, and counting, "1-2-3-4/1-2-3," as they moved, instead of adding the numbers first. I (G. D.) wanted to scream, "You can't do that. This is an adding game. You have to add!" I did show restraint, however, and in time, the kids stopped this inefficient behavior.

Dinosaurs and XYZ

When making homemade games, consider contents that appeal to children. Games with appealing contents are almost certain to be "hits" with kids, especially those with a fantasy theme and topics that are popularized by the media. Dinosaurs seem to be permanently fascinating to young children, and football is accepted with enthusiasm in the fall.

Consider the desirability of games that need no introduction. As stated earlier in the chapter, the kids in the class felt grown up and proud when they could invent the rules of a game without our help. We believe that this sense of competence and power affected a game's popularity.

Huckleberry Hound Concentration

Encourage discussions regarding scoring when children are interested. Children have definite ideas about how to total their scores when this is important to them. The teacher can encourage discussions about how to count the points. With a pair of 3's, for example, some want to count it as 3, while others want to count it as 3 + 3.

Put and Take

Consider other possibilities before writing point values on the chips. Although in Chapter 7 we suggested writing point values on the chips, there are times when that may be a bad idea. For example, if kids want to change the point system of the chips from 1, 2, and 10, to 1, 5, and 10, it will be impossible if the chips are already marked. Another possibility would be to write the numbers on masking tape. The tape can later be removed if the children want to change the point values.

Teachers may also want to use four colors of chips for the values of 1, 2, 5, and 10.

Ask, "How (or when) do we know we won?" from time to time. Because kids love to watch the spinner, they often play and play, without any interest in counting their points. By casually asking such a question, the teacher can encourage them to find out how close they are to the number required to win the game.

Let kids struggle through making change. It is difficult to sit by and watch kids struggle as they exchange a blue (10-point) chip for yellow and red ones. But they need to do it on their own, and here, too, the teacher needs to keep silent.

Double *Parcheesi* and *Sorry*

The teacher may want to conduct a discussion about doubles before introducing the games. As noted in Chapter 10, March section, I (G.D.) conducted a discussion about doubles before the introduction of Double *Parcheesi*. We think this discussion helped "set the stage" for this type of game, as the children found out that they had to skip a number each time the addend increased by 1. They found out, for example, that when the addends went from 5 to 6, the total increased from 10 to 12.

Be on the lookout for mistakes such as 7 + 7 = 13 and 9 + 9 = 19. The first error occurs because the children know 6 + 6 and add only 1 more. Likewise, 9 + 9 = 19 occurs because they know 10 + 10 and subtract only 1. As previously stated, our intervention would be limited to saying, "Do you agree?"

> NOTE: It may appear to the reader that we ask "Do you agree?" only when we see a mistake. We often ask this question when the answer is correct.

Piggy Bank

Let the kids peck. It is very painful to watch the eternal pecking when kids only have to know 4 + 1 and 3 + 2. The pecking is part of their development. They will stop it eventually, I (G.D.) promise!

Be on the lookout for trial and error based on proximity. Children often try to make pairs by putting cards together two by two only because they happen to be next to each other. For example, there may be a 2 and a 4 on the table, and a player may then turn over a 3. He will first try the 2 and the 4, by pecking, and then the 4 and 3, and declare that there is nothing he can take. In a classroom, another player is likely to point out the possibility of the 2 and 3.

Watch for three levels of determining the winner. At the lowest level, some children do not care or say that they don't know how to count their money. Others count the number of cards instead of counting their money. The middle-level player counts his money, more or less by pecking. When he says his total is 22, the teacher may be tempted to correct his pecking, knowing that his total has to be a multiple of 5. (This correction would seem to the child like the arbitrary imposition of something that does not make sense.) The highest-level players count by 5's or engage in premultiplication by grouping together all the 1's, all the 2's, all the 3's, and so on.

Tens with Playing Cards

Be patient about pecking. This game, too, particularly lends itself to pecking. At the risk of being repetitive, we would like to warn the reader about the need to be patient.

Be on the lookout for certain combinations that are easier than others. We have found that the easiest combination to remember is 9 + 1, with 1 + 9 being slightly more difficult. These are followed by 5 + 5 and 8 + 2. The most difficult ones are 7 + 3 and 6 + 4, and children need the most time to find these combinations.

Tens

Give the children plenty of time for their turns. This game is much more difficult than it initially appears, particularly because of the many possibilities to consider. Thus, kids need lots of time to look over the pieces both on the table and in their possession.

Be on the lookout for troubles with the green pieces. Although the two shades of green on the pieces appear quite different to us, many children had difficulty distinguishing them. Their question to us, "Do these greens go together?" was usually answered by other children, and we thus did not have to get involved.

Punta

Do not make kids sort cards before beginning the game. Children will sort their cards on their own if and when they feel the need to do so. If they do not, they should not be made to sort them. Instead, the teacher may want to say that *she* needs to do it for herself to be able to play. This may cause the children to think about the benefits of sorting.

Give children time to think and encourage the exchange of ideas. There is a lot to think about in Punta, and children need time to consider all the possibilities available to them. While the game is in progress, the teacher can and should encourage the players to discuss how they have made certain combinations, by questions such as, "What cards did *you* use to make 9?"

Make the Biggest Number

Encourage discussion among players. Conversations such as the following should particularly be encouraged: One player drew a 0 for his first card and said he was going to lose because 0 was the smallest number. Another player quickly corrected him by explaining that if he drew a 9, he could make 90, and that was a big number.

It is often useful to go through the game step by step with lower-level children. We noticed that lower-level children were able to play this game with a little help from us. (Refer to Chapter 10, April section, for a discussion of step-by-step help.) The fact that lower-level children can thus be helped shows how easy it is for first graders to learn how to "spell" two digit numbers.

The teacher may want to consider modifying this game to "Make the Smallest Number." The teacher would know best when the time is appropriate for the introduction of this change.

Guess My Number

The teacher may want to be the first recorder. In this way, the kids can have an example to imitate. The teacher should, however, use the kids' ideas. For example, when I (G.D.) first recorded the guesses, I asked the kids how to indicate "more" and "less." They told me to write "m" for "more," and "l" for "less" (see Figure 8.3).

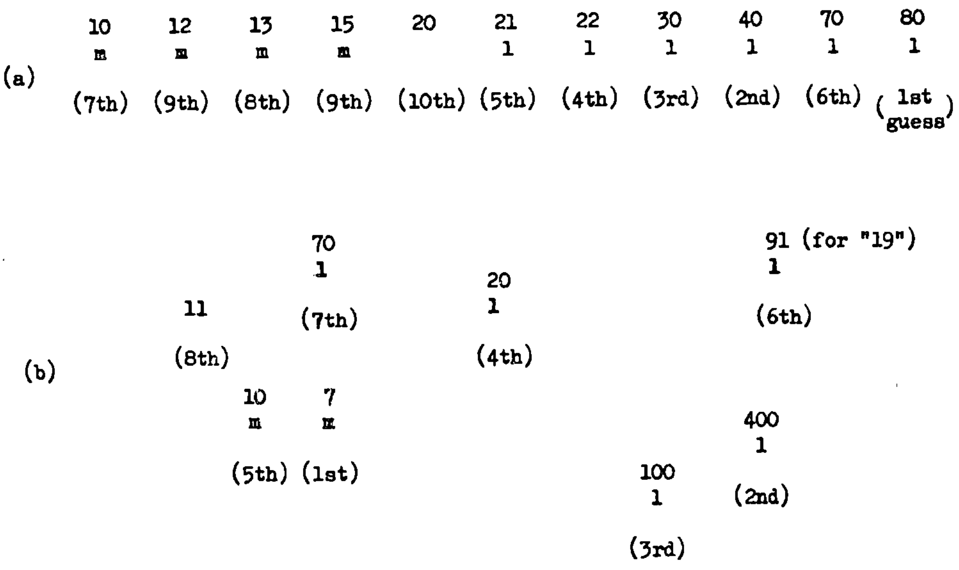

	10	12	13	15	20	21	22	30	40	70	80
(a)	m	m	m	m		l	l	l	l	l	l
	(7th)	(9th)	(8th)	(9th)	(10th)	(5th)	(4th)	(3rd)	(2nd)	(6th)	(1st guess)

(b)

```
                    70                                    91 (for "19")
                    l                                     l
          11                        20
                    (7th)           l                     (6th)
          (8th)                     (4th)
              10    7
              m     m                                      400
                                                          l
          (5th) (1st)                           100
                                                l     (2nd)
                                              (3rd)
```

FIGURE 8.3. Two ways of recording information in Guess My Number.

Do not make children use space on the board with a seriated organiza-tion.   Although I (G.D.) placed the numbers on the board as shown in Figure 8.3a, by using space with a seriated organization, the kids did it their own way on the next day, as can be seen in Figure 8.3b. As Piaget said, children imitate adults in their own ways, at their own level of development.

Don't insist on children's recording guesses on the board if they prefer not to do so.   This game is a particularly good activity for writing numbers. Good discussions come up about how to write the "teens," for example, when someone writes 71 for 17 and 91 for 19. The writing of numbers over 100 also gives rise to interesting discussions. Many children want to write 1002 for 102, and 10045 for 145. One child spontaneously went to the board and kept a record of the numbers correctly guessed. The following "invented spelling" remained on the board when she was finished:

Thes	53
ard	132
the	99
winr	

In spite of all these advantages of using the blackboard, some children prefer not to write the guesses and should not be made to do so.

The teacher may want to divide the class into two or three groups with the ranges in numbers up to 10, 30, and 100.   The three ranges of numbers will provide games of varying levels of difficulty. However, we do not recom-mend that the teacher assign the kids into the groups. We suggest, instead, that the kids make the choice. The division of the class into two or three groups works particularly well if there is an adult to sit near each group while a child is the leader. In this way, the adult can be of help when and if this is necessary.

Be on the lookout for astute comments to discuss either at the time or after the game.   One day in our class, for example, the kids had determined that the number in question was more than 2 and less than 30. Someone then guessed 20. Another immediately said that that was not a good guess because 20 was not in the middle. This kid was almost using division of range. In this case, we think that this comment was worth discussing, even though it was not understood by most of the class. It still presented a strategy that most kids had not considered. An idea that thus came from a child is often beneficial in some way. Even if the numerical reasoning is not understood, some children get the message that the teacher values children's ideas that emerge unexpectedly. This message encourages creative, independent thinking, as opposed to the cranking out only of "right" answers.

Part IV

HOW THINGS APPEARED
TO THE TEACHER

Chapter 9

From Skepticism
to Conviction

by Georgia DeClark

How were the children ever going to learn math? What would I say to questioning parents? Could I convince my principal when I was not convinced myself that games were the better way to learn? How would I justify games to the other teachers who were busily passing out worksheets to their children? What have I gotten myself into? These were among the questions I kept asking myself after reluctantly agreeing to *try* using a game-oriented curriculum for math.

When Connie asked in August, 1980, if I was willing to throw out of my math program all direct instruction and worksheets, and use instead only situations in daily living and group games, my answer was "No, I cannot promise to make that drastic a change right now, but I will do the best I can to *try* using games instead of worksheets."(At that time I did not even realize the value and importance of situations in daily living and could only focus on games.)

Intellectually, I had more or less accepted Piaget's theory of logico-mathematical knowledge, which I had studied for two years while working on a master's degree. In practice, however, I was still not convinced that instruction was unnecessary in this domain. Understanding the research had not been easy for me, and I was not an easy person to convince. As a stubborn skeptic, I *had* to see more proof for myself.

This chapter is written to communicate the seemingly endless struggle and frustration in putting Piaget's theory into practice; it is written for those teachers who find it extremely hard to accept what this book has to say. I would like them to know that as painful as it was for me to become convinced, in retrospect, it was truly worth the struggle.

Before my Piagetian training, I had taught math for five years in a fairly conventional way. That is, I basically followed the standard series. There were always some pages in the children's book that I skipped because they were either ridiculously easy or hard and not worth our time. Children predictably had problems with specific sections of the book such as those dealing with missing addends. I sensed that these "math concepts" were inappropriate for first grade, but feeling that I was expected to teach them anyway, I tried explaining the idea in my own way. After seeing a room full of blank faces each time I tried, I decided to skip those pages as well.

In retrospect, I questioned much of what the children and I were expected to do. I was not all that convinced of what I was doing because it did not "feel" right. I was not sure how they learned or why they continued to make the same errors on their worksheets. But I did not have to be convinced, as everyone else was teaching in the same way. Also, I did not have to defend what I was doing, since no one was challenging me or raising any questions. In my past training, I was told "this is how you teach," without any understanding of *how children learn,* and it became clear after five years of experience that my "teaching" did not necessarily result in children's learning.

When I consented to *try* using games for math, I did so with apprehension. Although it sounded very exciting, I was worried that I could not make changes as quickly as Connie wanted me to. I also worried that if I felt the need to fall back on worksheets, the children's work would not be interesting enough for her to observe. *It was because of Connie's support and willingness to work with me that I agreed to try to change*. She respected my need to change and to move at my own pace, acknowledging that my autonomy was an important factor in the outcome of the research. The agreement we made as we began the school year was that all the decisions were mine to make, and that if I felt the need to fall back on worksheets, Connie would respect my right to make such a decision. I am certain that there are many teachers who could (and hopefully will) make a similar change on their own. But for me, it was Connie's guidance, presence in the classroom, and willingness to analyze in depth what was happening from week to week that made it easier for me to say, "I will try."

AT THE BEGINNING

As I nervously began the school year with all sorts of doubts, encouraging things happened. First of all, the children *loved* the games. They could organize themselves and begin to play games within two minutes. Their autonomy surprised me; they could not only sustain the play but also make decisions without needing my help or approval. Also, they thought much more actively in games than while completing worksheets.

In explaining my intentions for a game-oriented math program to my principal, I was pleased to get his support. In essence, his response was that

I could teach in whatever way I preferred, as long as I reached my goals by the end of the year. My concerns about the other teachers proved to be unnecessary, too, as they were busy worrying about their own beginning-of-the-year problems.

My fears about September's Parent Night proved unfounded as well. In explaining my program to the parents, I confidently described the children's involvement with games. (If only they had known how I *really* felt!) I said that, by and large, the children were already thinking at a higher level than what they would be doing if they were using the traditional book. I went on to say that the children would continue with games instead of worksheets, and I encouraged the parents to ask their children to play the games with them at home. In retrospect, I avoided discussing why games were better than worksheets because I did not feel that I had an argument strong enough to convince the parents. Luckily, they did not challenge my plan.

Despite the fact that everything seemed to be "rolling along" fairly smoothly as the school year progressed, I continued to be skeptical. So many questions still kept coming to mind. How could I evaluate the children's math for the report cards? What about written math? How were they going to do vertical addition when they only played with dice and cards? Why were they choosing such easy games when they were capable of playing higher-level games? Should I push them? Was I getting around to see all the children to monitor their progress? My Piagetian training had raised so many questions that I was not sure of anything any more. I saw that some of my old ways were ineffective, but I had not constructed new beliefs.

If I had just relaxed and observed the children playing games, I would have seen answers to my questions. But instead, I let the empiricist part of myself take charge. On October 29, I gave an addition worksheet (just for curiosity's sake, I told Connie). Of course, the children completed it with ease, just as Connie had tried to reassure me they would. I gently "encouraged" them to play higher-level games, which did not work well. They did so out of obligation, with no enthusiasm. A few weeks later, however, when the same children chose the higher-level games *by themselves,* they played them with much more vigor.

The testing we did in October produced some encouraging results and interesting information (refer to Table 5.1). In this test, the children were shown two dice with numerals and were asked to give the sum. The table shows the percentage of children who gave the correct answer immediately to each question. I realized by looking at this table that I did not need to worry as much as I had done, as the children were doing fine. They were indeed all learning sums, *without any direct instruction from me*.

I was particularly interested in the results because they revealed how the children were constructing sums in an order significantly different from the one given in many math texts. For example, certain "doubles" (2 + 2, 5 + 5, and 3 + 3) turned out to be easier than "sums through 5," the first addition unit typically taught in a traditional program. Also, 6 + 1 turned out to be much easier (80 percent) than 2 + 3 (28 percent). (The 6 + 1 problem is included in the "sums through 10" unit, which comes after the "sums through 5" section in conventional books.)

THE CONTINUED STRUGGLE

As the year progressed, I began to relax—a little. I was pleased to see the children choosing the more difficult games that corresponded to their developmental levels. They decentered and argued about who won the games, negotiated rules to meet their needs, and showed a strong motivation to add numbers *for themselves*. Many teachers would have been delighted to see the progress and would have been convinced about the value of games, but not a true skeptic. I still worried about whatever was not perfect. For example, Connie and I observed even the higher-level children pointing to and counting each dot on both dice to know the total. We were so irritated by this behavior that we referred to it as "pecking." I was annoyed because, according to our October testing, these children already knew the sums. Connie tried to reassure me that the children would give up the pecking when they did not need to do it, but I was not satisfied. I felt the need to intervene, which I later realized made *me* feel better but did nothing for the children. We tried encouraging the children to use dice with numerals rather than those with dots. But when given the choice, they chose the dice with dots. I did not know then that most of the pecking would stop by March.

By December, I was pleased with the success I saw with the games and wanted to encourage parent involvement. I had a volunteer parent program in operation in the classroom where mothers came to the class and played games with the children. It was usually at this time that I explained to the parents the value of arguing and negotiating in games, and the fact that a high level of noise indicated a true involvement in games and not pandemonium. My explanation generally came after I saw a look of "mild horror" on the faces of the visiting parents as they reacted to the noise level in the room. Once they saw how involved the children were in the games, they were satisfied and needed no further explanations. To encourage additional parent involvement, I sent notes home, describing in detail several of the card games we played at school. I encouraged the parents to spend some time over the holidays playing card games with their children.

I continued to struggle with my empiricist background, even in January, when I again worried about written representation. Although Connie had told me that once children had constructed the logico-mathematical knowledge of addition, the writing would be easy, I had not seen it for myself and was not satisfied. I felt the need to include a game called Colorful Dot Adding Game. The game was actually more of a glorified worksheet than a game (as can be seen in Photograph 9.1). It consisted of three rows of eight addition problems, with answers written on twenty-four bottle tops. The sums did not exceed 10. The player(s) were to take turns reading the problems and putting the right bottle top under each problem. I needed to make this game (or nongame) for my own satisfaction. And just as Connie had predicted, the children did not need it, nor did they particularly like it. Again, she was very patient and let me come to my own conclusion.

The oscillation between frustration and satisfaction seemed intermina-

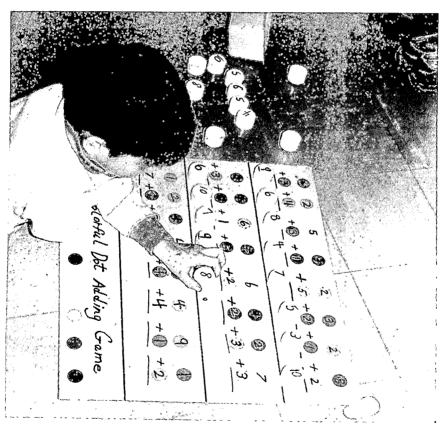

Photograph 9.1.   Colorful Dot Adding Game

ble—until the testing was repeated in January. It was a huge relief to see how well the children were doing, as can be seen in Table 5.1. Even Connie seemed a little surprised at the encouraging results, when all along I thought *she knew* what would happen and *I* was the only one to be amazed.

The + 1's and 1 +'s turned out to be very easy, followed by the + 2's and 2 +'s. Thus 5 + 2 was significantly easier in January (58 percent) than it was in October (8 percent). The one aspect of the children's construction of addition that particularly impressed me was the ease with which they used what they knew to figure out the unknown. For example, if a child did not know what 5 + 6 was, I said, "You know what 5 + 5 is. Does that help you?" Almost immediately, the child said, "Oh, it has to be 11, 'cause 5 + 5 is 10, and 5 + 6 would have to be one more." I had *never* seen this type of thinking when children did worksheets.

Now that I was feeling good about the children's progress based on the results of January's testing, I had to find another cause for worry. I chose subtraction. I knew that according to traditional first grade math, the children should learn subtraction, but something did not "feel" right. I knew intuitively from past experience that subtraction was always more difficult than addition, but felt the responsibility to at least present it to the children. In a class discussion, I told them they would be doing a lot of subtraction in second grade and I wanted them to know how to do it. I wrote the subtraction problem

$$\begin{array}{r} 4 \\ -2 \\ \hline \end{array}$$

on the board, explaining that it meant, "If you have 4 of something and you take away 2 of them, how many do you have left?" Some children did not seem to have any trouble with the example, but others were lost. I continued with several more examples until everyone seemed to have figured out his own way of solving the problems. At that point, Connie and I found that once a sum became "second nature" to children, they could automatically do the corresponding subtraction. For example, Marty told us that 4 − 2 was 2 "because 2 + 2 is 4." I felt a little better to know that children would construct subtraction on their own and decided not to impose it any further. I could see that by pushing subtraction too soon, I was imposing something on them that was counter to their natural way of thinking. This feeling was confirmed by the fact that the one subtraction game we introduced in February stayed on the shelf, untouched after the first few days.

By early April, I was finally more or less convinced that children learn more from games than from worksheets. However, I was plagued by new questions. How and when should I intervene in games and situations in daily living? What should I do when the children lose interest in games? How could I foster, or should I foster, more situations in daily living so the children would think about numbers? It was very difficult for me to recognize math in daily living and take time from other things to stop and discuss problems that came up. I acknowledged that situations in daily living were excellent ways of having children think about numbers. However, my empiricist training stressed that the teacher was the all-knowing problem solver and it was too disruptive to stop any classroom activity to discuss math in a practical situation. When I did bring the group together to work on a problem, I did see positive results. It was just a matter of realizing that the interruption was as valuable (if not more valuable) as whatever the children were doing beforehand.

I had to deal with the problem of declining interest in games, when in mid-May the children became tired of games. Of course, I was frustrated and wanted to push them into playing, but decided that they had done a lot of hard game playing and did not need pressure from me. Instead, I tried to concentrate on math in daily situations. I continued to worry about how the children would cope in second grade, since they would all be working in the traditional math program. But I told myself that if they could *think* about numbers, that was the best preparation they could have.

THE OUTCOME

As the school year came to an end, I was pleased—and finally convinced! Even the two lowest-level children blossomed! All the children *had* really constructed addition for themselves. I was satisfied with the June test results and confident that the children were "off to a good start" in math (refer to Table 5.1). I was ready to support and defend games to other teachers, parents, or administrators, if necessary. As it turned out, however, the parents were very pleased with the outcome and supportive of the program. They made comments such as, "I am so glad my child likes math and math games. I never understood math when I was in school, and I still hate it. I can barely balance my checkbook!" Several parents even promoted the game-oriented curriculum by recommending my class to parents of kindergarteners. When I showed the test results to several other primary teachers and explained how our children *thought* about numbers, they gave responses such as, "Gee, I wish I could do something like that. There is so much about the regular math program that the kids do not like."

I began the second school year with a very different perspective. I *knew* that games were much better than worksheets, and I looked forward to an opportunity to tell any interested listener why it was so. I was in a much better position to explain all the advantages that games had over worksheets, and I had specific anecdotes as well as statistical data to use in my explanation. Because I was convinced, I did not feel the least bit intimidated by anyone who challenged my program.

I still had worries, but they were very different from those I had had the previous year. For example, I was concerned about the development of the lower-level children. Also, I wanted to make sure that I was meeting the needs of the more advanced children in the class. But those were concerns I had every other year I taught anyway. I was still bothered by some of the problems that we had identified in the first year, such as the children's pecking, but I did not feel the frustration of not knowing if and when it would end. By and large, I spent the year enjoying the children as I watched them have fun with games. Even *I* could change!!

CHAPTER 10

A Month-by-Month Account of Using the Games

by Georgia DeClark

In Chapter 7, we gave descriptions of many games organized in terms of arithmetic, under headings such as "Addition," "Set Partitioning," and "Comparing Numbers." Since teachers must think more in terms of a month-by-month or week-by-week organization than the one used in Chapter 7, I decided to write this chapter.

I had a choice between writing about the first or second year of our work. We groped a lot during the first year and made a number of mistakes. The second year was much better because it was based on what we had learned. For example, we introduced Double War in November of the first year but knew by the second year that first graders could play it in September. Also, we introduced Subtraction Lotto in February of the first year and found out that it was a failure not worth repeating.

I decided to write about the first year because my purpose was to give not a "recipe" but a "feel" for how the games were used in the classroom and how we invented games, experimented with them, and evaluated them as a function of what children did with them. I wanted to communicate a way of thinking to teachers so that they would benefit from my experience.

If I sound calm, objective, and at times even confident in this chapter, it is because I wrote it after the second year, when I had already undergone the metamorphosis from skepticism to conviction, as decribed in chapter 9.

SEPTEMBER

Before the school year began, I considerd what games to have in the classroom. I wanted games that were fun for the kids and not too difficult. Therefore, I chose *Tic Tac Toe* and a Concentration game with *Huckleberry Hound* cards.

Another consideration was to provide games for the kids who already had experience with addition. For them, I chose Hop to It and *Piggy Bank*, a game of set partitioning, that is, $5 = 5 + 0$, $4 + 1$, or $3 + 2$.

Because I was curious to see if any children had had experience playing any card games, I set out six decks of playing cards without saying anything. I also provided a box of five hundred counting chips, just to see what the kids would do with them. I soon noticed that many kids played War and Go Fish without my introducing either.

Later in the month, I introduced Card Dominoes and Concentration with playing cards, neither of which turned out to be very popular. I will now comment on what happened with each game.

Tic Tac Toe

Tic Tac Toe was the game most frequently played in September. Many children already knew how to play it and played it quickly. All the children seemed eager to participate, and I often noticed many onlookers standing around the two players sitting on the floor. The spectators often discussed among themselves where the players should move and were anxious to offer unsolicited advice.

I noticed that generally the children did not decenter much. That is, they did not take their opponent's point of view and strategies into consideration before they moved. This often resulted in their being unable to think of moves that would have prevented the opponent from winning.

Concentration with *Huckleberry Hound* Cards

The children seemed to enjoy this game and played it well together, usually two at a time. They did not notice the point value printed at the upper left-hand corner of each card and tried only to find the matching pictures. When they finished the game, most children were not at all concerned with who had won, and very few considered comparing the number of cards they had collected.

War

In past years, I took out the face cards and explained the "ace" as having the value of "1." However, because so many children had already played War at home with the face cards included and knew the convention of a jack > a 10, a queen > a jack, a king > a queen, and an ace as the card with the most value, I decided to leave all the cards in the deck.

The relationship of "greater than" was one which seemed very easy for all the children. Dealing the cards, however, was not as easy. Most of the children had some difficulty dealing them in the usual way, that is, one card at a time, alternately, to the two players. Very often, the dealer began dealing in this way but soon became distracted and lost track of who had received the last card. Since these interruptions often occurred five or six times while dealing the full deck, the players usually ended up with unequal numbers.

Another method of "dealing" that occurred equally often involved the dealer's merely picking up what appeared to be half of the deck, giving it to the opponent, and then taking the other "half" for himself. Although this was obviously the less accurate way, it was perfectly acceptable to the children to do it that way. I never recall one incident where one of the players complained about possibly not having the same number as the other one.

Although they clearly knew the object of the game was to have *more* cards than the opponent at the end of the game, they did not see any need to have the same number at the beginning. That is, "dealing" meant giving cards to the players, and "winning" meant having more cards at the end of the game. It did not occur to them that if they had fewer cards in the beginning, they had less chance of winning at the end.

To determine the winner, they sometimes set the two stacks of cards side by side and compared their heights. If that was okay with them, it was okay with me.

Hop to It

This game was one of the first in which the children added two numbers. They usually organized themselves into groups of two or three. Many seemed to have had previous experience with board games, since the game generally went smoothly, without problems (e.g., not knowing in which direction to move the markers and not remembering the order for taking turns).

The children had the option of using conventional dice with dots or dice with numerals. For some, addition was relatively new. These children counted the dots on both dice. A very few who did not need to count dots generally preferred the dice with numerals. Having both kinds available, the kids could choose the kind that was more comfortable for them. I was pleased to see that, by and large, the children did change their choice from the dice with dots to those with numerals by the end of the year.

Concentration with Playing Cards

The children were not as interested in playing this variation as they were with the *Huckleberry Hound* cards. My interpretation is that playing cards contain only numbers for the most part, and the pairs are very similar (e.g., a 3 is very similar to a 4). With *Huckleberry Hound* cards, the children matched pairs of pictures which differed considerably and in more interesting ways. The game with playing cards may thus have seemed too dry in content, too difficult and/or too long.

Piggy Bank

Piggy Bank was not played as often as I had hoped, possibly because of the way in which it was introduced. I introduced it by playing it with three or four children, while a few others watched. After playing the game several times with a different group each time, I announced to the class that certain children knew how to play the game and that if someone wanted to play, he/she should ask those who knew. Unfortunately, the children who knew the game seemed to have difficulty in explaining it to the others. It often resulted in the kids' becoming frustrated and impatient and the game dissolving before it really got started.

When I observed *Piggy Bank* being played, I noticed that the children pointed to and counted each penny on the cards, hoping to get to 5.

When the game was completed, the children rarely checked to see who had won. When they did check, it was by counting their cards. (Five cents can be made either with two cards (e.g., a 2 and a 3) or with a single card (e.g., a nickel). Again, in this situation, I did not intervene to show the kids the "right" way to determine the winner.

Go Fish

Like War, this game needed no introduction, since the kids already knew how to play it. However, it was not played frequently.

Card Dominoes

The issue of how best to introduce a new game was one which I struggled with throughout the year. This question seemed significant with regard to Card Dominoes (Kamii and DeVries, 1980), in that I have wondered if its introduction had something to do with its lack of popularity.

I introduced this game differently from *Piggy Bank*. I asked three volunteers to play with me as the rest of the class watched. Our foursome sat on the floor, surrounded by the others as I explained the game. We played part of the game so that the children could get an idea as to how it was played. Unfortunately, some of the kids thought they could not see unless they were almost on top of me and the other players. There was, consequently, a certain amount of pushing, nudging, and the like for everyone to be in a prime location.

Another problem involved the players' inability to hold all twelve cards in their hands. Because they could not see all the cards at a glance, they each took what seemed like an eternity to the onlookers to try to find the necessary cards. The onlookers were impatient as they unmercifully harassed any player taking too long for his/her turn.

The game was not played very often, and when it was, I did not see it played through to completion.

OCTOBER

I introduced three new games, Football, *Benji,* and Sevens. The first two became instant successes, but Sevens was hardly ever played. I will comment on the three new games and proceed to the ones already discussed.

Football

I made and introduced the football game for several reasons. I noticed how interested the kids were in the football games they saw on television and played at recess and after school. Thus, I speculated that this content would be well received. In addition, I wanted a game that could later be modified to involve subtraction. I planned to first introduce it so the kids thought about the relationship of "greater than." In the modification for subtraction, the kids would consider the difference between the two numbers, that is, the relationship of "greater than by so many points." If the difference was three or more, the player would automatically score a touchdown, whereas if it was less than three, he would move only one line.

As I expected, Football was an instant success. It was so popular that the kids often organized themselves into a line to wait for their turns to play it. Unfortunately, at the time, I did not think about a more efficient way to keep track of who was next, such as the use of a sign-up sheet.

Because the children could tell with ease which number was "greater," the games progressed quickly. They cheered when one of the players scored a touchdown, but no one seemed interested in keeping track of the number of games won.

Benji

The kids loved *Benji* and played it *all* the time. My interpretation was that, like Football, its content was very attractive to the kids. They enjoyed doing several things at each turn, such as throwing the dice and reading a card. Before introducing it, I made new instruction cards which had more appropriate beginning reading vocabulary and were easier than the ones which came with the game. (See Chapter 7 for further detail.) The game was generally played with three, four, or five players, and once a player won, the kids usually stopped playing instead of continuing to see who won next.

Some of the kids argued about specific rules such as whether or not a player could take two cards during his turn if he landed on a picture again. Usually, they were able to come to an agreement without seeking my help.

Sevens

This game was not popular.[1] I showed it to Brad, Steve, and Marty, and played several games with them. I then announced to the class that those boys knew a new game and would show anyone who was interested. Only a couple of kids asked to be shown. Although the three boys explained the game very well, the new players did not continue with it. It was after our individual testing of the kids near the end of the month (refer to Table 5.1) that we understood why Sevens was unpopular. Most of the combinations that total seven (2 + 5, 5 + 2, 3 + 4, and 4 + 3) were too difficult at that time.

Concentration with *Huckleberry Hound* Cards

Some kids became more interested in winning than in September, and many compared numbers of pairs at the end of the game. Since they were not interested in comparing the number of points won, it is not surprising that they did not look for cards with higher point values.

Piggy Bank

Piggy Bank was more popular than when introduced. In this game, too, the kids began to be more interested in finding out who won. However, as stated before, they did so by counting cards rather than the amount of money banked.

Tic Tac Toe

The children decentered a little more than they had in September and consequently were better able to anticipate and block an opponent's move.

---

1. A first grade teacher in Selma, Alabama, reported that Sevens was not entirely unpopular in her classroom. According to her observation, this game was played often by the developmentally more advanced children.

They tended not to think about a diagonal win, and generally won their games with vertical and horizontal lines. The pace of the game was faster than earlier in the year, but neither the players nor the observers had difficulty keeping up with the moves.

Other Games

Concentration with playing cards, Card Dominoes, War, and Go Fish were hardly ever played. Although I tried to revive Card Dominoes by playing it with the children, they still did not choose to play it.

The popularity of War decreased substantially, probably because it became too easy and boring. Even when I asked the kids if they wanted to play the game with me, they usually said, "No, it's not a fun game any more." I was pleased to see that kids did choose games that were appropriate.

NOVEMBER

The most significant thing I observed in November was the progress in the children's thinking and in the way they played the games. I will first discuss the changes in Concentration with *Huckleberry Hound* cards and *Piggy Bank*. I will then comment on two new games introduced in November— Double War and Uncover.

Concentration with *Huckleberry Hound* Cards

The children became very interested in determining who won. Many showed interest in "big numbers" by counting the number of cards, rather than the number of pairs, as they did in October.

Early in the month, I was pleased to hear two girls arguing about who won. Before my Piagetian training, I did not see any value in the children's arguing. I considered arguments to be disruptive and annoying, and thought it was necessary to intervene and impose *my* solution. I failed to realize that this way of dealing with children's arguments reinforced their heteronomy, because I was unintentionally encouraging the kids to depend on me to make and enforce the rules. As I became more familiar with Piaget's theory, I saw the importance of their arguing their points of view. I thought the girls' argument itself indicated advances in their thinking. (I still need to "bite my tongue" to avoid intruding in their argument.)

Ann counted her cards and said she had 20, since she found ten pairs. Carol said that she had seven pairs and that Ann was cheating. When I asked them if they thought they could come to an agreement, Ann told Carol, "You're supposed to count all your cards because then you'll have a bigger number." Carol took Ann's advice and counted up to 14. Ann was smug as she recounted her cards and said, "I have 20 and you have 14. I still win." I doubt that either Carol or Ann made the relationship between seven and ten pairs and 14 and 20 cards, but I was pleased that (a) they were interested in comparing big numbers to find the winner, and (b) they could work together to come to a mutually acceptable agreement.

Later in the month, I observed some kids adding up the points on the cards. This way of determining the winner brought about new kinds of arguments. That is, some kids wanted to count a pair of 3's as 3, whereas others wanted the same pair scored as 6. Again, the kids settled their own arguments and thought a lot about numbers, and I was very excited to see that happen.

Piggy Bank

I enthusiastically observed the children making progress in the way they determined who won. Although many kids continued to count the number of cards, a few tried to add the amount of money they banked. I was pleased that these few worked hard at something that was obviously difficult for them. They tended to add the coin values by starting with 1. That is, they picked up a card with two pennies and said, "1-2," picked up another card with four pennies and went on to count, "3-4-5-6," instead of counting-on from 2 or 4. They generally had trouble with the cards with one nickel, often needing to ask how many pennies there were in a nickel.

I was encouraged by their hard work and determination. I could see that the strong motivation to add numbers came from the children and not from me. That is, they really worked at playing games for themselves and not to get rewarded with a gold star, smiling face, or other type of artificial "motivator" from me.

Double War

Connie introduced this game to all the kids in the class by playing it with two kids at a time. It was very well received, as evidenced by its being played very frequently.

After its introduction, almost all kids pointed to, and mechanically counted each "dot" on their two cards, without much thinking. That is, they did not compare their combination with their opponents', even when these were as obvious to me as 4 + 4 versus 2 + 1. Very few kids reasoned logically to determine who had the larger total when they had combinations such as 2 + 3 versus 2 + 4.

Cathy, one of the sharpest children in the class, was one of the few who made the relationship between different combinations equaling the same number. For example, she knew immediately that a 3 + 3 combination and a 2 + 4 combination meant Double War, since, according to her, "If you took a dot from this 3 and put it by the other 3, it would be just like the 2 and 4."

Double War often drew a crowd of spectators as *Tic Tac Toe* had done earlier in the year. Its instant success and continued popularity, combined with the quick decline in popularity of War, was more proof that children choose more difficult games as their thinking progresses to higher levels.

Uncover

This game, played moderately frequently, was well accepted. Some kids seemed quickly to have noticed the different combinations which equaled the same number. For example, when kids rolled a 5 + 3 and a 4 + 4 on consecutive turns, they commented after the second roll, "You already uncovered 8, except with two other numbers."

Many children surprised me by keeping track of who was ahead in two different ways—some by counting the boxes still covered and others by referring to the original total of 10. For example, Jackie watched as I played this game with another girl. She looked at my side of the board and noticed that I had two boxes still covered. My opponent had three of them. Jackie said, "Mrs. DeClark, you're winning 'cause you already uncovered eight boxes, 'cause 8 + 2 is 10."

Other Games

I was pleased to see both *Benji* and Football played very frequently, but did not see anything in the children's play that was significantly different from October.

Because I never saw the children play Concentration with playing cards or Go Fish in November and in any subsequent months, I will be making no more comments regarding them.

DECEMBER

This was a month filled with holiday projects, songfests, parties, and programs, and there was little time left for games. I chose not to introduce any new ones, since there would not be enough time for them anyway. With that in mind, I used my energies to try to resolve a problem. I will first discuss it as I saw it in *Piggy Bank,* Double War, and *Benji*. Then, I will comment on some experimentation Connie and I did with subtraction in Football.

Piggy Bank

This game was not played very often. When it was, I was not happy with what I saw. Almost all kids pointed to and counted every penny on the cards in their attempts to bank 5 cents. The term "pecking" that Connie and I used to refer to this behavior expresses our irritation.

My displeasure was based on the fact that most of the kids already knew these sums according to Connie's October testing (refer to Table 5.1). I wanted the kids to pick up the two cards totaling 5 instead of pecking when easy combinations such as 4 + 1 turned up. They must have needed to peck, since they did it regularly, so I reluctantly decided not to intervene at this time.

Double War

The kids continued to play this game *all* the time. However, I did not see much progress with regard to pecking. As was the case with *Piggy Bank*, the kids knew many sums which came up on the cards. But they continued to behave like "counting machines" and did not show any inclination to think to determine whose total was more.

In our attempts to reduce the pecking, Connie and I both tried unobtrusively to intervene and suggest more intelligent ways. For example, we might say, "I know a way of telling who won without counting. Do you want me to tell you?" If they said they did not want to know, we did not push it. But they usually wanted to know. We showed them, with a 4 + 1 and a 4 + 3 combination, for example, that since the 4's were the same, we needed only to compare the 1 with the 3. With a 2 + 1 and a 4 + 3 combination, we pointed out that since 2 + 1 was less than 4, it did not matter what the other number was.

We could tell by watching the kids' faces if they understood our reasoning. Almost all of them understood without any trouble. For a few turns, they went through the same kind of comparison. However, all of them soon reverted back to pecking. The lesson we learned was that it is better not to push kids beyond the method that is comfortable for them. They may model us for a short while, but if they have not made the relationships for themselves, they will approach the problem in a way that works best for them.

Benji

This game continued to be an all-time favorite. I became frustrated, however, when I observed kids counting the dots on the dice, just as they pecked in *Piggy Bank* and Double War. These were the advanced kids like Marty and Cathy, who knew the sums. I was not bothered by the slower ones' counting, but always felt an urge to intervene with the others.

To do away with the pecking problem, Connie and I decided to add a pair of dice with numerals to the existing ones that had dots. We tried to encourage those advanced kids to use the new dice, and kept the original pair in the box for those who needed to peck. I later observed that the new dice were not used very often, and the kids who used the dice with dots almost always pecked. The moral of the story: Let the *kids* decide when to move on to something more difficult. Just as kids give up crawling when they prefer to walk, they will give up pecking when they prefer a more efficient way.

Football

I was pleased to see how well the kids were generally doing in addition. However, I felt anxious about their lack of work in subtraction. They had done virtually nothing in that area, and I knew the kids in the traditional first grade math programs had already begun this work. Therefore, Connie and I decided to experiment with four of the brightest kids in the class to see if they could handle subtraction. Connie explained the rule that if the difference between the cards was 3 or more, that meant an instant touchdown. For example, if a 5 and a 2 were turned up, the player with the 5 scored a touchdown. If a 5 and a 3 were turned up, however, the player with the 5 could move only to the next line.

When Steve played with Marty, Steve had no idea what Connie meant by the difference between two numbers. At every flip of the cards, he looked to Connie for help or waited for Marty to give his opinion. Marty, on the other hand, understood the idea and by and large did all the comparing throughout their game.

When Ed and Cathy played, Ed was the stronger player. He was able to determine the difference each time the cards were turned up. Cathy could also figure the difference, but it was more difficult for her and she did need some help.

It seemed more natural for the kids to use addition than subtraction, as evidenced by Marty's comment on 4 versus 1: "The difference is 3, 'cause 1 + 3 = 4." Because subtraction thus seemed unnatural and hard for three of the four most advanced kids in the class, we decided to wait before trying it with the others.

JANUARY

With the new year came new games, new relationships made, and, unfortunately, the same old pecking problem. The new games I introduced were Coin War, Tens with Playing Cards, and Colorful Dot Adding Game, to which I referred in Chapter 9. I added more cards to Football and Double War and will comment on these additions. The pecking problem with respect to *Benji* and *Piggy Bank* will be discussed next, followed by an analysis of the problem. After discussing that, I will conclude with comments on some new relationships the children made in the Concentration game with *Huckleberry Hound* cards.

Coin War

This game was invented for several reasons. First, coins and their values are supposed to be introduced to first graders in the district. In addition, I knew that kids had an interest in money. Connie and I also thought that a game format would be more natural to teach this social (conventional) knowledge than "teachy" instruction.

The kids enjoyed the game and played it quite often, but it did not seem easy for them to look at the card and know at a glance the total value of the coins (refer to Figure 7.6b). This difficulty provided me with the opportunity to show the kids the advantages of counting by 2's, especially for the cards with many pennies. Unfortunately, however, the kids did not care about my way and continued to peck anyway. I decided to "bite my tongue" and not to push them. (As mentioned in Chapter 7, we changed the spatial arrangement as shown in Figure 7.6a during the second year, with a maximum of five pennies in the left-hand column. This arrangement enabled the children to look at three pennies and immediately know that there were eight.)

Tens with Playing Cards

This game was very popular, partially because of its appeal to spectators. Very often I saw at least three or four onlookers advising the players of a pair of cards totaling 10.

Football

In my desire to have the kids become familiar with two digit numerals, I brought out a set of cards with numerals from 11 to 50 and showed them to Marty, Steve, Brad, and Carl. They knew just what to do with the cards, and two of them began playing right away in the same way as before, that is, with the player getting the higher number moving one line. The kids did surprisingly well, and their knowledge of two digit numerals seemed almost second nature. With the new set of cards, Football was played even more frequently. I suggested leaving the original set of small numbered cards in the box in case someone preferred to play with them.

Double War

I was delighted to note that many kids began to think about number combinations more and pecked less during January. They could look at ace + 2 and 4 + 2 combinations, for example, and know who was the winner. Because they were doing well, I added the 5 through 9 cards, so the sums became much greater. At first, I was afraid that including the higher numbers might bring about even more pecking, but was surprised to find that the kids generally continued to look and think rather than pecking.

Benji

Since it appeared as though pecking was here to stay, I decided not to worry about the majority of the class. As hard as I tried to ignore the problem, however, I found myself intervening with the sharper kids, such as Susie, who knew all the sums. When I noticed one of the more advanced kids pecking, I would wait until he rolled the dice, hold my hand over the dice, and say, "Now, what is 4 + 2?" Almost always, the child would immediately say, "6." I would just smile and say, "That's using your head." I am not sure if this did any good for the children, but it made me feel a little better.

Piggy Bank

Even though I knew that children were capable of regulating their own difficulty level and that I should be patient with their pecking, I was anxious to give some kids a little "push" to stop the pecking they did not need to do. Connie and I designed a variation of this game to solve this problem and planned to introduce it in February. It would be exactly the same as *Piggy Bank* except that the new deck would have numerals instead of coins. I was anxious to see what difference the numerals would make.

Remarks

Since pecking continued to be a problem in January, Connie and I tried to understand why we saw less of it in Double War than in *Benji* and *Piggy Bank*. She pointed out that in *Piggy Bank* and *Benji,* the kids had to know the exact sum. That is, in *Piggy Bank,* kids needed to know whether or not two cards totaled 5. In *Benji,* similarly, they needed to know the exact number of steps to take. In Double War, by contrast, they needed only to know who had more. Thus, there was less need to peck.

Concentration with *Huckleberry Hound* Cards

I noticed that the number of points scored became much more important than it had been earlier in the year. The kids openly discussed their strategies for looking for the cards with the higher point value, since that would result in a higher score. By and large, they totaled their score by counting each number of the pair, that is, scoring 6 for a pair of 3's. This is in contrast to November's play, when more kids compared the number of cards or pairs they had found.

Other Games

Card Dominoes, Hop to It, and Uncover were never played in January or any subsequent months.

FEBRUARY

There was no sense in my going crazy over the pecking problem because it certainly did not decrease much in February. In my comments on *Piggy Bank,* I will discuss what I reluctantly observed. Two new games, Ladybug Bank, and Dinosaurs, however, brought a ray of hope. After discussing these new games, I will continue with an analysis of what happened with Double War. In February, I began to focus some of my attention on an approach to subtraction different from what Connie tried in December. The outcome was a new game, Subtraction Lotto.

Coin War

I did not have to bet money to know what the kids were doing when they played this game. Pecking, of course! I was pleased to note, however, that many kids began to add pennies to nickels quickly. That is, when they saw a card with a nickel and three pennies, for example, they said, "5/6-7-8" with confidence.

Piggy Bank

Thank goodness we planned to introduce a different version of this game (called Ladybug Bank), because everyone's continued pecking was driving me crazy. I had all I could do to not become angry and say something to the kids out of frustration. I just walked away from the games, cringing because I knew that they knew those sums.

Ladybug Bank

This game, created to combat the pecking problem by using numerals instead of coins, was a suprising success. I silently celebrated when I watched the children pick up the pairs of cards quickly without *any* pecking!

The unusual name of Ladybug Bank was suggested by one child and accepted by all others. One child had chosen to put a decorative sticker of ladybugs on the back of each card. I thought it was a strange name for a game, but I was only the teacher who would have been outvoted if I had objected.

The shelves were getting so cluttered with games that I suggested putting some away. The *Piggy Bank* deck was one of the games the kids voted to keep on the shelves. However, from the time that Ladybug Bank was introduced, almost all kids preferred it over *Piggy Bank*. All this was intriguing because I seemed to be succeeding in stopping the pecking simply by introducing a different material (which the kids were free to reject). It is hard to know when kids need to peck and when they don't. With the introduction of Ladybug Bank, what seemed to be a strong need (to peck) disappeared immediately.

Dinosaurs

The other new game for February, Dinosaurs, was created for the purpose of encouraging children to mentally regroup numbers. That is, Connie and I read in Hatano (1980) that Japanese first graders did not "peck" or "count-on" when adding. Instead, they mentally regrouped numbers around 10 and 5. For example, when they added 8 + 7, they regrouped around 10, and thought about the problem as 8 + 2 + 5. We liked the number 5 as an intermediary higher unit because it is a perceptual number, and a natural one in the sense that we have five fingers on each hand. Since the numbers 6 through 9 are harder to think about than 1 to 5, we agreed that it would be easier for the kids to think about numbers in this way:

$$6 = 5 + 1$$
$$7 = 5 + 2$$
$$8 = 5 + 3$$
$$9 = 5 + 4$$
$$10 = 5 + 5$$

With these ideas in mind, I made the board game with a format similar to *Benji* (refer to Photograph 7.5). Instead of dice, however, I provided the cards shown in Figure 7.1b for the kids to draw. After a short introduction to the idea of 5 +, the kids were immediately able to know the number at a glance, without pecking.

A new problem presented itself, however. As can be seen in Photograph 7.5, the kids egocentrically wanted to read the cards, only for themselves. There was, consequently, no interaction among the kids regarding the 5 + cards. The same held true for the instruction cards that the kids read when they landed on the picture of the dinosaur. The sharing of opinions about those cards, however, was not as important as with the 5 + cards. To make the number observable by all the players, we introduced the die in Figure 7.1a.[2] The kids did not seem to care whether they used cards or a die, and the game continued to be as popular with the die as it was with the cards.

Double War

Although this game was played moderately frequently, I had hoped it would be more popular than it was. The addition of the 5 to 9 cards seemed overwhelming for the kids, since it increased the total number of cards from 32 to 72. I think that 72 cards was a little too unmanageable, and maybe that is why the kids did not choose this game as often as I had hoped.

Another aspect of the additional cards was the total sum. With the 5 to 9 cards, there was the possibility of adding 8 + 9 and 7 + 8, for example. Since the kids had not had the opportunity to think about regrouping the

---

2. After using one side of the cube for each of the numbers 6–10, there was an extra side left over. We put a second 5 + 3 on it, since that one seemed to be the most difficult one to recognize immediately.

numbers greater than 5 to their advantage, as in the Dinosaurs game, the problems were too difficult.[3]

Subtraction Lotto

I was anxious to provide opportunities for subtraction but was aware that the difference between two numbers had been too difficult even for the sharper kids in the class in December. Consequently, Connie and I decided to try subtraction through "take away." Since Marty had figured out subtraction in terms of addition, we decided this way would be most natural for the other kids as well. We thus chose subtraction problems consisting of sums that were easy for the majority of the class, according to Connie's January testing (Table 5.1). For example, we chose 4 − 2 because we knew that 2 + 2 was very easy for the children.

I planned an involved introduction for this game, since the kids had had little exposure to subtraction at school. However, that proved to be unnecessary because many kids shouted out the answers as soon as the caller read the problems. I was pleasantly surprised to see the ease with which the kids played this game.

MARCH

In March, the kids made a great deal of progress. There was a dramatic drop in pecking, and I will comment on that as seen in *Benji* and Ladybug Bank. In Tens with Playing Cards, the children became very proficient at making totals of 10. On the basis of that, I introduced two new games, Tens Concentration, a card game, and *Tens*, a commercially available game. I was also pleased with the kids' work with doubles in a new game we made up called Double *Parcheesi*. In another new game, Punta. I was both pleased and surprised to see how well some kids partitioned and added numbers. The lack of interest in Subtraction Lotto, however, was disappointing.

Benji

Early in the month, the kids gave me their approval to take out the dice with dots and leave only those with numerals. I "explained" that I needed the first pair for something else. The children did not seem at all disturbed

---

3. In 1981–82, we added the 5–9 cards in two stages, the 5 and 6 cards first and the others later. Both groups were added after the introduction of the TILE dice.

by the switch and breezed through the addition without showing any need to peck. This example is similar to February's discussion of Ladybug Bank, in that it illustrates how a change in material can so dramatically affect the way the children add two numbers. The disappearance of the dice with dots did not affect the popularity of this game.

Ladybug Bank

I was surprised to see that this game was as popular as it was, since it seemed too easy for the children. However, its popularity lasted only throughout the first part of March. It was easy to see how sure the children were of the sums to 5. They immediately put together the pairs equalling 5, apparently without even thinking.

Tens with Playing Cards

This game, too, moved along very quickly, indicating that the kids were sure of the combinations that make 10. There were a few kids who needed to peck in this game, but most could figure out the pairs in their heads if they needed to do any figuring at all.

Tens Concentration

This game was well received by the kids, especially the ones who knew with confidence the combinations that make 10. Their job was obviously much easier if they only had to remember where the cards were, instead of having to figure out which number they needed to make a total of 10.

Tens

The children worked very hard at playing this game, even though it was not as easy as the previous two games. There was a lot to think about with each turn. The players had to match the colors as well as the numbers totaling 10. In addition, the possibilities to consider increased with each piece that was added. With so much to take into account, I was pleasantly surprised to see them play the game to completion. On one occasion, I played one game with them which lasted for 35 minutes. Only one of the players left the game before it was completed. During our play, we attracted many spectators, who, by the end of the game, were anticipating moves and telling me what I would need to draw from the pile to be able to use a piece.

Double *Parcheesi*

I introduced the idea of doubles by writing the following on the board:

1	2	3	4	5	6	7	8	9	10
$+1$	$+2$	$+3$	$+4$	$+5$	$+6$	$+7$	$+8$	$+9$	$+10$

As the class discussed what answers to write, several children quickly noticed the 2, 4, 6, 8, . . . pattern. We talked about the "counting by 2's" idea, and they quickly told me the rest of the answers.

I then introduced the game of Double *Parcheesi*, using a 10-sided die instead of a conventional cube. I told the kids that by doubling the number rolled, they could get to the end much faster. It caught on well, the kids enjoyed the game, and they had no trouble with the doubles.

Punta

The kids and I loved this game. It was not easy for them, however, to become accustomed to the way the game was played. That is, when they looked at the TILE cards to see what number they were supposed to make, many kids wanted to use only two cards to do so, rather than using as many as was necessary. For example, if they were supposed to make 8, they said they could not use their 3, if they did not have a 5 card. They could not immediately think of using two 3 cards and two 1 cards. It did not take long, however, before they began to think about many possible combinations.

Although the children did not regroup numbers around 10 and 5 as we thought they might, I did see evidence of their using what they knew to make a total (and I was thrilled to see this happening!). For example, Ann was quite amused to see that she could make 12 with 5 + 1 and 4 + 2, since 6 + 6 = 12. She was also interested in what everyone else had for their combinations. It made perfect sense to her that Ed used 3 + 3 + 3 + 3 to get to 12, again since 6 + 6 = 12.

Because the Punta game used combinations to 12, we needed to change the arrangement of the TILE cards from that used on the die in the Dinosaurs game, where the numbers ranged only from 6 to 10. I was a little worried that the kids might have trouble with the new arrangement shown in Figure 10.1, but this worry proved to be unnecessary. Many kids needed to count the 8 and 9 TILE cards, but 6, 7, and 10 were easily recognized. When they counted a 9, they did so in a counting-on way, that is, 5/6-7-8-9.

Subtraction Lotto

I was disappointed to see that this game was not played more often. I was surprised as well, since it was instantly successful in February. I wonder if

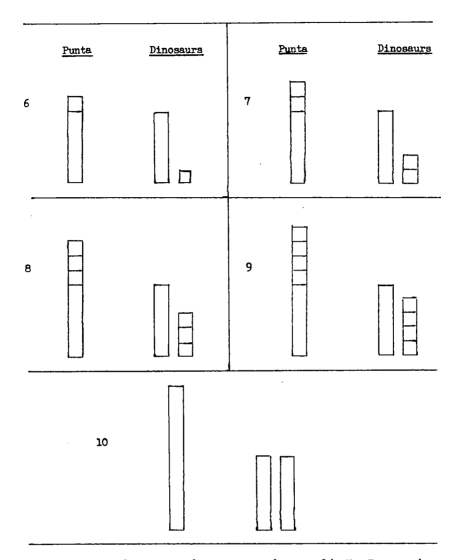

FIGURE 10.1.   The 1, 2, 3, and so on, arranged on top of the 5 in Punta, rather than beside it as they were in Dinosaurs.

the organization part of it was too much of a bother to the kids. That is, there needed to be agreement as to who would be the caller, who would use the blue card, and so forth, before the game could begin. Maybe this was too much for the kids and they preferred to play something that needed less arguing.

In addition, the kids did not have much to do while playing. For example, there was no rolling the dice, reading·a card, or moving a piece. I guessed that these factors might have had something to do with its lack of popularity.

Other Games

Piggy Bank and Colorful Dot Adding Game were never played in March or any subsequent months.

APRIL

For reasons unknown to me, the interest in games dropped significantly in April. By and large, the only ones played very often were new ones. I will first discuss the new games that were popular: *Put and Take, Sorry,* XYZ, and Make the Biggest Number. I was pleased to see the continued popularity of Punta and Double *Parcheesi* as well. There was, however, a new variation of Double War, Double War with Subtraction, which never became popular.

Put and Take

From its very beginning, this game was extremely popular. My guess is that it was because the kids were active and had something to do while they were playing. I was pleased to hear them interact with each other about the way they should play. For example, when one of the girls spun a "Take 3," she began to take three yellow chips (worth 1 point each). Another player commented that she should take a red chip (worth 2 points) and a yellow one "because there are a lot of red ones in the cup and it's the same if you do it either way."

Sorry

This, like Double *Parcheesi,* was a game which we introduced to promote the learning of doubles. Many of the kids were familiar with the *Sorry* game they played at home, which used cards to determine the moves. We were not interested in the cards, since the directed moves were arbitrary and did not involve thinking about number. We used the ten-sided die as in Double *Parcheesi.* Since April was a slow month for games, I imagine this game was popular because of its novelty.

XYZ

We created this game to give the children another opportunity to think about numbers above 5 as 5 plus another number. We made two dice, one with the numeral 5 on every side, and the other with the numerals 1, 2, 3, 4, 4, and 5 on each of the sides, as shown in Photograph 7.6. In that way, the children would always add a number to 5.

The game was well received. With respect to the 5 + aspect of the game, the kids did well. I rarely saw them add the 5 to the smaller number. Usually, they counted-on, if necessary, so that a 2 + 5 roll was treated as 5/ 6-7.

Make the Biggest Number

The idea for this game came rather casually as I was worrying that some kids were still not sure of how to read and write two digit numbers such as 18 and 81. Knowing that the children could not understand place value, I wanted them to know that the 40's come before the 50's and the 50's are less than the 60's.

The lower-level children were occasionally unsure of the best way to arrange their two numerals to make the biggest number. But usually if I talked them through it, by saying, for example, "Let's see, a 3 and a 5. Would it be better for you to have 35 or 53?" that was all they needed. They then seemed sure about the way they wanted to arrange their cards. The zero cards confused many of the average kids at first. When they drew a 0, they said that they were going to lose that hand. But the sharper kids were quick to point out that it depended on the other card, and that if they got a 9, they could make 90.

I particularly liked this game because the kids did a lot of talking with each other about written numbers, and it was easy for me to see how they thought about two digit numbers.

Punta

Although this game was one of the few that was played often in April, for many of the kids, it was not easy. I was pleased that they worked so hard and did not give up on it, as they might have done with something else that they found too difficult. Nancy, a lower-level child, for example, had to count every number when she tried to make a sum. That is, for a 12, she started with a 6 card, counted, "1-2-3-4-5-6," and then randomly picked another card from her hand and continued with "7-8-9," and so on. It did not occur to her that she could use number combinations that she already knew.

I did intervene a lot with the lower-level kids, but they did not seem too bothered with my questions. For example, when a 12 came up and I saw Nancy randomly pick up a 6 card and begin to count another one randomly picked up, I would stop her and say, "Okay, how many more do you need to make 12, if you already have 6?" She usually counted on her fingers, tapping one at a time on the table edge as we counted-on, "7-8-9-10-11-12." I concluded with, "So what number would you need with your 6?" She smiled and said, "6." I do not know if this intervention was helpful to Nancy, but it made *me* feel a little better!

Double *Parcheesi*

I assume that Double *Parcheesi* was still new enough to the kids to maintain their dwindling interest in the games in April. They chose this game often and usually played with three or four players, rather than just two. The doubles came quickly and seemed to be remembered easily. However, the playing of Double *Parcheesi* did not automatically help develop the kids' ability to make relationships based on the doubles. That is, I did not see the evidence that their knowing 6 + 6 necessarily helped them when they worked on 6 + 7. Nancy's knowing the doubles in this game did not seem to help her when she played Punta either.

Double War with Subtraction

When I introduced this game in the beginning of April, I did not get the feeling that it was going to be one of the more popular games. The kids did stick with it fairly well, but it was easy to see that playing the game was much more difficult than Double War with addition. The children almost always relied on using their fingers to figure the difference.

With worksheets in the past, it seemed as though the kids naturally thought about addition and often did addition on a subtraction page. I used to think that if the kids paid a little more attention to the " + " and " − " signs, that was all they needed to do. But now I think that addition is so much more natural to them that subtraction really *is* more difficult.

MAY/JUNE

As the school year came to a close, I worried about what the kids would be doing in second grade and how I could best "prepare" them. I thought that if they could actively *think* about the problems they faced, that was the best preparation I could give them. I often found myself intervening in their play to help facilitate their thinking, as discussed in Punta and XYZ. At the same time, I enjoyed observing the ease with which they played Make the Biggest Number and *Put and Take*. I was pleased to see that by May, the children who played Double *Parcheesi* did have an easy time with the doubles.

Punta

Punta continued to be a popular game. By this time, most of the kids saw the advantage of sorting their cards before playing. For some of the kids, the regrouping of numbers was almost second nature. Ed, for example, saw 11 as 5 + 6 and could break these numbers down even further, if necessary, without any difficulty. Nancy, on the other hand, still started with 1 and usually chose cards randomly to try to make her total. Kate, a lower-level child, played several times with the more-or-less "regulars" (Marty, Ann, Skip, and Carol) and stuck with it, even though she was struggling. She did not have any trouble reading the TILE cards, but would look at all the cards in her hand and seem overwhelmed. I helped her through each turn, by asking her if she knew of some numbers that would add up to the number on the TILE card. It was clear that this was not a very effective approach with Kate, since she could only start with 1 and count-on from there. Sometimes, it appeared as though something "clicked" and she followed my line of thinking. At other times, however, she looked very confused. It was easy for me to see when I was helping and when I was not.

I came away from this experience feeling a little bit better about my eternal question concerning when it is desirable to intervene and when it is not. In this case, I tried several approaches, could sense what the child understood, and stopped trying to push when she appeared confused. The answer to my question is that there is no set rule that works in every situation.

XYZ

The issue of intervention again came up as I was playing this game with Jill and Jan. The game was going along smoothly, but I was slightly bothered by the fact that the girls were mindlessly moving their pieces along when a bit of thinking was entirely possible. I figured that these two particular girls were autonomous enough to put me in my place if I got too "out of line," so I started interrupting them before they could merrily count along. Jan was on the 30 box and rolled a 5 + 5. She started counting and moving her piece one by one, at which time I interrupted and said, "If you think about it, can you figure out where you should end up?" Without any hesitation, she said, "I know, it's 40." Evidently, she did not need to count out her move, one by one, since she could figure out where to put her piece. Feeling rather successful with my first attempt, I tried the same thing with Jill. She was on the 70 box and rolled a 9 combination. When I interrupted her as she began to count and move one by one, she said without much delay, "It has to be 79, 'cause 70 + 10 would be 80 and it's 1 less."

In this situation, I felt that my intervention was worthwhile, since, later in the game, they tried to figure out where to put their pieces rather than counting one by one. However, my decision to try this could not have been cataloged in an "intervention handbook." A teacher has to try to intervene and look for evidence to know if the intervention was helpful. If the kids seem confused, it is best to drop the attempt.

Make the Biggest Number

This was one of the most popular games at the end of the year. The kids played it quickly and with much confidence. For example, they laughed when the numbers 10 and 99 came up, as if they were aware of the big difference between the numbers.

I was very pleased with their interest, particularly when I noticed that several of the kids made their own deck of cards and played at their desks and at home.

Put and Take

This was still very popular at the end of the year. It was usually played only by two people at a time, and this seemed to cut down on the arguing. It was a good game to foster the thinking about 10's, and many of the kids could glance at their blue pile of chips and know that they had thirty, forty, and so on. The kids were, by and large, proficient at using the 1's chips with the 2's chips. For example, if they had to make a 5, it appeared easy for them to take two red chips and a yellow one (red = 2 points, yellow = 1 point).

Double *Parcheesi*

Although this game was not played very often, I did notice that when it was, the same kids were involved, usually the girls. And it seemed obvious to me which ones had played this game and *Sorry* when the end-of-the-year testing came up. The doubles were very easy for those who had been playing Double *Parcheesi*. For others who had not played as often, 7 + 7, 8 + 8, and 9 + 9 were not easy.

Part V

EVALUATION AND PROSPECTS FOR THE FUTURE

CHAPTER 11

Evaluation
of the Program

When Georgia and I talk about the work reported in this book, people often ask how our children turn out by the end of first grade in comparison with children traditionally taught. They seem satisfied when we tell them that the performance of the two groups, insofar as sums are concerned, is roughly the same.[1] But I must qualify that conclusion and comment upon the relationships among evaluation techniques, educational goals, and the learning theories on which teaching is based.

I will argue that the evaluation tools we used to assess children's progress (a highly restricted, time-limited test of sums) were inadequate, and that measures more sensitive to children's thought processes ought to have been used. The problem was that no such measures existed. A new breed of evaluation procedures that can capture aspects of knowledge building needs to be created. In this regard, I will give examples of children's thinking and reasoning that emerged during the testing sessions that the specific outcome measures did not record. These aspects of thinking are central, not only in knowledge building in mathematics but also in other areas of development as well.

I will offer some suggestions regarding what should be included in a more adequate evaluation for the benefit of others who may wish to pursue this topic. But let me begin by describing the procedures used to gather the comparative data; I will also discuss the differences in test results between two cohorts of children (1980–81 and 1981–82).

TESTING

It was necessary during the first year of our work (1980–81) to find out from time to time if our children were indeed learning sums. Therefore, we tested the children in October, January, April, and June on their knowledge of the sum of two numbers depicted on dice. (As stated in Chapter 5, in this

---

1. This statement was made before the analysis of the second-year data.

test, we showed two dice with numerals on them and asked children individually how many points they would have if they got those numbers.) The order in which the questions were posed is given in Table 11.1. Each child's response to each question was recorded in a protocol.

The results of these tests have already been presented in Table 5.1. It will be recalled that this table includes only the percentages of children who immediately gave correct answers from memory.[2] The criterion of immediacy was the giving of the answer within 2 seconds. All the incorrect answers and the correct ones given after a long reaction time were excluded from this table. Correct answers obtained by counting were excluded both because they took too long and because they did not come from memory.

It can be seen in Table 5.1 that our children kept learning sums throughout the year; the percentages of correct, immediate responses increased steadily. The hypothesis that children can learn sums on their own, without any instruction, can thus be said to have been confirmed. All the children committed the easy sums to memory (i.e., certain doubles and " + 1's"). By extrapolating from Table 5.1, we can expect almost all children to know all

TABLE 11.1.   The Order of Test Items

1. 2 + 2	11. 4 + 2	21. 5 + 4
2. 5 + 5	12. 3 + 2	22. 6 + 2
3. 3 + 3	13. 2 + 4	23. 3 + 6
4. 4 + 4	14. 5 + 6	24. 4 + 5
5. 6 + 6	15. 5 + 3	25. 3 + 4
6. 4 + 1	16. 2 + 5	26. 6 + 3
7. 5 + 1	17. 5 + 4	27. 4 + 6
8. 6 + 1	18. 2 + 6	28. 6 + 5
9. 1 + 4	19. 5 + 2	29. 3 + 5
10. 2 + 3	20. 4 + 3	30. 1 + 5

2. I used the criteria of correctness and immediacy because the basic hypothesis I was testing was that children could learn sums on their own without any direct instruction in first grade.

the sums with addends up to 6 before long. The sums that were relatively difficult at the beginning of the year (e.g., 6 + 5) remained relatively difficult at the end of the year.

At the end of the school year, we became curious about two other questions: How would our children do with addends larger than 6, and how would they compare with the other first graders in the same school, who had been given traditional instruction with workbooks, worksheets, and flashcards? There were only twelve other children of the same age in an ungraded primary unit, and we decided to test them.[3] For brevity, these children will be called the "control" group, and those in Georgia's class will be referred to as the "experimental" group.

As can be seen in Table 11.2, our children did slightly better on certain items and slightly worse on others, but did not differ on the whole from the "control" group. More specifically, the two groups did equally well with the easy sums, the "control" group did slightly better on the more difficult ones involving addends up to 6, and the "experimental" group did slightly better with addends larger than 6.

While there were no appreciable quantitative differences between our children and the "control" group, the qualitative differences were striking. The children in the "control" group were mentally and socially passive. They only gave answers and hardly ever volunteered to say anything else. When asked how they got particular answers, they either redid what they had just done or responded by saying, "I don't know" or "I thought it (in my head)." Only one of the twelve children gave a reasoned statement once to describe how he got 9 + 9 = 18: "10 + 10 is 20; so 9 + 9 is 18."

The children in the "experimental" group made many varied relationships and spontaneously talked about them during the test. Following are the kinds of relationships they made:

- *Relationship between what they wanted to know and what they knew.* When asked about 9 + 9, Ed said, "If 8 + 8 is . . . . 18!" (This answer, incidentally, is an example of one not included in Table 11.2. Ed took time to think out loud and, therefore, did not give the answer within 2 seconds.)

   When asked about 9 + 9, Ann asked, "What was the 8 + 8 one?" and looked at Georgia's notes. Upon seeing that Georgia had recorded 16 for 8 + 8, Ann said, "18. If you know that 8 + 8 = 16, you know to skip another one, and it *has to be* 18." (This answer, too, was excluded from Table 11.2, as it did not meet the criteria for inclusion.)
- *Relationship between intuitive thinking and an answer arrived at through a more precise procedure.* When asked about 5 + 7, Bob said, "5 + 5, 17,

---

3. All the testing in June, 1981, was done by Georgia DeClark.

TABLE 11.2.   Comparisons of Experimental and Control Groups

	June, 1981			June, 1982		
	"Exp." N=24	"Control" N=12	Difference	Experimental N=21	Control N=20	Difference
2 + 2	100%	100%	0%	95%	95%	0%
5 + 5	100	92	8	95	100	− 5
3 + 3	100	100	0	90	100	−10
4 + 1	100	100	0	90	100	−10
6 + 1	100	100	0	90	100	−10
5 + 1	100	100	0	95	95	0
1 + 4	100	100	0	95	100	− 5
2 + 3	100	92	8	81	100	−19
5 + 2	100	92	8	81	100	−19
4 + 4	96	100	−4	90	95	− 5
1 + 5	96	100	−4	90	100	−10
6 + 6	88	75	13	52	85	−33
4 + 2	88	83	5	76	95	−19
3 + 2	88	92	−4	81	100	−19
2 + 5	88	92	−4	76	100	−24
6 + 2	88	83	5	71	85	−14
2 + 6	88	67	21	67	90	−23
6 + 3	79	67	12	48	95	−47
4 + 5	75	92	−17	71	100	−29
2 + 4	75	92	−17	71	100	−29
5 + 4	71	83	−12	81	100	−19
4 + 3	71	83	−12	76	80	− 4
3 + 4	71	75	−4	52	90	−38
4 + 6	67	50	17	52	95	−43
5 + 3	63	83	−20	67	100	−33
3 + 6	63	67	−3	62	90	−28
3 + 5	63	75	−12	71	100	−29
6 + 5	54	58	−4	43	70	−27
5 + 6	50	58	−8	76	85	− 9
9 + 1	100	100	0	95	100	− 5
7 + 2	100	83	17	81	90	− 9
1 + 10	100	92	8	90	90	0
10 + 10	100	75	25	95	95	0
2 + 8	88	67	21	86	90	− 4
7 + 3	83	67	16	76	80	− 4
9 + 2	79	67	12	81	90	− 9
9 + 9	63	58	5	48	80	−32
8 + 5	54	42	12	57	80	−23
8 + 8	54	42	12	38	65	−27
7 + 7	50	50	0	52	85	−33
5 + 7	50	58	−8	52	75	−23
7 + 8	38	25	13	33	45	−12

NOTE: The data for June, 1981 are reprinted from C. Kamii, *Number in Preschool and Kindergarten* (Washington, D.C.: National Association for the Education of Young Children, 1982).

no, it should be less, 12." Our children's thinking was thus never divorced from their intuition. The "control" children, on the other hand, never revealed any evidence of intuitive "feelings."
- *Compensation.* When asked about 5 + 7, Brad said, "If you take 1 from 7 and put it with 5, that's 6 + 6, and that's 12."
- *Commutativity.* When asked about 2 + 8, Brad said, "You could do it backwards like 8 + 2, that's 10."
- *Relationship between one answer and another.* When asked about 7 + 3, Ann said, "10. Two 10's in a row." A term more often used was "again." For example, after 1 + 10 and 10 + 10 came 9 + 2, and the children in the "experimental" group often said 9 + 2 made "11 again."

When they were asked how they got certain answers, too, our children reacted much more actively than the "control" children. They responded with a variety of descriptions and/or arguments and often corrected themselves in the process. Below are some examples, beginning with a conversation about a correct answer.

- When asked what 7 + 8 was, Jill replied, "15." She explained that she got this answer because 7 + 7 was 14, and one more had to be 15.
- Carol had said that 9 + 9 was 17. When asked to explain how she got 17, she exclaimed, "18! It's 18!" Our children sometimes deduced that if 8 + 8 = 16, 9 + 9 had to be one more than 8 + 8, and later corrected themselves.
- Steve had quickly used his fingers before saying that 5 + 7 = 11. When asked how he got 11, he said, "It might not be 11. I had 5 + 5. I added; no, it's 12."
- When asked what 7 + 8 was, Brad counted on fingers and announced, "11." Georgia asked him how he got 11, and he explained, "7 + 4 = 11, 4 more is, oh, it's 15." He thus corrected himself while trying to explain how 7 + 8 could be changed to 7 + (4 + 4).

The most striking statement came from Martha, one of the low-level children who blossomed toward the end of the year. Georgia tried to help her when she had sat for a while, not saying anything about 5 + 6. When Georgia asked, "Would it help to know 5 + 5?" Martha firmly responded: "Wait. I have to think it in my own head."

Our children were thus mentally more active and autonomous than the "control" group. The fact that they each thought in their own ways can be seen in the wide variety of their responses. They often used the examiner's notes and checked their answers against their intuition. Our children hardly wrote anything in arithmetic, but they often asked us to read what we had written. The children in the "control" group used pencils but did not seem to think about the utility of what had been written.

Piaget often talked about young children's intuitive thinking, which becomes "articulated" during the preoperational period, before children "group" operations. The education of intuition is usually not discussed by math educators, but a constructivist approach emphasizes it because more precise cognitive processes grow out of it. The children in the "control" group thought in superficial, uninvolved, and mechanical ways. While they had memorized sums and had techniques for producing correct answers, they seemed not to feel any ownership of, or responsibility for, their thinking and had no desire to explain how they got their answers.

The variety of awkward verbal expressions found in the "experimental" group also attests to the fact that our children each invented their own ways. For example, Ann said while trying to do 9 + 9, "If you know that 8 + 8 = 16, you know to skip another one, and it *has to be* 18." In this sentence, "another one" and "it" were not used very clearly, but the underlying ideas were perfectly clear. Like Ann, our children often said "it *has to be*," which was their way of expressing logical necessity. When children construct deductive generalizations for themselves, they can deduce their own conclu- sions with certitude.

Brad's words for commutativity were "you could do it backwards." As Gréco (1962) demonstrated, children can figure commutativity out on their own between 6 and 8 years of age, without having it taught. Like Brad, our children were often pleased with the relationships they had invented and wanted to talk about them. "You could do it (2 + 8) backwards like 8 + 2, that's 10," is too long an answer for inclusion in Table 11.2, but it is truly the product of a child's own construction.

The reader may rightly object that the "experimental" children were more talkative because they were tested by their own teacher. But these qualitative differences were found again at the end of the second-year replication (1981–82), when an external examiner was asked to test both groups.

The reader may be asking if our children could manage worksheets. As stated in the Introduction of this book, Georgia gave four worksheets between September, 1980, and April, 1981, and found that her pupils who had committed sums to memory had absolutely no trouble writing the answers in the appropriate places. (She quickly explained what the " + " sign meant, and where the answer had to be written, and the children understood her immediately.) The only children (one or two) who had trouble with worksheets were also the ones who had trouble in games.

In 1981–82, I wanted to replicate the experiment of the first year with a new group of first graders in Georgia's class. This second year started with two full first grade classes, because another school had been closed and

Georgia's school absorbed the children who would otherwise have attended it. The teacher of the other first grade class was also transferred from that school, and she agreed to have her class serve as the control group.

Only 21 and 20 children respectively are included in the data analysis (Table 11.2). Those who joined the class later and those who left the class during the year were excluded from the sample. The children were assigned to the two classes by the school principal, presumably randomly. The two groups seemed very similar in September, 1981, on the pretest.

It can be seen in Table 11.2 that the control group did extremely well in the posttest in June, 1982, and the percentages of children who gave the correct answer immediately were 90 or higher on almost all the items involving addends up to 6. There were no differences between the two groups on four easy items (2 + 2, 5 + 1, 1 + 10, and 10 + 10), but the control group had higher percentages on all the others.

Let us examine each group separately, beginning with the experimental group. It can be said that the sums that were relatively easy in June, 1981, were also relatively easy in June, 1982 (namely, the small doubles, the " + 1's," and the "1 +'s," the " + 2's" and "2 +'s," and 10 + 10).

Table 11.3 includes a comparison of the 1981 and 1982 experimental groups. It can readily be seen that the differences were slight but consistent. The percentages of the first year were consistently higher. These differences can be explained by the fact that we had three low-level children during the second year who did not blossom as the low-level children had done during the first year. (One of them should chronologically have been in kindergarten but was in Georgia's class because of her parents' insistence.) The first year's group also had a few more very "sharp" children than the second year's. Small samples are thus unfortunately influenced by a few individuals. Work of these individuals, however, supported the theory of constructivism: Each child developed from his initial level; low-level children used what they had to develop beyond their level, and high-level children in the same classroom used what they had to go much further.

Curious about how our children failed to meet the criteria for inclusion in these tables, I decided to examine individual cases. While the control group was uniformly strong in 1982 (except for one child who frequently counted on fingers), the experimental group could be divided into two subgroups— the higher-level two-thirds (14/21) and the others (7/21).

Eight of the two-thirds responded just like the children in the control group, quickly and correctly. Four others were similar but intermittently took a few seconds too long, sometimes by thinking out loud. (Our children never had any timed tests, and we did not tell anyone that reaction time was a criterion used in our tests.) Two other children also behaved like the control children except that they relaxed completely toward the end and

TABLE 11.3.   Comparisons of Two Experimental and Two Control Groups

	Experimental Groups			Control Groups		
	June, 1981 N=24	June, 1982 N=21	Difference	June, 1981 N=12	June, 1982 N=20	Difference
2 + 2	100%	95%	− 5%	100%	95%	− 5%
5 + 5	100	95	− 5	92	100	8
3 + 3	100	90	−10	100	100	0
4 + 1	100	90	−10	100	100	0
6 + 1	100	90	−10	100	100	0
5 + 1	100	95	− 5	100	95	− 5
1 + 4	100	95	− 5	100	100	0
2 + 3	100	81	−19	92	100	8
5 + 2	100	81	−19	92	100	8
4 + 4	96	90	− 6	100	95	− 5
1 + 5	96	90	− 6	100	100	0
6 + 6	88	52	−36	75	85	10
4 + 2	88	76	−12	83	95	12
3 + 2	88	81	− 7	92	100	8
2 + 5	88	76	−12	92	100	8
6 + 2	88	71	−17	83	85	2
2 + 6	88	67	−21	67	90	23
6 + 3	79	48	−31	67	95	28
4 + 5	75	71	− 4	92	100	8
2 + 4	75	71	− 4	92	100	8
5 + 4	71	81	10	83	100	17
4 + 3	71	76	5	83	80	− 3
3 + 4	71	52	−19	75	90	15
4 + 6	67	52	−15	50	95	45
5 + 3	63	67	4	83	100	17
3 + 6	63	62	− 1	67	90	23
3 + 5	63	71	8	75	100	25
6 + 5	54	43	−11	58	70	12
5 + 6	50	76	26	58	85	27
9 + 1	100	95	− 5	100	100	0
7 + 2	100	81	−19	83	90	7
1 + 10	100	90	−10	92	90	− 2
10 + 10	100	95	− 5	75	95	20
2 + 8	88	86	− 2	67	90	23
7 + 3	83	76	− 7	67	80	13
9 + 2	79	81	2	67	90	23
9 + 9	63	48	−15	58	80	22
8 + 5	54	57	3	42	80	38
8 + 8	54	38	−16	42	65	23
7 + 7	50	52	2	50	85	35
5 + 7	50	52	2	58	75	17
7 + 8	38	33	− 5	25	45	20

either counted or thought out loud. It can thus be said that two-thirds of our children, all high-level ones, essentially did not differ from the control group.

The other third responded in a variety of ways, indicating that when they are not taught to behave in certain ways, lower-level children do a variety of things that suit their personalities and intellectual levels. Three "specialized" in one kind of behavior or another, two by constantly counting on fingers and one by never using them. This child took a long time instead, either to think or to count in an unobservable way. The other four did different things for different questions, such as counting, thinking out loud, and responding immediately (not always correctly). When asked 6 + 5 = ?, for example, Betty said, "6 + 4 = 10, so plus 5 is 11." When asked about 5 + 3, she immediately answered "7." After being asked how she had gotten this answer, she counted on her fingers, found 8 as the total, and declared, "I don't care if it's within 1." (I had never heard such a statement from a first grader. Usually in school math, a small error is considered an error just like a big one.)

The control groups of 1981 and 1982 are also compared in Table 11.3. It can be observed that the percentages for the second-year group are consistently higher. They are very close to 100, and these figures can probably be attributed to the teaching that the second-year group had received. It must be noted, however, that even when children are directly and conscientiously instructed, the naturally harder items (7 + 8 and 8 + 8) are harder to memorize than naturally easier ones.

The difference between the control and experimental groups in Table 11.2 can thus be said to have been produced mainly by the low-level children. In June, there were seven low-level children in the experimental group and only one in the control group. If we assume (albeit without confidence) that the groups had the same kinds of children with the same distribution in September, we can say that low-level children become able to perform better on the posttest if they are instructed directly in first grade. My own conclusion, however, is that it is better to encourage low-level children to get to a higher level in their own ways. The children in the experimental group had a variety of different approaches to the problems, and I prefer to let them invent their own ways individually than to instruct them in how to give right answers at an earlier age.

The significant finding from Table 11.2 for me is that the advanced two-thirds in the experimental group turned out like the control children, without any lessons, worksheets, flash cards, or adult pressure. Although these children looked similar on the test, my own speculation based on the quality of their thinking is that they built a better foundation for future learning because they truly invented their own arithmetic. This is only a hypothesis that needs to be tested in a long-term study.

The testing and data analysis presented above were done more for research than for evaluation. It is important to know what sums children are learning, if any. However, since the optimal speed of this acquisition is not known, these data cannot be used directly to evaluate the "teaching" reported in this book. As the data must also be interpreted in the socio-emotional context within which arithmetic is learned, considerable work remains to be undertaken. We turn next to a discussion of some of the directions in which this work might proceed.

DIRECTIONS FOR FURTHER WORK

The "proof of the pudding" in developmental education lies in long-term effects, that is, in children's math in grades 3, 7, and beyond. Since development is deeper and more general than specific surface learnings, it takes longer than a year or two to occur. I will discuss two aspects of the long-term evaluation of the results of our "teaching."

Long-Term Effects in Arithmetic

Math educators are familiar with the difficulties commonly found in elementary math. "Carrying" and "borrowing," fractions, and decimals are only a few of the well-known computational problems. Many children know computation well but have no idea whether to add, subtract, multiply, or divide when faced with "story" problems. These difficulties should diminish when children have a better foundation. Since logico-mathematical knowledge is constructed by each child through the coordination of relationships *he* constructed before, a good foundation is absolutely necessary for its further development. While a good foundation is *necessary*, it is not *sufficient*. A good foundation cannot result in further construction if it is "put on hold" by poor teaching.

Our children went into second grade and immediately started to receive the kind of traditional instruction that almost all second graders receive in the United States. The foundation they had developed in Georgia's class was quickly "put on hold" as can be seen in the following example. In September, Nancy and her classmates were given a worksheet containing subtraction problems such as 9 − 5. (The children Georgia had had were mixed with all the other second graders from the same school and the other one that had been closed, and the children were randomly assigned to two classes.) Nancy did some of the problems by counting on fingers and had to

stay in the room during recess, until she finished her work. She ended up
zooming through it and joined her classmates on the playground.

By December, Nancy was doing "subtraction up to 20" by mindlessly
counting the letters of the alphabet on her desk. To do $17 - 9$, for example,
she counted the letters to "Q," then from "A" to "I," and then from "J" to "Q."
The teacher was satisfied with the correct answers thus produced.

By March, Nancy was doing double-column subtraction such as the
following:

$$
\begin{array}{ccc}
71 & 65 & 44 \\
-37 & -17 & -28 \\
\hline
46 & 52 & 24
\end{array}
$$

These are common errors. When I asked Nancy why she had subtracted the
bottom number from the top in the first column, but did the opposite in the
second column, she explained with a straight face that that was the way one
was supposed to do them. After some unsuccessful attempts at probing, I
finally ended up telling her, "I thought you were supposed to borrow," and
she exclaimed, "Oh, YEAH!!!"

Most of the other children from Georgia's class, as well as from other first
grade classes, were behaving in similar ways in the second grade. Double-
column subtraction could be done only through tricks, as place value was
still too hard to understand. Long-term evaluation of our teaching thus
seemed impossible without better teaching in second grade and beyond. I
remain convinced that children would construct arithmetic without the well-
known difficulties if they were encouraged to think *in their own ways*.

The point I am trying to make is this: The "proof of the pudding" of our
work in first grade arithmetic must be sought in the reduction or disappearance of difficulties commonly found in grades 3, 5, 7, and beyond. However,
this evaluation can be done only in longer-range research that includes
constructivist teaching in subsequent grades.

Evaluation in children's arithmetic also needs to take into account the
contextual features of the classroom that contribute to children's feelings of
confidence and desire to make sense of their experiences. Georgia and I can
vouch for the fact that we did not create a single case of budding math
phobia. But beyond that, our children *reinvented* (created for themselves)
important parts of arithmetic. Most of them reinvented commutativity;
others struggled with a problem of proportionality (what happens if the boys
vote for the boys and the girls vote for the girls, when there are ten boys and
fifteen girls in the class). The children who were slower in arithmetic also
had the self-confidence to raise their hands whenever there was something
they did not understand. The children felt free to learn from and to
challenge not only each other but also the teacher.

If children insist on understanding everything they do in arithmetic, they build a solid logico-mathematical foundation naturally. Unfortunately, traditional schools teach ready-made algorithms and unwittingly make children pretend to know what they are doing. "Understanding math" becomes confused with "obediently learning proper procedures." How many adults dared to ask while they were in elementary school why

$$\frac{3}{4} \div \frac{3}{5}$$

had to be solved through multiplication?

How to assess children's confidence and initiative is a question yet to be answered. I hope that someone in evaluation research will take it up and give it the time it deserves. Meanwhile, the anecdotes about situations in daily living related in Chapter 7 should suggest that our children had confidence and came up with relationships of all kinds throughout the day. Even Martha, a low-level child, refused Georgia's help and said, "Wait. I have to think it in my own head."

Long-Term Effects in the Development of Autonomy

In the chapter on autonomy as the aim of education, Piaget (1948, Chapter 4) discussed math education at great length, saying that intellectual and moral development cannot be separated in a classroom. Here is what he said more generally:

> Education constitutes an indissoluble ["indissociable" in the original] whole, and it is not possible to create independent ["autonomous" in the original] personalities in the ethical area if the individual is also subjected to intellectual constraint to such an extent that he must restrict himself to learning by rote without discovering the truth for himself. . . . Conversely, if his ethics consist exclusively in submission to adult authority, and if the only social exchanges that make up the life of the class are those that bind each student individually to a master holding all power, he will not know how to be intellectually active (p. 107).

Speaking of the importance of peer interaction for the development of critical thinking, he went on to say the following:

> No real intellectual activity could be carried on . . . without free collaboration among individuals—that is to say, among the students themselves, and not only between the teacher and the student. Using the intelligence assumes not only continual mutual stimulation, but also and more importantly mutual control and exercise of the critical spirit, which

alone can lead the individual to objectivity and to a need for conclusive evidence (pp. 107–108).

This suggests that children's arithmetic should be evaluated in the context of the following three aspects of autonomy, both in first grade and subsequently:

1. Children's relationships with adults (with respect to authority, rules, affection, mutual respect, trust, etc.)
2. Their relationships with peers (the ability to coordinate points of view, leadership, community feelings, etc.)
3. Their relationship to learning (curiosity, confidence, alertness, etc.).

The socio-affective attitude surrounding arithmetic that I discussed previously is part of the third aspect (relationship to learning). The key element cutting across all three aspects is mental activity. There can be no arithmetic in a Piagetian sense without mental activity, and this activity is stimulated by peer interaction and interaction with adults in which children's own ways of thinking are encouraged.

The method of data collection might be observation in real life. A way to assess autonomy in relation to adults might be to ask the teacher to leave the room. A class that continues to function with no change in children's behavior can be said to be autonomous. I mentioned a child during group time in Chapter 8 who raised his hand asking the teacher to wait because he had a conflict to resolve with another child. This is a highly unusual behavior in a classroom and reflects a high degree of autonomy, both in relation to the adult and to peers. In Chapter 2, I also mentioned a child who said that it was not necessary to vote for the other alternative because "13 + 13 = 26, and we have only 24 kids today." These all supply anecdotal evidence reflecting the kinds of relationships we want children to have with adults, peers, and learning.

A new theory of learning thus leads to the conceptualization of new objectives and the need for evaluation along new dimensions. Traditional achievement tests can no longer be used as the principal instrument for evaluating educational practices.

Traditional educators assume that children's minds, like empty glasses, have to be filled up to a certain level in first grade, a bit more in second grade, and so on throughout their school career. This assumption leads to an unfortunate approach to evaluation based on test scores: the more correct answers a child learns to give in one year, the better his education can be said to have been.

Knowing one hundred sums by the end of first grade in no way guarantees that the child has built a solid foundation for higher-level mathematics. It may well be that children who have learned fewer sums more slowly and autonomously in first grade have built a more solid foundation for later learning. A good foundation is particularly important in mathematics because in logico-mathematical knowledge, all subsequent constructions are made with previously built elements, created by each individual from within, through reflective abstraction. Sums can be memorized as specific bits of input as if they were social, conventional, arbitrary knowledge. But such learning provides a poor foundation for understanding other arithmetic operations, as well as algebra and higher mathematics later on. It also proves tangential to being able to solve problems in real life involving numerical reasoning.

Adults often say that math was their worst subject, that they never understood it in school, and that they memorized tricks and formulas to somehow get by. While many schools give achievement tests nowadays, very few people are putting these tests into relationship with the widespread fear of math. Fear of math is the result of educators' basing their means and ends on the presumption that educational objectives can and ought to be defined one by one, separately. In this compartmentalized common-sense approach, arithmetic is considered apart from reading, and the three R's are conceived separately from children's social, emotional, and moral development.

First graders' grabbing of erasers when asked how they got a particular answer on a worksheet is an early symptom of math phobia. This problem is particularly severe for minority children and girls. Grieb and Easley (1983) pointed out that in universities, there are very few blacks and women enrolled in math courses. Their longitudinal individual case studies are beginning to show that already in kindergarten, girls and children from minority groups may be more vulnerable to adult approval while working on math problems. The children they found to be confident and indifferent to adult approval are white middle-class boys, whom they called "Pale Male Mathematics Mavericks."

. Students' sense of alienation at school is reflected in vandalism, truancy, absenteeism, and apathy. Children who feel listened to and respected are unlikely to smash windows or stay aloof from classroom activities.

Let us take voting as an activity flowing from arithmetic conceived in the context of autonomy. The children in Georgia's class voted constantly on issues ranging from going out to recess to giving a pet to the class next door. The counting of votes belonged to arithmetic, but the greater educational value may well have lain in children's emotional, social, and moral development. Our children argued about the whys of every decision they were allowed to make. After ten years of this kind of schooling, adolescents might have greater courage to stand up for what they believe to be right rather than following the will of peers.

Evaluation must thus first begin with the evaluation of objectives. If an educator's goals and objectives are inadequate, everything else he does will be of little value. The recent hysteria about test scores would not be so tragic if test scores had not become our objectives. Achievement tests were made to *assess* achievement. Within the past ten years in America, however, they have become the very objectives of education. American education is thus caught up in a gigantic enterprise of chasing its own tail, unaware that their objectives are based on the wrong theory about how children learn. Human beings are not empty glasses to be filled with 10 cc's of math, 10 cc's of reading, and 10 cc's of writing in first grade. They are highly complex organisms with their own intelligence and motivation.

I close with Erlwanger's (1975) clinical interviews that illustrate the different conclusions that can be reached through different theories and methods of data collection. As can be seen in the following account, the teacher basing her judgment on tests thought Mat was making above-average progress, but Erlwanger arrived at a diametrically opposed conclusion. Mat was a fifth grader with an IQ of 121 attending a school using an individualized instruction program in mathematics. He had been in this program since the second grade. It was the now familiar kind consisting of an initial diagnostic test, booklets containing exercises, and tests to evaluate mastery of each level. An adult checked the answers against a key before letting the child go on to the next booklet. The interview concerned the addition of $\frac{3}{4}$ and $\frac{1}{4}$. Mat had two answers:

(i) $\frac{3}{4} + \frac{1}{4} = \frac{4}{8} = \frac{1}{2}$; (ii) . . . "If I divide this [circle] into 4 . . . and then add this [shading $\frac{3}{4}$:] . . . and this [shading $\frac{1}{4}$:] . . . it's a whole." He then wrote $\frac{3}{4} + \frac{1}{4} = 1$. . . .

Erlwanger: But when you did it the other way . . . you had $\frac{1}{2}$ . . . how come?

M: *I don't know! That's the way it is.*

E: What method did you use when you got $\frac{4}{8}$?

M: I . . . uh . . . added the numerators and then the denominators . . . [and] . . . *that's the one they taught me* . . . . I think it was [level] E fractions.

E: How does this really work then . . . that . . . here you are doing it one way . . .

M: [Interrupting] *You get a different answer every method you use.*

E: And then how do you decide which answer is right?

M: *It depends on which method you are told to use. . . . And you use that method and you come out with the answer. And that's what answer is in the key. . . .* (p. 250)

When faced with a choice between the two answers, Mat ended up choosing ". . . the one where you add the denominators and numerators, because that's what method they've taught me to do it, in my booklet, and they didn't teach me to do it with diagrams." For Mat, mathematics was thus a vast system of methods for heteronomously finding answers, and the answer he got depended on the method he used! He had more confidence in the method he thought he had been taught (solution i) than in his own ability to think (solution ii).

There is thus much more to evaluation than tests. Evaluation, too, has a long way to go, and its validity depends on the validity of the theory on which it rests.

CHAPTER 12

Prospects
for the Future

Public schools have been in trouble for some time, and problems are known to be particularly acute in math and science education. The solutions to these problems, proposed by professional educators and reiterated in legislative and agency pronouncements at all levels of government, have been the familiar ones that have reappeared from time to time. The National Commission on Excellence in Education (1983), for example, recommended raising high school graduation requirements, lengthening the school year, giving more homework, raising teachers' salaries, and improving their preparation (requiring more content and less methods courses). "Back to basics" with its systematic testing and intensive direct teaching is the conservative panacea offered at the moment.

For the most part, "innovations" in math education have consisted of ways and means of teaching children more, earlier, and/or more efficiently. Regardless of the specifics of curricular changes suggested, almost all have shared the empiricist assumption that math can be *transmitted* from the outside. The so-called "modern math" was an attempt to transmit the results of centuries of construction in prepackaged form. Cuisenaire, Dienes, and Montessori materials, as well as teaching machines and the latest of the technological innovations, the computer, have generally been conceived of as devices to transmit "math concepts" to children with dispatch.

A constructivist approach to the teaching of arithmetic is different. It is based on a comprehensive, and to date most adequate, scientific theory of how children learn. It is a pedagogy that asks teachers to decenter and to think about their practice from the standpoint of how children learn and come to understand, rather than how children can be made to behave, whether that behavior be social (conduct) or cognitive (test results) in nature. Constructivism suggests that human beings cannot be made to learn very well through imposed exercises, fear of tests, and obedience.

Piaget's theory is as revolutionary today as the heliocentric theory was in 1543. From the geocentric (egocentric) perspective, it was perfectly obvious that the sun revolved around the earth. Copernicus was laughed at when he described a motion that went counter to the evidence of common sense and experience. Piaget's theory is likewise counterintuitive and rejected by many psychologists and educators. It is very hard to become convinced that children learn 2 + 2 = 4 by themselves, rather than being taught this apparent "fact." It is also very hard to become convinced that ready-made answers, learned quickly from the outside in, are educationally unsound in the long run.

What is the likelihood that the ideas presented in this book will influence those charged with the education and welfare of society's future adults? It seems useful to delineate four groups who are involved in children's education: teachers, parents, school administrators, and university professors in schools of education. In my experience, teachers and parents have been by far the most receptive to the notions considered in this book. School administrators have constituted the conservative end of the spectrum.

To be sure, some teachers are resistant to change. But others have been constructivist in attitude, prior to being introduced to the gentleman from Geneva and before having any inkling of the accumulated body of research. When I suggest at professional meetings that games are better than worksheets for first grade arithmetic, these teachers understand immediately. They also express relief and delight at finally understanding why place value and missing addends are so hard to teach. Some teachers remain skeptical until they study their own pupils with previously unasked questions. What convinces them is not what I say but what they observe in their own classrooms, day after day.

Parents are initially guarded in their reactions to educational innovation. Georgia and I presented our plan, rationale, and data from the previous year during parents' night in September of the 1981–82 school year. All the parents accepted our plan, albeit without enthusiasm. The most negative reaction we heard was: "My child is very bright. Since we are both college graduates, our child can afford to play for a year."

Parents' support, however, began to come the next day. One father sent playing cards that his company gave away. Volunteer mothers made cards and board games, and were very interested to know how their children learned arithmetic and autonomy with these materials. At Christmas, I received warm words of appreciation about how much their children enjoyed playing the games. By the time I left to go to Geneva in April, a few mothers had told me they wished their older children had had such a pleasant introduction to math.

Georgia received inquiries from parents of kindergarteners about the possibility of getting them into her class the following year. Parents understand what is good for their children. They know which of their children go to school enthusiastically every morning and which do not. The fact that Georgia had already been respected and trusted for five years in the same school played an enormous role in parents' acceptance. Over the two years, only one mother felt compelled to tutor her child at home.

When a teacher knows what she is doing and can justify her practice with theory and scientific evidence, parents trust her professional knowledge and judgment. Just as they trust physicians' scientific training, parents trust teachers who know the findings of contemporary research. Very few parents demand that older treatments be used when more recent discoveries point the way toward new cures.

The people who are the closest to children are the most enthusiastic about this type of teaching. But both of these groups soon become frustrated by a variety of administrative barriers. For parents, hesitation begins when they ask what will happen to their children after the first grade. Georgia could do nothing about the rest of the system, and she could do nothing about many things in first grade either. She felt compelled to conduct reading groups by following the prescribed series that came with workbooks. The practical daily consequence was the problem of noise. She knew that the children were making perfectly normal noise when they played games, but she could often not hear the children reading to her. The result was the eternal "shhhh . . . shhh . . . shhh . . ." that always worked only for a little while. If I had known more about the teaching of reading, I would have nagged her into experimenting with that, too!

A teacher's day is interrupted by many "special" events. Gym, music, other branches of humanities, the program for the gifted, the weekly trip to the library, assemblies, and so forth were part of the school day for Georgia's class, too. Since none of the other teachers had heard of autonomy, our children had autonomous math and heteronomous everything else! Gym could have been an ideal time to keep score, invent games, and negotiate rules. Art projects could have been opportunities to learn measurement, physics, and chemistry by reading instructions and thinking about alternative ways to produce desired effects.

Administrators have a great deal of power, and the combination of their power and ignorance has made many constructivist teachers leave public schools. Principals and curriculum specialists tend to punish teachers who do not use traditional, prescribed methods. Among the forces converging to keep them conservative are that education is virtually a state monopoly, with little competition and a guaranteed clientele and revenues, and that educational policies are ultimately determined by common sense rather than scientific debate and long-range considerations.

Faced with public dissatisfaction, most public school administrators have lined up behind achievement tests and behavioral objectives, which the public understands. When test scores improve, the public is mollified. The decision to make educational objectives out of tests is sadly and mistakenly supported by public opinion. But try to imagine a physician whose knowledge of scientific advances is fifty years behind the times! Try to imagine a business executive who bases his policy decisions on common sense rather than on market research! Educators ought first to educate themselves, and then assume leadership in educating the public.

The case of British primary education, which may be the best in the world today, suggests the role of administrative freedom in advancing the profession. In England, principals (headmasters and headmistresses) have almost complete freedom to make curriculum and personnel decisions for their own schools. One principal may thus have "family grouping" in his school, while the one nearby operates with traditional age groups. It is this freedom to decide that encourages these principals to be well informed. When a principal is free to decide, he is responsible for the decisions he makes, and this responsibility necessitates knowledge. Just as children become responsible and desirous of more knowledge when they have to take a stand, principals become better informed and more progressive when they are autonomous.

In schools of education, the prospects for constructivist education are promising. Many younger professors are willing to make the effort to study a difficult theory. Once a scholar finally understands Piagetian theory, there is little likelihood that he will revert to a more limited perspective. I am one among many former associationists who have adopted Piagetian theory. I know of no Piagetians who have moved in the opposite direction.

The work reported in this book needs to be subjected to further scientific scrutiny. Constructivist education and constructivist teaching are far from being fully articulated, in math as well as in other subjects. Further research is sorely needed.

Traditional practices unfortunately do not have to be justified, no matter how bad they may be. The burden falls on the innovators to justify and prove themselves. How soon constructivist education becomes a reality in American public schools may in the end depend less on research findings than on the willingness of educators to enter into conflict with established views. Constructivist ideas clash squarely with pre-Piagetian notions, and individuals who operate within the boundaries of tradition and the established reward system are protected by them. That an increasing number of people are willing to stand up against the established views is a hopeful sign that attests to human beings' urge to go beyond the past.

Bibliography

PUBLICATIONS

Ackermann-Valladão, E. *Construction d'égalités à distance (collections discrètes)*. Unpublished paper, 1982. (Available from the author at the University of Geneva.)

Allardice, B. S. *The development of representational skills for some mathematical concepts*. Unpublished doctoral dissertation, Cornell University, 1977.

Brun, J. *La représentation symbolique d'opérations additives en situation d'interaction et de communication*. Paper presented at the meeting of the International Group for the Psychology of Mathematics Education, Grenoble, 1981.

Carpenter, T. P. *The effect of instruction on first-grade children's initial solution processes for basic addition and subtraction problems*. Paper presented at the meeting of the American Educational Research Association, Boston, 1980.

Carpenter, T. P., Hiebert, J., & Moser, J. M. *The effect of problem structure on first-graders' initial solution processes for simple addition and subtraction problems* (Tech. Rep. 516). Madison: Wisconsin Research and Development Center for Individualized Schooling, October, 1979.

Carpenter, T. P., & Moser, J. M. The development of addition and subtraction problem-solving skills. In T. P. Carpenter, J. M. Moser & T. A. Romberg (Eds.), *Addition and subtraction: A cognitive perspective*. Hillsdale, N. J.: Erlbaum, 1982.

Christofides-Henriques, A., & Maurice, D. *La recherche des raisons dans le contexte d'une série numérique*. Unpublished manuscript, 1982. (Available from the authors at the University of Geneva.)

Conne, F. *Recherche sur la lecture de l'écriture équationnelle chez des enfants de 7 ans*. Research report to the Fonds National Suisse de la Recherche Scientifique, 1981. (Available from the author at the University of Geneva.)

Danzig, T. *Number: The language of science*. New York: Free Press, 1967. (Originally published in 1930.)

Duncan, E. R., Capps, L. R., Dolciani, M. P., Quast, W. G., & Zweng, M. J. *Modern school mathematics: Structure and use*. Teacher's annotated ed., rev. ed. Boston: Houghton Mifflin, 1972.

Erlwanger, S. H. Case studies of children's conceptions of mathematics—Part I. *The Journal of Children's Mathematical Behavior*, 1975, *1*, 199–277.

Ferreiro, E., & Teberosky, A. *Literacy before schooling*. Exeter, New Hampshire: Heinemann, 1982.

Furth, H. G. *Piaget and knowledge*. (2nd ed.) Chicago: University of Chicago Press, 1981.

Fuson, K. C. *Counting solution procedures in addition and subtraction*. Paper presented at the Wingspread conference on number, Madison, Wisconsin, 1979.

Fuson, K. C. An analysis of counting-on solution procedure in addition. In T. P. Carpenter, J. M. Moser & T. A. Romberg (Eds.), *Addition and subtraction: A cognitive perspective*. Hillsdale, N. J.: Erlbaum, 1982.

Giannoni, J. *Card games for kids*. New York: Golden Press, 1974.

Gibb, E. G. Children's thinking in the process of subtraction. *Journal of Experimental Education*, 1956, 25, 71–80.

Gimbayashi, H. Mathematics and math education. In K. Hatano and H. Gimbayashi (Eds.), *Logic and psychology of school subjects: 4. Mathematics*. Tokyo: Meijitosho, 1969.

Ginsburg, H., & Opper, S. *Piaget's theory of intellectual development*. (2nd ed.) Englewood Cliffs, N. J.: Prentice-Hall, 1979.

Golick, M. *Deal me in!* New York: Jeffrey Norton Publishers, 1973.

Gréco, P. Recherches sur quelques formes d'inférences arithmétiques et sur la compréhension de l'itération numérique chez l'enfant. In P. Gréco, J. B. Grize, S. Papert, et J. Piaget, *Problèmes de la construction du nombre* (Etudes d'épistémologie génétique, XI). Paris: Presses Universitaires de France, 1960.

Gréco, P. Une recherche sur la commutativité de l'addition. In P. Gréco et A. Morf, *Structures numériques élémentaires* (Etudes d'épistémologie génétique, XIII). Paris: Presses Universitaires de France, 1962.

Grieb, A., & Easley, J. A primary school impediment to mathematical equity: Case studies in rule-dependent socialization. In M. Steinkamp and M. S. Maehr (Eds.), *Women in science*. Greenwich, Conn.: JAI Press, 1983.

Gwynne, F. *The king who rained*. New York: Windmill Books, 1970.

Hatano, G. *Mental regrouping strategy for addition: An alternative model to counting-on*. Paper presented at the meeting of the National Council of Teachers of Mathematics, Seattle, 1980.

Hatano, G. Learning to add and subtract: A Japanese perspective. In T. P. Carpenter, J. M. Moser & T. A. Romberg (Eds.), *Addition and subtraction: A cognitive perspective*. Hillsdale, N. J.: Erlbaum, 1982.

Ibarra, C. G., & Lindvall, C. M. Factors associated with the ability of kindergarten children to solve simple arithmetic story problems. *Journal of Educational Research*, 1982, 75, 149–155.

Inhelder, B., & Piaget, J. *The early growth of logic in the child*. New York: Harper & Row, 1964. (First published in 1959.)

Inhelder, B., & Piaget, J. De l'itération des actions à la récurrence élémentaire. In P. Gréco, B. Inhelder, B. Matalon et J. Piaget, *La formation des raisonnements récurrentiels* (Etudes d'épistémologie génétique, XVII). Paris: Presses Universitaires de France, 1963.

Inhelder, B., Sinclair, H., & Bovet, M. *Learning and the development of cognition*. Cambridge, Mass.: Harvard University Press, 1974.

Kamii, C. Teachers' autonomy and scientific training. *Young Children,* 1981a, *36,* 5–14.

Kamii, C. Application of Piaget's theory to education: The preoperational level. In I. E. Sigel, D. M. Brodzinsky & R. M. Golinkoff (Eds.), *New directions in Piagetian theory and practice.* Hillsdale, N. J.: Erlbaum, 1981b.

Kamii, C. Piaget for principals. *Principal,* 1981c, *60,* 12–17.

Kamii, C. *Number in preschool and kindergarten.* Washington, D.C.: National Association for the Education of Young Children, 1982.

Kamii, C., & DeVries, R. Piaget for early education. In M. C. Day & R. K. Parker (Eds.), *The preschool in action.* (2nd ed.) Boston: Allyn & Bacon, 1977.

Kamii, C., & DeVries, R. *Physical knowledge in preschool education.* Englewood Cliffs, N. J.: Prentice-Hall, 1978.

Kamii, C., & DeVries, R. *Group games in early education.* Washington, D.C.: National Association for the Education of Young Children, 1980.

Kamii, M. *Place value: Children's efforts to find a correspondence between digits and numbers of objects.* Paper presented at the Tenth Annual Symposium of the Jean Piaget Society, Philadelphia, 1980.

Kamii, M. Children's ideas about written number. *Topics in Learning & Learning Disabilities,* 1981, *1,* 47–59.

Kamii, M. *Children's graphic representation of numerical concepts: A developmental study.* Unpublished doctoral dissertation, Harvard University, 1982.

Kohlberg, L., & Mayer, R. Development as the aim of education. *Harvard Educational Review,* 1972, *42,* 449–496.

Locke, J. *Essay concerning human understanding.* Oxford: Oxford University Press, 1947.

McKinnon, J. W., & Renner, J. W. Are colleges concerned with intellectual development? *American Journal of Physics,* 1971, *39,* 1047–1052.

National Commission on Excellence in Education. *A nation at risk: The imperative for educational reform.* Washington, D.C.: United States Department of Education, 1983.

O'Brien, T. C. Introduction to SEEDBED. *SEEDBED* (published by Teachers' Center Project, Southern Illinois University at Edwardsville), 1980, No. 5, i–ii.

O'Hare, E. Piaget, the six-year-old and modern math. *Today's Education,* 1975, *64,* 33–36.

Perret, J.-F., Theurillat, M., Jeanneret, H., Lorimier, M., & Schwaerzel, J. *Numération: Compter ou coder? "Le jeu de l'oie"* (IRDP/R 81.01). Neuchâtel, Switzerland: Institut Romand de Recherches et de Documentation Pédagogiques, June, 1981.

Perret-Clermont, A.-N. *Social interaction and cognitive development in children.* New York: Academic Press, 1980.

Piaget, J. *The moral judgment of the child.* New York: Free Press, 1965 (first published in 1932).

Piaget, J. *The origins of intelligence in children.* New York: Norton, 1963 (first published in 1936).

Piaget, J. *The psychology of intelligence.* Patterson, N. J.: Littlefield, Adams & Co., 1963 (first published in 1947).

Piaget, J. *To understand is to invent*. New York: Grossman, 1973 (first published in 1948).

Piaget, J. Problèmes de la construction du nombre. In P. Gréco, J. B. Grize, S. Papert et J. Piaget, *Problèmes de la construction du nombre* (Etudes d'épistémologie génétique, XI). Paris: Presses Universitaires de France, 1960.

Piaget, J. *Recherches sur la contradiction. 1/ Les différentes formes de la contradiction* (Etudes d'épistémologie génétique, XXXI). Paris: Presses Universitaires de France, 1974a.

Piaget, J. *Recherches sur la contradiction. 2/ Les relations entre affirmations et négations* (Etudes d'épistémologie génétique XXXII). Paris: Presses Universitaires de France, 1974b.

Piaget, J. *The grasp of consciousness*. Cambridge, Mass.: Harvard University Press, 1976 (first published in 1974).

Piaget, J. *Recherches sur la généralisation* (Etudes d'épistémologie génétique, XXXVI). Paris: Presses Universitaires de France, 1978.

Piaget, J., & Inhelder, B. *Memory and intelligence*. New York: Basic Books, 1973. (First published in 1968.)

Piaget, J., & Szeminska, A. *The child's conception of number*. New York: Norton, 1965. (First published in 1941.)

Reyes, A. G., & Vargas Suarez, J. A. *El numero y la solucion de problemas aritmeticos* (Un punto de vista piagetiano). Unpublished thesis, Universidad Nacional Autonoma de Mexico, Facultad de Psicologia, 1979.

Romberg, T. A., Harvey, J. G., Moser, J. M., Montgomery, M. E., & Dana, M. E. *Developing mathematical processes*. Chicago: Rand McNally, 1974.

Schell, L. M., & Burns, P. C. Pupil performance with three types of subtraction situations. *School Science and Mathematics*, 1962, *62*, 208–214.

Schubauer-Leoni, M. L., & Perret-Clermont, A.-N. Interactions sociales et représentations symboliques dans le cadre de problèmes additifs. *Recherches en Didactique des Mathématiques*, 1980, *1*, 297–350.

Schwebel, M. Formal operations in first-year college students. *The Journal of Psychology*, 1975, *91*, 133–141.

Sinclair, A., Siegrist, F., & Sinclair, H. *Young children's ideas about the written number system*. Paper presented at a NATO conference, University of Keele, 1982. Also in D. Rogers & J. Sloboda (Eds.), *The acquisition of symbolic skills*. New York: Plenum, 1983.

Sinclair, H., Stambak, M., Lézine, I., Rayna, S., & Verba, M. *Les bébés et les choses*. Paris: Presses Universitaires de France, 1982.

Smith, D. E., & Karpinski, L. C. *The Hindu-Arabic numerals*. Boston: Ginn, 1911.

Suydam, M. N., & Weaver, J. F. Research on mathematics learning. In J. N. Payne (Ed.), *Mathematics learning in early childhood*. (Thirty-seventh yearbook.) Reston, Virginia: National Council of Teachers of Mathematics, 1975.

Taylor, H. Mary Bowman's second grade. *Newsletter of Dialogues in Mathematics Education*, 1983, *2*, 2–3.

Thoburn, T., Forbes, J. E., Bechtel, R. D., & Nelson, L. D. *Macmillan mathematics*. New York: Macmillan, 1978.

Tohyama, H. *Wakaru Sansuh*. Tokyo: Yuhgen Kaisha, 1965.

Wirtz, R. *New beginnings: A guide to the Think-Talk-Read Math Center for Beginners*. Monterey, Calif.: Curriculum Development Associates, 1980.

COMMERCIALLY MADE GAMES

Benji. Mulberry Square Productions, 1976. All rights reserved by House of Games Corporation Limited, Bramalea, Ontario.
Huckleberry Hound. Commack, N. Y.: EDU-CARDS, 1961.
Parcheesi. Bay Shore, N. Y.: Selchow & Righter, 1975.
Piggy Bank. Commack, N. Y.: EDU-CARDS, 1965.
Put and Take. Minneapolis: Schaper Manufacturing Co., 1977.
Sorry. Salem, Mass.: Parker Brothers, 1972.
Tens. Bramalea, Ontario: House of Games Corporation, 1975.
Tic Tac Toe. Publisher unknown (discontinued).

About the Author

Constance Kazuko Kamii is Professor in the School of Education at the University of Alabama in Birmingham. She previously held a joint appointment in the College of Education, University of Illinois at Chicago and in the Faculty of Psychology and Sciences of Education, University of Geneva, Switzerland. Following receipt of her Ph.D. from the University of Michigan in 1965, she was a research fellow under Jean Piaget at the International Center of Genetic Epistemology and the University of Geneva.

Index